Public Vows

$\mathscr{P}$UBLIC $\mathscr{V}$OWS

A HISTORY OF MARRIAGE
AND THE NATION

NANCY F. COTT

NEW HANOVER COUNTY
PUBLIC LIBRARY
201 CHESTNUT STREET
WILMINGTON, NC 28401

HARVARD UNIVERSITY PRESS

Cambridge, Massachusetts

London, England

2000

Copyright © 2000 by Nancy F. Cott

All rights reserved

Printed in the United States of America

Library of Congress Cataloging-in-Publication Data

Cott, Nancy F.

Public vows: a history of marriage and the nation / Nancy F. Cott

p. cm.

Includes bibliographical references and index.

ISBN 0–674–00320-9 (hardcover : alk. paper)

1. Marriage—United States—History. 2. United States—Social life and customs. I. Title.

HQ536 .C757 2000

306.85'0973—dc21   00-031898

CONTENTS

INTRODUCTION

*M*arriage is like the sphinx—a conspicuous and recognizable monument on the landscape, full of secrets. To newcomers the monument seems awesome, even marvelous, while those in the vicinity take its features for granted. In assessing matrimony's wonders or terrors, most people view it as a matter of private decision-making and domestic arrangements. The monumental public character of marriage is generally its least noticed aspect. Even Mae West's joke, "Marriage is a great institution . . . but I ain't ready for an institution yet," likened it to a private asylum. Creating families and kinship networks and handing down private property, marriage certainly does design the architecture of private life. It influences individual identity and determines circles of intimacy. It can bring solace or misery—or both. The view of marriage as a private relationship has become a public value in the United States, enshrined in legal doctrine. In 1944 the U.S. Supreme Court portended a momentous line of interpretation by finding that the U.S. Constitution protected a "private realm of family life which the state cannot enter."[1]

At the same time that any marriage represents personal love and commitment, it participates in the public order. Marital status is just as important to one's standing in the community and state as it is to self-understanding. Radiating outward, the structure of marriage organizes community life and facilitates the government's grasp on the populace. To *be* marriage, the institution requires public affirmation. It requires public

1

knowledge—at least some publicity beyond the couple themselves; that is why witnesses are required for the ceremony and why wedding bells ring. More definitively, legal marriage requires state sanction, in the license and the ceremony. Even in a religious solemnization the assembled guests know to expect the officiating cleric's words, "By the authority vested in me by the state of . . . I now pronounce you husband and wife."

In the marriage ceremony the public recognizes and supports the couple's reciprocal bond, and guarantees that this commitment (made in accord with the public's requirements) will be honored as something valuable not only to the pair but to the community at large. Their bond will be honored even by public force. This is what the public vows, when the couple take their own vows before public witnesses. The public sees itself and its own interest reflected in the couple's action.[2]

In the form of the law and state enforcement, the public sets the terms of marriage, says who can and cannot marry, who can officiate, what obligations and rights the agreement involves, whether it can be ended and if so, why and how. Marriage prescribes duties and dispenses privileges. The governmental apparatus in the United States has packed into marriage many benefits and obligations, spanning from immigration and citizenship to military service, tax policy, and property rules. Husbands and wives are required to care for and support each other and their children. Social Security and veterans' survivors' benefits, intestate succession rights and jail visitation privileges go to legally married spouses. Even though state governments, not federal authorities, have the power to regulate marriage and divorce, a 1996 report from the U.S. General Accounting Office found more than *one thousand* places in the corpus of federal law where legal marriage conferred a distinctive status, right, or benefit.[3]

From the founding of the United States to the present day, assumptions about the importance of marriage and its appropriate form have been deeply implanted in public policy, sprouting repeatedly as the nation took over the continent and established terms for the inclusions and exclusion of new citizens. Political authorities expected monogamy on a Christian model to prevail—and it did, not only because of widespread Christian faith and foregoing social practice, but also because of positive and punitive laws and government policy choices. Political and legal authorities endorsed and aimed to perpetuate nationally a *particular* marriage model: lifelong, faithful monogamy, formed by the mutual consent of a man and a woman, bearing the impress of the Christian religion and the English common law in its expectations for the husband to be the family head and economic provider, his wife the dependent partner. Because mutual consent was intrinsic to it, this form of marriage was especially congruent with American political ideals: consent of the parties was also the hallmark of representative government. Consent was basic to both marriage and government, the question of its authenticity not meant to be reopened nor its depth plumbed once consent was given.

Public preservation of marriage on this model has had tremendous consequences for men's and women's citizenship as well as for their private lives. Men and women take up the public roles of husbands and wives along with the private joys and duties. These roles have been powerful, historically, in shaping both male and female citizens' entitlements and obligations. Molding individuals' self-understanding, opportunities, and constraints, marriage uniquely and powerfully influences the way differences between the sexes are conveyed and symbolized. So far as it is a public institution, it is the vehicle through which the apparatus of state can shape the gender order.

The whole system of attribution and meaning that we call *gender* relies on and to a great extent derives from the structuring provided by marriage. Turning men and women into husbands and wives, marriage has designated the ways both sexes act in the world and the reciprocal relation between them. It has done so probably more emphatically than any other single institution or social force. The unmarried as well as the married bear the ideological, ethical, and practical impress of the marital institution, which is difficult or impossible to escape. Karl Llewellyn, a legal theorist of the mid-twentieth century, was referring to marriage when he observed, "The curious feature of institutions is that to society at large they are a static factor, whereas to the individual they are in first instance dynamic. Society they hold steady: they are the received pattern of its organization and its functioning. The individual . . . is moulded dynamically by and into them." Llewellyn emphasized that the institution of marriage was "a device for *creating* marital going concerns."[4]

Whether or not marriage is as natural as is often claimed, entry to the institution is bound up with civil rights. Marriage is allowed or disallowed by legislators' and judges' decisions. The separate states from Maine to California, which have the power to regulate marital institutions as part of their authority over the local health, safety, and welfare, determine who gains admittance. Consequently, marriage has also been instrumental in articulating and structuring distinctions grouped under the name of "race." In slaveholding states before the Civil War, slaves had no access to legal marriage, just as they had no other civil right; this deprivation was one of the things that made them "racially" different. Long after the era of slavery, a white person and an African American did not have the civil right to marry each other in the majority of states (not only in southern states). A white and an Asian wishing to marry in many western states found themselves similarly tabooed. Marriage law thus constructed racial difference and punished (or in some instances, more simply refused to legitimize) "race mixture." Sixteen states still considered marriage across the color line void or criminal as recently as 1967, when the U.S. Supreme Court overruled them.[5] It is striking, too, as the history in the following chapters will unfold, that the marital nonconformists most hounded or punished by the federal government were deemed "racially" different from the white majority. They were Indians, freed slaves, polygamous Mormons (metaphorically nonwhite), and Asians. Prohibiting divergent marriages has been as important in public policy as sustaining the chosen model.

By incriminating some marriages and encouraging others, marital regulations have drawn lines among the citizenry and defined what kinds of sexual relations and which families will be legitimate. On the contemporary scene, same-sex couples have made their exclusion conspicuous. By contesting their deprivation, they have thrown a spotlight on marriage as a matter of civil rights and public sanction. Excluded or policed groups such as same-sex couples (or, in the past, slaves, or Asians who believed "proxy" marriages valid, or native Americans who had non-Christian traditions) have readily understood that they, as minorities, may have to struggle for equal status on the terrain of marital regulation. The majority, meanwhile, can parade the field, taking public affirmation for granted. Aspiring minority groups (ex-slaves during Reconstruction are a good example) have often tried to improve their social and civil leverage with conventional marriage behavior, recognizing that the majority has an investment in the sanctity of marital roles, whoever holds them.[6]

No modern nation-state can ignore marriage forms, because of their direct impact on reproducing and composing the population. The laws of marriage must play a large part in forming "the people." They sculpt the body politic. In a hybrid nation such as the United States, formed of immigrant groups, marriage becomes all the more important politically. Where citizenship comes along with being born on the nation's soil as it does here, marriage policy underlies national belonging and the cohesion of the whole. Therefore the federal government has incorporated particular expectations for marriage in many initiatives, and especially in citizenship policies, even though there is no federal power to regulate marriage directly (except in federal territories). At least three levels of public authority shape the institution of marriage. The immediate community of kin, friends, and neighbors exercises the approval or disapproval a couple feels most intensely; state legislators and judges set the terms of marriage and divorce; and federal laws, policies, and values attach influential incentives and disincentives to marriage forms and practices.[7] The United States has shown through its national history a commitment to exclusive and faithful monogamy, preferably intraracial. In the name of the public interest and public order, it has furthered this model as a unifying moral standard.

Secular rather than religious authorization of marriage has been a consistent tradition in the United States. This was not inevitable, but rather a latter-day outcome of a specific history of church-state conflict in Christian Europe. Following upon the birth of Christianity, the Catholic Church had to endeavor for far more than a millennium to put the norm of faithful, lifelong monogamy in place and to bring its adherents' marital behavior under ecclesiastical administration; then European monarchs succeeded for the most part in wresting this regulatory control from the Church.[8] Kings of would-be nations in England and Europe sparred with the Church for three centuries for control over marriage because they saw this power as decisive for the social order. Typically, founders of new political societies in the Western tradition have inaugurated their regimes with marriage regulations, to foster households conducive to their aims and to symbolize a new era—whether in colonial Virginia, revolutionary France, the breakaway republic of Texas, or the unprecedented Bolshevik system in the Soviet Union.[9] Modern sovereigns generally want to prescribe marriage rules to stabilize the essential activities of sex and labor and their consequences, children and property.

Because the United States established no national church, but said it would separate church and state and observe religious tolerance, state control flourished. The author of the preeminent nineteenth-century legal treatise on marriage and divorce showed his commitment to state authorization by calling marriage a "civil status"; he dismissed as "too absurd to require a word of refutation . . . the idea that any government could, consistently with the general well-being, permit this institution to become merely a thing of bargain between men and women, and not regulate it." The Christian religious background of marriage was unquestionably present and prominent. It was adopted in and filtered through legislation.[10] For Americans who envisioned marriage as a religious ceremony and commitment, the institution was no less politically formed and freighted; yet they were unlikely to object to secular oversight when both the national and the state governments aligned marriage policies with Christian tenets. Echoing and reinforcing the religious dictates of "Christian civilization" in the United States, public rules on marriage have had an especially large potential to influence citizens' views. At the same time, civic decision-making has remained paramount. State legislators altering the terms of marriage have often found cover in divine mandate or the law of nature—when nullifying marriages that crossed the color line, or creating unequal statuses for husbands and wives, for example—yet they have not hesitated to exercise their own jurisdiction.

Not only Christian doctrine but also the ancient common law of England deeply inflected the legal features of marriage in the United States. "Domestic relations" in the common law included the relative privileges and duties of husbands and wives, employers and employees, and masters and slaves. Political ordering began in the household and influenced all governance and representation inside the household and out. Marriage itself served as a form of governance. In the longer Western political tradition on which the common law drew, a man's full civil and political status consisted of his being a husband and father and head of a household unit, representing himself and his dependents in the civic world. Wives and children did not represent themselves but looked to the male head of household to represent and support them, in return for which they owed their obedience and service. A man's headship of a family, his taking the responsibility for dependent wife and children, qualified him to be a participating member of a state.[11] The political tradition thus built on monogamous marriage; the two complemented each other.

Under the common law, a woman was absorbed into her husband's legal and economic persona upon marrying, and her husband gained the civic presence she lost. Marriage decisively differentiated the positions of husband and wife. The wife's marital dependency so compromised her ability to act for herself in public that single women, too, being potential wives, were often treated as lacking civic independence. Even though most American states supplanted the common law with their own legal codes by the early 1800s—and the social hierarchies represented in the common law were contested at every subsequent point—central assumptions about marriage, such as the essential unity of the married pair, continued to orient the minds of lawyers and statesmen and to flow into legal decisions and the culture at large. In the 1850s it was not surprising for an essayist to observe: "The husband acquires from the union increased capacity and power. He represents the wife in the political and the civil order." So many generations of statesmen regarded this model of marriage as a foundation of the American way of life that the influence of the common law extended into the mid-twentieth century. As recently as 1996, congressional debate on the Defense of Marriage Act reiterated long-lived official insistence on traditional marriage as a necessary pillar of the nation.[12]

The public face of marriage can be sought in the legal record, which reveals more than the letter of the law. The legal apparatus in the United

States, encompassing elections of legislators and judges, production and interpretation of legislation, methods of enforcement, achievement or failure of consensus about law's justice, and resort to the Constitution, has always strongly colored the political culture and social expectations.[13] Reading the legal record for cultural and social insights need not conflict with awareness that the law represents coercive power: quite the opposite. In shaping an institution like marriage, public authorities work by defining the realm of cognitive possibility for individuals as much as through external policing. Law and society stand in a circular relation: social demands put pressure on legal practices, while at the same time the law's public authority frames what people can envision for themselves and can conceivably demand.[14] Reflecting the majority consensus, legislators, judges, and most other public spokesmen in the history of the United States have shown remarkable concurrence on the basic outline of marriage as a public institution. Judges have reviewed but only very rarely have struck down legislators' enactments. When there has been conflict, the issue has usually been competition between federal and state-level authorities, not the elevated status of lifelong monogamy.

Yet challenges and disruptions have occurred. In recent decades they have proliferated. Marital behavior always varies more than the law predicts. Men and women inhabit their marital roles in their own ways, not always bending fully inside the circle of civil definitions, but bringing new understandings into the categories of "husband" and "wife." Unless the legal order is deeply hypocritical, however, the majority of the people conform more than they resist. By definition, in a representative government the majority do not feel coerced as they follow the marital model instigated by public authority. Dissidents or minority groupings *are* likely to feel the force of the law, while the majority absorb and mirror the force of moral regulation silently exerted by public symbols and governmental routines. The more that marriage is figured as a free and individual choice—as it is today in the United States—the less the majority can see compulsion to be involved at all. Like the sphinx with its riddles, the institution of marriage, shadowing the public landscape with its monumental bulk, confounds as much as it shows.

1

AN ARCHAEOLOGY
OF AMERICAN MONOGAMY

*I*n the beginning of the United States, the founders had a political theory of marriage. So deeply embedded in political assumptions that it was rarely voiced as a theory, it was all the more important. It occupied the place where political theory overlapped with common sense. Rather than being "untutored," or "what the mind cleared of cant spontaneously apprehends," Clifford Geertz has pointed out, common sense is "what the mind filled with presuppositions . . . concludes." Kinship organization, property arrangements, cosmological and spiritual beliefs give rise to common sense, so that it varies from culture to culture.[1] The common sense of British colonials at the time of the American Revolution was Christian; Christian common sense took for granted the rightness of monogamous marriage. Moral and political philosophy (the antecedent of social science) incorporated and purveyed monogamous morality no less than religion did.[2] Learned knowledge deemed monogamy a God-given but also a civilized practice, a natural right that stemmed from a subterranean basis in natural law.

Yet at that time, Christian monogamists composed a minority in the world. The predominance of monogamy was by no means a foregone conclusion. Most of the peoples and cultures around the globe (so recently investigated and colonized by Europeans) held no brief for strict monogamy. The belief systems of Asia, Africa, and Australia, of the Moslems around the Mediterranean, and the natives of North and South

America all countenanced polygamy and other complex marriage practices, which British and European travel writings on exotic lands recounted with fascination. Anglo-America itself was set down in the midst of polygamist and often matrilineal and matrilocal cultures. No doubt Christians in Britain, Europe, and America at the time thought monogamy was a superior system, but it had yet to triumph.

As a result, while no one involved in founding the new nation would have disputed that Christian marriage should underpin the society, political thinkers and moral philosophers at the time were conscious of monogamy as a system to be justified and advocated. European political theorizing had long noted that legal monogamy benefited social order, by harnessing the vagaries of sexual desire and by supplying predictable care and support for the young and the dependent. The republican theory of the new United States assumed this kind of utilitarian reasoning and went beyond it, to give marriage a political reason for being. From the French Enlightenment author the Baron de Montesquieu, whose *Spirit of the Laws* influenced central tenets of American republicanism, the founders learned to think of marriage and the form of government as mirroring each other.[3] They aimed to establish a republic enshrining popular sovereignty, ruled by a government of laws, and characterized by moderation. Their Montesquieuan thinking tied the institution of Christian-modeled monogamy to the kind of polity they envisioned; as a voluntary union based on consent, marriage paralleled the new government. This thinking propelled the analogy between the two forms of consensual union into the republican nation's self-understanding and identity.

Although the details of marital practice varied widely among Revolutionary-era Americans, there was a broadly shared understanding of the essentials of the institution. The most important was the unity of husband and wife. The "sublime and refined ... principle of union" joining the two was the "most important consequence of marriage," according to James Wilson, a preeminent statesman and legal philosopher. The consent of both was also essential. "The agreement of the parties, the essence of every rational contract, is indispensably required," Wilson said in lectures delivered in 1792. He saw mutual consent as the hallmark of marriage—more basic than cohabitation. Everyone spoke of the marriage *contract*. Yet as a contract it was unique, for the parties did not set their own terms. The man and woman consented to marry, but public authorities set the terms of the marriage, so that it brought predictable rewards and duties. Once the union was formed, its obligations were fixed in common law. Husband and wife each assumed a new legal status as well as a new status in their community. That meant neither could break the terms set without offending the larger community, the law, and the state, as much as offending the partner.[4]

Both the emphasis on consent and the principle of union seamlessly adapted Christian doctrine to Anglo-American law. Even before the Protestant Reformation, the Church had made consent more important than consummation in validating marriage. The legal oneness of husband and wife derived from common law but it matched the Christian doctrine that "the twain shall be one flesh," having exclusive rights to each others' bodies. James Wilson noted this congeniality. Christian doctrine expected heterosexual desire to be satisfied exclusively within marriage and so demanded sexual fidelity of both partners. The Bible also made the husband the "head" of his wife—his wife's superior—as Christ was head of the church. In the spiritual domain of immortality of the soul, however, Christianity equalized wives and husbands; that did not end marital hierarchy, but it required respect for the wife's position. Anywhere on the wide and shifting spectrum of Protestantism in the early republic, from deism to Anglicanism, these basic Christian beliefs about marriage were in place.

As Wilson emphasized, the common law turned the married pair legally into one person—the husband. The husband was enlarged, so to speak, by marriage, while the wife's giving up her own name and being called by his symbolized her relinquishing her identity. This legal doctrine of marital unity was called *coverture* and the wife was called a *feme covert* (both terms rendered in the old French still used in parts of English law). Coverture in its strictest sense meant that a wife could not use legal avenues such as suits or contracts, own assets, or execute legal documents without her husband's collaboration. Nor was she legally responsible for herself in criminal or civil law—he was. And the husband became the political as well as the legal representative of his wife, disenfranchising her. He became the one *full* citizen in the household, his authority over and responsibility for his dependents contributing to his citizenship capacity.

The legal meaning of coverture pervaded the economic realm as well. Upon marriage a woman's assets became her husband's property and so did her labor and future earnings. Because her legal personality was absorbed into his, her economic freedom of action was correspondingly curtailed. This was basic to the economic bargain of marriage, essential to marital unity, and preeminent in daily community life. The husband gained his wife's property and earning power because he was legally responsible to provide for her (as well as for himself and their progeny). The wife in turn was obligated to give all her service and labor to her husband. By consenting to marry, the husband pledged to protect and support his wife, the wife to serve and obey her husband. The body of marriage was understood to rest on this economic skeleton as much as on sexual fidelity.

Because marriage and the state both were understood to be forms of governance—of the husband over the wife, the ruler over the people—in the sixteenth and seventeenth centuries it was easy to think of them analogously. Shakespeare drew on this accepted rhetoric in *The Taming of the Shrew*. Kate, the title character, not only became chastened and reformed by the end of the play, but also advised other recalcitrant wives to obey their husbands:

> Such duty as the subject owes the prince
> Even such a woman oweth her husband,
> And when she is forward, peevish, sullen, sour
> And not obedient to his honest will,
> What is she but a foul contending rebel
> And graceless traitor to her loving lord?[5]

Kate justified wifely obedience by reciting the many benefits and protections a husband was obliged to give to his wife, including laboring to support her. Marriage governed the wife, but it also governed the husband. Like a good prince, a husband had to behave in certain ways to deserve his name and was not an unconstrained wielder of power.

John Winthrop, the leader of the Massachusetts Bay colony, similarly used an analogy between marriage and secular government when he wanted to defend the power of the ruling magistrates over the restive colonial populace in the 1630s. He maintained that in both marriage and government, freedom of choice coexisted with a corollary necessity to obey once the choice was made. "The woman's own choice" in marriage, he said, "makes such a man her husband; yet being so chosen, he is her lord, and she is to be subject to him, yet in a way of liberty, not of bondage." The freemen of the colony had likewise exercised choice in establishing the political order, by electing the magistrates—"it is yourselves who have called us to this office, and being called by you, we have an authority from God," he emphasized. Consequently, the freemen were obliged to bow to the magistrates' authority.[6]

At the time Massachusetts Bay was founded, European monarchs liked to claim that royal power over subjects was authorized by God, as much as the power of fathers and husbands over their families was.[7] Winthrop's emphasis on the freemen's consent showed him to be somewhat more liberal. Like monarchists, however, he saw marital governance and political governance as linked along the same continuum; they occupied the same spectrum and each contributed to the other's stability. The Puritan leaders of Massachusetts Bay so seriously expected family, church, and state authority structures to be interlocking that they made infractions against the Fifth Commandment, "Honor Thy Father and Thy Mother," part of their criminal law. They interpreted the commandment as a directive not only to children but also to wives to respect and obey their husbands, to congregants to respect and obey their ministers, and to subjects to respect and obey their king and magistrates. An unruly wife, congregant, or child threatened *all* lines of authority in church and state; one convicted of disrespect would suffer public punishment, being made to stand in the stocks wearing an identifying sign and reciting the Fifth Commandment.[8]

By the 1760s, however, few Britons in the American colonies believed that monarchs governed by divine right handed down from the first father, Adam. Most of them had come to think that government authority derived from men's consent and intention to preserve their own interests. A revolution in theory and practice had challenged the patriarchal theory of political legitimacy, by radically differentiating the authority of family heads from that of political rulers and denying that the two occupied the same continuum. During the power struggle between king and Parliament leading to Britain's Glorious Revolution of 1688, parliamentary supporters argued that political authority did not come naturally, as parental authority did. Legitimate political authority had to be purposely constructed by individuals' collective consent to be governed, because these individuals had inherent natural rights to defend. In the view of John Locke and other theorists, individuals would give their consent and thus form a governing social contract in order to gain the advantages of social order and collective protection, endowing a ruler with power but also setting limits on it. The people's consent to be governed bound them to obey. If the ruler abused his power and broke the social contract, however, then rebellion among the governed might be reasonable.[9]

This transformation underlay the political theory justifying the American Revolution. When colonial Americans were imagining their way toward independence they nonetheless often interpreted Great Britain's imperial relations with the colonies in terms of familial analogies.[10] Since children typically first confront authority, hierarchy, and reciprocal rights and duties in a family setting, use of a family model to think about justice in the polity has never become entirely irrelevant.[11] Rebellious colonists used both parent-child and husband-wife analogies in their rhetoric—the first in order to make the break with Great Britain, the second more often to model the political society to be. These analogies remained forceful in considerations of political authority despite the way that social contract theory had broken the direct link between patriarchal authority and legitimate government.

Contractual thinking about authority was so appealing, in fact, that it became knit into views of the ideal family. In an era when the natural rights of individuals were being heralded, even parental and husbandly authority seemed to require justification other than nature or custom. The eighteenth-century Scottish moral philosophers favored by colonial revolutionaries contended that reciprocal rights and responsibilities bound husbands and wives, parents and children, magistrates and subjects, masters and servants, *all,* just as they did the ruler and the citizens.[12] Thus the child should obey the parent because the parent guarded and supported the child, not simply because generational hierarchy was in place. In corollary, the parent who was abusive or negligent might not deserve obedience.

Belief in a father's natural dominion had once justified kingly absolutism, but American revolutionaries used the analogy between familial and governmental authority to reinforce ideals of contractualism and reciprocity as requirements for justice. When they protested against imperial harshness in the 1760s, American spokesmen portrayed the colonies as the abused offspring of a cruel and unfeeling imperial parent, who left the child no alternative but to disobey. John Adams, the Massachusetts revolutionary who would become the second president of the United States, wrote, "We have been told that . . . Britain is the mother and we are the children, that a filial duty and submission is due from us to her and that we ought to doubt our own judgment and presume that she is right, even when she seems to us to shake the foundations of government. But admitting we are children, have not children a right to complain when their parents are attempting to break their limbs, to administer poison, or to sell them to enemies for slaves?" Revolutionaries justified colonial independence with a family analogy of generational change, contending that Britain "took us as babes at the breast; they nourished us . . . [but now] the day of independent manhood is at hand." "A parent has a natural right to govern his children during their minority," another emphasized, "but has no such authority over them as they arrive at full age."[13]

When the colonies declared independence and joined together in a new nation, a marital metaphor became far more compelling than the parent-child reference so serviceable to interpret empire and colony. The method of the new nation was union and the essence of the national union was to be the voluntary adherence of its citizens. Allegiance was to be contractual, not coerced—to be motivated by love, not fear. Yet this chosen bond could not be a passing fancy of the moment. Individuals' loyalty and the states' allegiance to one another had to last if the new nation was to succeed. "Only in union is there happiness," the Revolutionary minister Jonathan Mayhew declared. Marriage, being a voluntary and long-sustained bond, provided a ready emblem. Understood to be founded on consent, marriage could be seen as an analogue to the legitimate polity.[14] And marital status permeated personal identity and civic role as national allegiance was intended to.

As an intentional and harmonious juncture of individuals for mutual protection, economic advantage, and common interest, the marriage bond resembled the social contract that produced government. As a freely chosen structure of authority and obligation, it was an irresistible model. The suitability of the marital metaphor for political union drew tremendous public attention to marriage itself in the Revolutionary era. Newspapers, essays, pamphlets, novels, stories, and poetry—including Thomas Paine's journalistic writings just at the time he wrote the incendiary pamphlet *Common Sense*—abounded with discussions of marriage choices and roles. This continued after independence. Essays and doggerel with titles such as "Thoughts on Matrimony," "On the Choice of a Wife," "Character of a Good Husband," "Praise of Marriage," "Reflections on Marriage Unions," "Matrimonial Felicity," "Conjugal Love," and "On the Pleasures Arising from a Union between the Sexes" defined marital companionship, advised on choice of mate, prescribed how to achieve fairness and balance between the partners. Many fictions centered on the consequences of husband and wife being well matched or mismatched.

In this flood of authorship, marriage appeared ideally as a symmetrical union. Marital relations were reenvisioned in terms of reciprocal rights and responsibilities rather than formal hierarchy. Not protection and obedience, not headship and subordination, but rather the "mutual return of *conjugal love*," "the ties of reciprocal sincerity" between husband and wife, defined a happy marriage. The ideal marriage was "the highest instance of human friendship," wrote the Presbyterian cleric and president of the College of New Jersey, John Witherspoon, shortly before becoming a signer of the Declaration of Independence. Therefore the couple should be equally suited in "education, tastes, and habits of life." Reason, virtue, and moderation were the keys in choosing a partner—not fortune, beauty, or momentary passion.[15]

This emphasis suggested some ongoing reevaluation of the hierarchy between husbands and wives in actual marriages but did not indicate that husbandly superiority had wafted away. Use of the analogy between marriage and government in the political atmosphere of 1776 stressed symmetricality between the partners, in order to highlight consent and reciprocality, but interest shifted in the more conservative post-Revolutionary period to the bond formed by the granting of consent. By consenting, the citizens delegated authority to their elected representatives, and the wife gave authority to her husband. In both instances governance based on consent was no less governance. The future lexicographer Noah Webster meant to dampen grass-roots political assertions in the 1780s when he likened a citizen's relation to his representative to a bride's unity with her groom. He implied that the representative was the more knowledgeable and judicious one of the pair, who should make the decisions, as most people assumed the husband was and did. The analogy cut both ways. A 1793 essayist who called himself "a real friend to the fair sex" urged wives to "chearfully [sic] submit to the government of their own chusing [sic]," arguing that "women by entering upon the marriage state, renounce some of their natural rights (as men do, when they enter into civil society) to secure the remainder." A wife gained "a right to be protected by the man of her own choice," just as "men, living under a free constitution of their own framing, are entitled to the protection of the laws," he contended. Like Shakespeare's Kate, he further advised that "if rebellion, insurrection, or any other opposition to a just, mild, and free political government, is odious, it is not less so to oppose good family administration."[16]

More than an analogy was involved in the public reiteration of the "loving partnership" between husband and wife. Actual marriages of the proper sort were presumed to create the kind of citizen needed to make the new republic succeed. It was not only that marriages and the families following from them brought a predictable order to society (although that was never unimportant). There were specifically political reasons imbedded in revolutionaries' thinking about human nature, human relations, and the possibilities for just government that put demands upon marriage. American revolutionaries' concern with virtue as the spring of their new government motivated this attention to marriage. The United States was a political experiment, an attempt to establish a republic based on popular sovereignty in a large and diverse nation. The character of the citizens mattered far more there than in a monarchy, Revolutionary leaders believed. In this they drew on Montesquieu's *Spirit of the Laws*, which categorized all governments as republics, monarchies, or despotisms, each with a distinctive source of sovereignty and a characteristic principle prompting the people to act conformably. Concern for honor drove monarchy; fear made despotism work.[17] In a republic, the people were sovereign, and the motivating principle was political virtue. The government would depend on the people's virtue for its success.

"Virtue," the political catchword of the Revolution, meant not only moral integrity but public-spiritedness.[18] Selfish, small-minded individuals narrowly seeking their own advancement would not do: citizens in a republic had to recognize civic obligation, to see the social good of the polity among their own responsibilities. How would the nation make sure that republican citizens would appear and be suitably virtuous? Marriage supplied an important part of the answer, at the same time that it offered a model of consensual juncture, voluntary allegiance, and mutual benefit. To complement (and mitigate) the individualistic foundation of social contract thinking, the revolutionaries turned to Montesquieu and subsequent moral philosophers who believed that human beings had to define themselves in relation to others and to seek companionship.[19] The conviction that the most reasonable and humane qualities of mankind arose in sociability rather than in isolation set the stage for American republicans to see marriage as a training ground of citizenly virtue.

Not everyone had to read political or moral philosophy for these themes to pervade late eighteenth-century Americans' political attitudes.

An essay called "Conjugal Love" in the *Massachusetts Magazine* of 1792 typically affirmed, "Reason and society are the characteristics which distinguish us from the other animals" and "these two privileges of man . . . enter into wedlock." Marriage played a salutary part because it served as a "school of affection" where citizens would learn to care about others. A 1791 paean to matrimony praised love for enabling man to "live in another," subduing selfishness and egotism: "In detaching us from self, it accustoms us to attach ourselves the more to others . . . Love cannot harden hearts, nor extinguish social virtues. The lover becomes a husband, a parent, a citizen." John Witherspoon urged marriage upon reluctant men in part because it stimulated a sociable attitude, whereas "continuing single to the end of life narrows the mind and closes the heart," he said. Witherspoon took for granted "the absolute necessity of marriage for the service of the state, and the solid advantages that arise from it." To Revolutionary-era readers, it followed that when "the tender feelings and soft passions of the soul are awakened with all the ardour of love and benevolence" by marriage, "man feels a growing attachment to human nature, and love to his country."[20]

Eighteenth-century assumptions about differences between the sexes made marriage the best site for nourishing these social virtues (rather than friendship between men, for instance). Male citizens had natural superiority in reason and judgment, it was assumed, but the social virtues lay in the "heart" or "affections," where women were presumed to excel.[21] Intimate interaction between the sexes in courtship and marriage would serve especially well to cultivate and exercise these qualities in men. Enlightenment political and moral philosophers and republican statesmen never neglected the presence of women—even though their main attention focused on male citizens—and their understanding of "manners" explained why. At that time, the word "manners" referred not simply to deportment but to habits and values, including morality, bearing, and character, which were conveyed by patterns of behavior and expression. Manners were understood to be learned behavior, although slow and difficult to change in adulthood. Because individuals inevitably and even unwittingly displayed their manners in social interactions, opportunities lay all around for moral education by exposure to good company. The presence of refined women promised benefit to male citizens. "The gentle and insinuating *manners* of the female sex tend to soften the roughness of the other sex," Henry Home, Lord Kames, noted in his *Six Sketches on the History of Man,* published in Philadelphia in 1776. Because women were assumed to be more pliable and impressionable than men by nature, they were also assumed to acquire polished manners more easily.[22]

In their campaign for virtue, Revolutionary-era Americans adopted this perspective. "Dissipation and corruption of manners in the body of the people" was as much a danger to "the liberties and freedom of our country" as was power-grabbing by rulers, warned a Fourth of July orator in 1790. He was sure that "in a republic, manners are of equal importance with laws"; and while men made the laws, "the women, in every free country, have an absolute control of manners."[23] John Adams showed himself enmeshed in this kind of thinking when, in France on a wartime diplomatic mission in 1778, he visited the residence of Madame de Pompadour. She had been mistress to the French king Louis XV. Imagining the covert machinations of the king at her residence, Adams reflected,

> The Manners of Women, are the surest Criterion by which to determine whether a Republican Government is practicable in a Nation or not. The Jews, the Greeks, the Romans, the Swiss, the Dutch, all lost their public Spirit, their Republican Principles and habits, and their Republican Forms of Government, when they lost the Modesty and Domestic Virtues of their Women. What havock *[sic]* said I to myself, would these manners make in America? Our Governors, our Judges, our Senators, or Representatives and even our Ministers would be appointed by Harlots for Money, and their Judgments, Decrees and decisions be sold to repay themselves, or perhaps to procure the smiles *(and Embraces)* of profligate Females.

If the company of good women could refine and polish, so could bad company degrade and corrupt the republican citizen. Adams's reasoning that "the manners of Women were the most infallible Barometer, to ascertain the degree of Morality and Virtue in a Nation" led him into a brief for monogamous fidelity. He recorded his conviction that "the foundations of national Morality must be laid in private Families. In vain are Schools, Accademics [sic] and universities instituted, if loose Principles and licentious habits are impressed upon Children in their earliest years . . . How is it possible that Children can have any just Sense of the sacred Obligations of Morality or Religion if, from their earliest Infancy, they learn that their Mothers live in habitual Infidelity to their fathers, and their fathers in as constant Infidelity to their Mothers."[24]

On this point, that republican success relied on faithfulness to monogamy, Adams was exceptionally articulate, but his convictions were not extraordinary. For him as for other Revolutionary-era leaders, marriage had several levels of political relevance, as the prime metaphor for consensual union and voluntary allegiance, as the necessary school of affection, and as the foundation of national morality. Revolutionary-era discussions of appropriate marriage partners and the usefulness of marriage in the republican social order assumed that household conduct was linked to political government. On this point American revolutionaries and constitutionalists were following Montesquieu, as they did also in their convictions about checks and balances, the rule of law, and moderation in government. Montesquieu's *Spirit of the Laws* had declared that the source of sovereignty in any government operated in reciprocal equilibrium with the people's motivation. Therefore, the "general spirit, the mores, and the manners" of a society, including household arrangements and relations between the sexes, materially affected political values. "Domestic government" and "political government" were "closely linked together."[25]

Montesquieu had first drawn the relation between domestic government and the political order in a cautionary satire, his epistolary novel *Persian Letters* (1728).[26] The novel took the form of letters written between two Persian travelers in France, Usbek and Rica, and the eunuchs and wives whom Usbek had left in his seraglio, or harem, at home. With Usbek gone, the harem (ruled by his delegated subordinates) became riven with jealousies and intrigues so intense as to cause the tragic suicide of his favorite wife. Motivated by fear and maintained by coercion, the harem embodied the spirit of despotism. The Persians' letters home also satirized the excesses and pitfalls of French honor, the motivating force for monarchy. Their commentary implied that a government of laws, characterized by political moderation and liberal treatment of women, would solve these problems.

Although Montesquieu's target was not non-Western cultures but despotic aspects of the French government (and the Catholic Church), his work initiated what became a formulaic Enlightenment association of polygamy with despotism. The harem stood for tyrannical rule, political corruption, coercion, elevation of the passions over reason, selfishness, hypocrisy—all the evils that virtuous republicans and enlightened thinkers wanted to avoid. Monogamy, in contrast, stood for a government of consent, moderation, and political liberty. Thus an American post-Revolutionary essay lauding the benefits of monogamous love contrasted the ways of the harem: "Behold in the seraglios human nature at the lowest point of abasement. Wretches there, maimed in body and in mind, know only to be cruel. They thirst for the misery of another to allay their own . . . To crush a feeling heart under the despotism which has proved fatal to themselves, is their only joy."[27]

From the perspective of the American republic, stock contrasts between monogamy and polygamy not only illustrated the superiority of Christian morality over the "heathen" Orient and reassured Christian monogamists in their minority position worldwide, but also staked a political claim. The philosophers and ethicists favored by leading men of the early United States endorsed monogamy outright and found both moral and political reasons to support it. For example, *The Principles of Moral and Political Philosophy* (1785) by William Paley, which became the most widely read college text on the subject in the first half of the nineteenth century, touted the private happiness and social benefits of monogamous marriage. An Anglican bishop and Enlightenment utilitarian at the same time, Paley was admired by the American political and literary elite. His defense of monogamy did not rest with divine law alone;

he examined arguments for and against such alternatives as fornication and cohabitation and found social reasons for believing formal marriage far superior. In comparison to monogamy, he contended, polygamy did "not offer a single advantage" but rather produced the evils of political intrigue, jealousy, and distrust, as well as "voluptuousness," abasement of women, and neglect of children. Paley's and similar prescriptive pronouncements about marriage and the public order, expounded by the jurist James Wilson in the 1790s and adopted by such important antebellum writers of legal treatises as Chancellor James Kent of New York and U.S. Supreme Court Justice Joseph Story, shaped the thinking of the bar and permeated American legal and political traditions.[28]

The thematic equivalency between polygamy, despotism, and coercion on the one side and between monogamy, political liberty, and consent on the other resonated through the political culture of the United States all during the subsequent century. Buttressing the social and religious reasons for Americans to believe in and practice monogamy, this political component also inhabited their convictions, all the more powerful for seeming self-evident. A commitment to monogamous marriage on a Christian model lodged deep in American political theory, as vivid as belief in popular sovereignty or in voluntary consent of the governed or in the necessity of a government of laws. This commitment would emerge when national circumstances demanded—and even when they did not.

2

PERFECTING COMMUNITY RULES
WITH STATE LAWS

*W*hile the political theory of the new nation depended on monogamy, the state legislatures actually set up the rules of marrying. And in front of these two levels of formal ordination of marriage in the United States stood a third, informal one. The most effective disciplining as well as honoring of marriage through the early nineteenth century (and even later, in the less populated areas) took place in the local community. Public direction of marriage took place simultaneously on all three levels, although an individual or couple might consciously apprehend only a fraction of it.

The most diffuse, least recognized of the three was the national authority exerted over marriage. Lacking specific regulatory power, the federal government had few visible avenues along which to implement its fundamental commitment to monogamy. It had little bureaucracy and few powers directly touching the population. A "midget institution in a giant land," in one historian's words, the federal government generally busied itself domestically with distribution—of land, offices, charters—rather than regulation. Besides establishing the national currency and tariffs, the federal government ran the post office. Between the 1810s and the 1840s, postal employees composed about three quarters of the federal work force.[1] The important federal tasks lay in foreign relations—conquering the continent, subduing native Americans, negotiating with

European colonial powers, and adding new states amidst the complexities of balancing slaveholding and free labor.

Even without regulatory power, however, the federal government could exert an impact on marriage through some policy pronouncements. Indian policy was one. The native Americans living on the continent had their own forms of political authority, sovereignty, and marriage practice. In the government's intentions to accustom native Americans to the sovereignty of the United States, or else remove them from the continent, marriage patterns could not be forgotten. For if monogamy founded the social and political order, then groups practicing other marital systems on American soil might threaten the polity's soundness. Native Americans did not share Christians' common sense about marriage. Most groups—notably the Iroquois, who dominated the eastern part of North America—did not make the nuclear family so fundamental an economic and psychological unit as Protestants did, nor did they generally recognize private property as such. Heterosexual couples were important, but they married within complex kinship systems that accepted premarital sex, expected wives to be economic actors, often embraced matrilocal residence and matrilineal descent, and easily allowed both polygamy and divorce with remarriage. Native American men generally hunted and the women were the agriculturalists, making their sexual division of labor dramatically different from what white Americans expected and associated with gender propriety—men working the fields and women caring for the house.

To Christian settlers, missionaries, and government officials, Indian practices amounted to promiscuity. Since first contact, they had derided Indian men for laziness and lack of manliness because they went out hunting and did not exert authority over wives and children, as heads of households, and did not own property or cultivate land.[2] To government officials, the native American marriage system represented an unintelligible foreignness. One wrote to the Office of Indian Affairs, "some of the Indians have several wives, who sometimes live in different towns, and at considerable distance from each other, they are allowed by the Indian to own property not subject to their husbands." He also mentioned the "facility with which they can at any time dissolve their marriage contracts." Similarly, a southern judge expressed wonder (or envy) that "under the laws and customs of the Creek tribe, a man was allowed to take a wife, and abandon her at pleasure, and that this worked an absolute dissolution of the marriage state." Another thought that "marriage among the Indian tribes must generally be considered as taking place in a state of nature."[3]

American officials sought to reform these baffling practices. If natives were to be regarded as trustworthy in negotiations over land and trade, their behaviors could not fly in the face of American morality. Prohibiting polygamy, valuing premarital chastity, reorienting the sexual division of labor and property-ownership and consequent inheritance patterns—all these behaviors hung on the institution of marriage. The federal government consistently encouraged or forced Indians to adopt Christian-model monogamy as the *sine qua non* of civilization and morality. The government's aims dovetailed with those of evangelical Protestant missionaries early in the nineteenth century, and the two groups often collaborated.[4] The Protestant religious revivals after 1800 reinvigorated earlier Quaker efforts to turn Indian families into male-headed nuclear households, farming rather than hunting. At this time, Anglo-American Protestants were sending missionaries around the globe, focusing attention on the contrast between "heathen" and Christian forms of marriage. Missionary discourse touted the benefits of lifelong monogamy and spousal obligation in Christian legal marriage and decried the personal indulgence, the lack of manhood, and the sexual degradation of women in the "heathen" model.[5]

Both political and religious officials assumed that native Americans' assimilation had to be founded on monogamous marriage, from which would follow the conventional sexual division of labor, property, and inheritance. Both envisioned that Indians could be educated to embrace Christian values. Indians were not seen as so different from white Americans that they could not *become* civilized. The government's selection of a Protestant minister, the Reverend Jedidiah Morse, to head a investigation among many different native American groups in 1820 exemplified the convergence of political and religious aims. Having been directed to learn what he could to maximize trading opportunities, and not to overlook information on the natives' "moral condition," Morse concluded his trip optimistic that "the marriage institution, in its purity," would serve as a vehicle of civilization among the natives. Their practice of polygamy would fade away if simply "discountenanced," because "this practice ever yields and vanishes before the light of civilization and christianity." Morse advocated intermarriage between white men and Indian women (once the women had some Christian education) to produce new generations who would merge with the American people. The federal Office of Indian Affairs leaned toward the same approach in dealing with Cherokees and Creeks in the old southwest. Like Morse, when government officials at this time mentioned intermarriage, they envisioned it as a prerogative of white men, and said nothing about Indian men marrying white women.[6]

Official views on the desirability of Indian-white marriage gave way to greater racial differentiation and distaste later in the nineteenth century, but the trajectory was not consistent. Federal policy continued to recognize marriage to a white American as evidence of an Indian's joining "civilized life." Because government purpose linked male headship of a family with property-holding and citizenship—a triumvirate built on monogamous marriage and its usual (European/English-derived) gender expectations—marriage was always relevant to land grants and citizenship. As the nation conquered the continent, the removal of Indians from their traditional location by violence or by treaty was usually accompanied by the government's offer of individual property and U.S. citizenship to heads of household who were willing to forgo tribal affiliations. It was always "heads of households"—not necessarily male, but *expected* to be male—who were offered this incentive.[7]

The federal government could pronounce what native Americans should do, and offer incentives and punishments, but state legislatures regulated access to legal marriage. States had the formal power to say who could marry whom and how, what marriages (if any) were invalid, what composed marital obligations, how a marriage could be terminated, and what were its consequences for divorced or widowed partners. To enforce boundaries understood as religious and also, increasingly, "racial," at least a dozen states at some time in their histories declared that marriages between Indians and whites would be null and void.[8] In those states such unions could only be informal. Most states required the issuance of a marriage license, a form of public oversight, before a marriage could take place; and they authorized only certain officials—though a rather broad group—to perform marriage ceremonies legally.

The state-level apparatus of formal control included the enforcement of laws by municipal and state officials and the decisions made in state courts as juries and judges resolved legal disputes.[9] In general, the states had little wish to burden marriage. Rather, in line with national ideals, state legislators wished to further monogamous relationships and the building of households around them. At the outset, state laws set a few, known boundaries—solemnization took a certain form; marriages could not be bigamous or incestuous or terminated at will; adultery and fornication were crimes. As time went on, state legislatures kept interposing the reality of their authority over marriage with new legislation. The most striking new laws before the Civil War expanded the grounds for divorce and compromised coverture.

The motivations for these laws arose from citizens and their local communities, yet the passage of any new law also demonstrated some assertion of the state itself as a self-conscious entity. The federal principles of the United States allowed each state to make its own rules on marriage and divorce, while the constitutional doctrine of comity meant the states had to respect one another's laws on marriage—a necessity where individuals crossed state lines so easily. No state operated in isolation. Differ as they might, they composed a recognizably national system. There was incentive for them to do so, because, as travel writers all reported, prevailing marriage patterns were seen as evidence of national character. Legislators paid attention to other states' actions on marriage and divorce; judges on state supreme courts looked to their brethren on the bench in other states, and cited their opinions as well as the U.S. Supreme Court when making decisions. Where states did disagree (for instance, on grounds for divorce, and hence recognition of an out-of-state divorce as valid), sharp contentions might arise, and intolerable ambiguity for individuals, since marital status fundamentally conditioned an individual's civic persona.

In the early United States, however, where the population spread out thinly under little state surveillance, the state apparatus was not likely to enter the life of a couple unless they were reported to authorities by neighbors. The "informal public" made up of family, kin, and neighbors exercised practical control of marriage formation, preservation, and termination. The local community had far more access to the circumstances of ongoing households and relationships than law enforcement officers—and even the largest cities did not have police forces before the mid-nineteenth century. State law set a framework that guided and influenced local communities, but because of its proximity, the community's ability to approve or chastise its members came first. It could easily be felt as more important than any law—more affirming when it echoed an individual's or couple's desire and more coercive when it did not. A community's shared belief in the morality and utility of its marriage practices forms part of its sense that it *is* a community. The informal public exercised the forces of approval or condemnation that shaped prospective and married couples' behavior.

Communities could be generous—thus marriages between Indians and whites and between their mixed progeny went on informally even where they were prohibited by law, at the sufferance of local communities.[10] Or they could be harsh. Daniel Carroll and Laura Smoak were one couple who found this out at first hand as a result of their illicit affair. He was a married man with children, she an unmarried women—both white—in a tiny town in South Carolina in the 1870s. The neighbors so disapproved of the lovers' continuing relationship that they called a public meeting to discuss it. There, forty-one of them signed a resolution warning Carroll to get out of town or else be indicted for breaking the state law against "habitual" sexual intercourse outside of marriage. Carroll took this warning as an opening to negotiate. He promised his neighbors that he would end his folly, if he could only stay, and continue to "protect his family" and try to see his lover's reputation restored. He even put his promise in writing for them—but his will power must have been weak, because he broke his promise. His neighbors then fulfilled theirs, making sure that the couple was indicted for "unlawful carnal intercourse." The local prosecutor bothered only with Carroll, not with the single woman. Carroll was the responsible party and had directly insulted the informal public's view of the sanctity of marriage, which was also the *official* view. A jury convicted Carroll and sentenced him to six months' imprisonment and a two hundred dollar fine. When he appealed the judgment, the Supreme Court of South Carolina upheld it, although his attorney had brought procedural objections that might have made his case had the court been so inclined. But it was not.[11]

In practice, state courts and local norms rarely diverged much on basics, because of the widespread shared common sense about marriage among the Christian population. Local practice throughout early American history displayed not so much conflict with state law as variation upon it. Localities tended to be pragmatic in their enforcement of marriage expectations. For the individual in a like-minded community, this kind of enforcement felt like freedom. State legislative codes could not be so flexible as neighbors or kin. Judges' opinions, on the other hand, were by their very nature interpretations; and "judge-made" case law, which predominated in the legal shaping of marriage, often followed the pragmatic direction of communities.[12]

State law could trump a local community's preferences, but the "informal public" exercised its marital jurisdiction over much of the underpopulated American landscape. That produced a varied scene of marital coupling, resembling native American practices more than missionaries and government agents would have cared to admit. White and nominally Christian Americans engaged in informal marriages, self-divorces, premarital unchastities, and bigamy, without suffering much for their sins despite the existence of prohibitory laws. Informal marriage, in which couples lived together as husband and wife without the requisite official license and ceremony—"self-marriage" or "common-law" marriage as it came to be called—was the most frequent irregularity. Despite stipulation of appropriate marriage ceremonies, informal marriage was common and validated among white settlers from the colonial period on. The dispersed patterns of settlement and the insufficiency of officials who could solemnize vows meant that couples with community approval simply married themselves. Acceptance of this practice testified to the widespread belief that the parties' consent to marry each other, not the words said by a minister or magistrate, mattered most. Neighbors' awareness of the couple's cohabitation and reciprocal economic contributions figured a great deal in establishing that a marriage existed between a man and woman, but consent was the first essential.[13]

In the northern colonies, by the eighteenth century it had become easy to find an appropriate secular or clerical official to conduct a ceremonial marriage. Informal marriage did not disappear in the north, but was more common in the Anglican southern colonies, where wedding ceremonies were supposed to be performed by a minister but the Church of England supplied few clerics. Proper ceremonies did not become at all frequent until after 1750. In longer-settled and more populous areas, festive weddings at home became an emblem of rank and wealth by the Revolutionary era, while common folks still married by making reciprocal promises (sometimes posting public notices called banns beforehand, indicating that a marriage was to take place so possible objections could be raised) and proceeding to live together.[14]

Informal practices continued as white immigrants fanned out to the south and west. Marriage frequently followed upon a sexual relationship between and man and a woman proving fruitful, rather than preceding it: pregnancy or childbirth was the signal for a couple to consider themselves married. A chaplain whom Colonel William Byrd brought on an 1728 expedition to survey the border between North Carolina and Virginia was called on to marry no one while he was asked to christen more than a hundred children. Byrd concluded that "marriage is reckon'd a lay contract in Carolina."[15] The great eighteenth-century lord of Carrollton in Maryland and his cousin Elizabeth Brooke cohabited for twenty years beyond their first child's birth before marrying. An Anglican minister in Montgomery County, Maryland, averred, "if . . . no marriage should be deemed valid that had not been registered in the Parish Book, it would I am persuaded bastardize nine tenths of the People in the Country."[16] The first time the itinerant Anglican minister Charles Woodmason married a couple in the Carolina backcountry, in the 1780s, he noted, "Woman very bigg [with child]." Subsequently he realized that this was a general state of affairs. As he saw it, "thro' want of Ministers to marry and thro' the licentiousness of the People, many hundreds live in Concubinage— swopping their Wives as Cattel, and living in a State of Nature, more irregularly and unchastely than the Indians." Many times he found himself baptizing "numbers of Bastard Children."[17]

Well into the nineteenth century, the practice of informal marriage persisted in the south, especially among poorer and backcountry whites. Although North Carolina law did not recognize informal marriage, the state's Supreme Court found itself having to declare as a general rule in 1827 and again in 1859 that "reputation and cohabitation" or "reputation, cohabitation and the declaration and conduct of the parties" would serve in court as adequate evidence of a marriage, unless the suit concerned adultery or bigamy.[18] Southern states—Virginia initially—led the way among the United States in revising common-law standards to enable children to be legitimated by their parents' subsequent marriage. Virginia also was first to change the judicial norm in the United States to allow a child born outside wedlock to inherit from his or her mother; most other states followed suit by the mid-nineteenth century. State and local governments providing poor relief had an interest in seeing that all children were supported by parents (wed or not) rather than becoming dependent on public largesse. Because the states intended to discourage irregular sexual relations, however, the status of the child born outside legal marriage was not fully equalized.[19]

One might imagine that white southerners would be eager to observe the legal niceties of matrimony, to distinguish themselves from slaves and maintain racial caste. African American slaves could *not* marry legally; their unions received no protection from state authorities. Any master could override a slave's marital commitment.[20] The slaveholding elite of the antebellum decades did make elaborate weddings into occasions to display wealth, reaffirm social networks, and mark the consolidation of properties; for women of their class, premarital chastity was a must. Nonelite white southerners, on the other hand, especially in more remote areas, continued to marry informally rather as slaves did, although they did so of their own accord and their reputable unions, unlike slave marriages, would be recognized in court.[21]

The denial of legal marriage to slaves quintessentially expressed their lack of civil rights. To marry meant to consent, and slaves could not exercise the fundamental capacity to consent. To be able to marry one had to be free enough to take on obligations, for consent in marriage meant acceptance of the responsibilities that came along with public definition and public honoring of the institution. This was impossible for a slave; his or her obligations as a spouse might be trumped at any time by the master's legal right of command. Slavery and marriage were so incompatible that a master's permission for a slave to be (legally) married was interpretable as manumission.[22]

The northern states that did not end slavery immediately during the American Revolution, but instituted a gradual emancipation, also recognized marriages among the slaves remaining. If the master agreed, a slave's marriage could be solemnized and regarded as valid. This state recognition was a sham, however, for public authorities did not in fact protect married slaves' rights in the face of a master's contrary demands. Even the Georgia minister and slaveholder Charles Colcock Jones, who called marriage a "divine institution," conceded that it "depends . . . largely upon the protection given it by the law of the land." State laws were not willing to give slave marriages that protection. During New York's long period of gradual emancipation, the state legislature recognized slave marriages but later stipulated that the marriage of a slave did not constitute manumission, which amounted to declaring that it was not legally binding.[23]

Southern elites were more consistent. Their marriage law for slaves exemplified the "natal alienation," or official kinlessness, that all modern writers have seen as a basic and characteristic deprivation in enslavement. In 1838 the Chief Justice of the North Carolina Supreme Court, Thomas

Ruffin, had to assess whether a slave couple could be understood to be united in "rightful and formal" marriage. He concluded that "concubinage, which is voluntary on the part of the slaves, and permissive on that of the master . . . in reality, is the relation, to which these people have ever been practically restricted, and with which alone, perhaps, their condition is compatible." Two decades later another North Carolina justice (subsequently Chief Justice) wrote more dismissively, "Our law requires no solemnity or form in regard to the marriage of slaves, and whether they 'take up' with each other, by the express permission of their owners, or from a mere impulse of nature . . . cannot, in contemplation of law, make any sort of difference."[24]

Nonetheless, it was to the advantage of masters to have slaves reproduce themselves and nurture their young, which became all the more indispensable after the national ban on importation of slaves in 1808. The economic success of slavery in the American south has been attributed to the high rate of family formation and natural reproduction of the slave labor force. How often masters forced certain slave men and women together is unclear, but some female ex-slaves testified to forced "breeding" or cohabitation that they found hateful. Self-marriage was more ordinary. Sexual intimacy frequently preceded marriage; given the enforced tentativeness of all slave relationships, "taking up" with a partner might last or might not. More fortunate slaves could create rich family lives for themselves, giving their marriages the respect that slaveholders withheld. Diverse and adaptable, in order to fit the demands of their situations, the families springing from marital relationships formed the heart and molded the culture of slave communities. About half of all slaves lived on large plantations, where the slave community consisted of a close-knit collection of simple families, built around couples, parents and children, and often grandchildren, yet embracing unmarried adults. For those on small farms, an "abroad" marriage where the slave husband and wife did not live together but saw each other at the owners' discretion was the only possibility. Since a slave woman's offspring became her owner's property, children of an "abroad" marriage lived with their mother, swelling the numbers of mother-headed families.[25]

Slaveholders encouraged coupling and family formation. Slave weddings frequently became plantation events where the pair went through a makeshift ceremony or "jumped the broomstick," and Christian slaves were even granted their wish to have a minister officiate, sometimes. What masters did *not* do was to honor the integrity of the marriages or families thus formed. When it suited them, they put all slave relationships in the character of temporary "taking up." Masters gave absolute priority to their own agendas for selling or moving slaves regardless of family relationships. They also felt free to use slave women sexually themselves, with no particular concern for the woman's feelings or for her marriage ties. Slave women on small farms not only had to look for partners from "abroad" but also were more likely to be exploited sexually by their masters and to bear their children.[26]

Churchmen exhorted masters to keep slave couples together, but did so ineffectually. Recognizing the fragility of his marital union, a religious slave recorded, "In May, 1828, I was bound as fast in wedlock as a slave can be. God may at any time sunder that band in a freeman; either master may do the same at pleasure in a slave." The congregations to which Christian slaves belonged often had to decide whether to discipline a member who had taken up with a new partner after being separated by sale or migration from a first who was still living. The second relationship was bigamous, in effect, and against God's law. Rather than answering hard questions about the clash between slavery and Christian monogamy, churches compromised by treating the forced separation like death. The slave had little choice in the matter.[27]

Informal marriage was by no means a strictly southern peculiarity or an American one. "Living tally" (cohabiting without solemnization) was common among working-class and industrial wage-earning populations in England and Scotland, partly because this consensual arrangement was understood to allow self-divorce. The birth record kept by a clergyman in a North Wales community showed that between 1766 and 1799, 60 percent of all the babies born were the offspring of "besom weddings," self-marriage arrangements in which the couple jumped over a broom placed aslant in the doorway, as slaves did on southern plantations. The couple could divorce within the first year by jumping back over the broomstick, while the man remained obliged to support any child born. British couples who married informally usually did so to escape the expense of legal ceremonies. A significant proportion of working-class couples in France, too, cohabited, and observers said this was to escape the high cost of religious and bureaucratic formalities. Probably one fifth of marriages in mid-century Paris were self-marriages.[28]

The costs of licenses and ceremonies were purposely low in the United States, and many states empowered a wider range of officials to solemnize marriages, yet as Americans and immigrants settled farther west and south in new areas of the continent, informal marriages continued to dot the landscape. The marriages between Anglo fur trappers or other adventurers and Mexican or native American women in former Spanish territory frequently were informal. Spanish law required marriage to be performed by a Catholic priest; when no priests were nearby, Catholics temporized. Texas instituted a unique system called "marriage by bond," to allow a substitute ceremony to serve until a priest arrived. No provision was made for non-Catholics, so those couples simply took vows before friends or sought a civil magistrate.[29]

Andrew Jackson, later president of the United States, married Rachel Donelson Robards this way in Natchez in 1791 when it was under Spanish rule. His political opponents impugned the marriage during the presidential campaign of 1828 and accused the couple of having committed adultery, not so much because of the tenuous form of the marriage as because of Rachel's situation at the time—married to another man. She believed that her first husband had obtained a legislative decree of divorce in December 1790 in Kentucky, but actually he had been granted only permission to sue for divorce, a fact that later emerged. He did obtain the divorce easily, on the ground of her adultery, once she began living with Andrew Jackson. The Tennessee community to which the Jacksons returned made no objections, however, and accepted them as validly married. The neighbors knew the story of Rachel's suffering at her first husband's hands. Exemplifying the flexible popular understanding of marriage, they accepted what she had done as justified.[30]

When couples married informally, or reversed the order of divorce and remarriage, they were not simply acting privately, taking the law into their own hands. Among slaves on large plantations as well as among free whites, a couple about to join or leave an intimate relationship looked for communal sanction.[31] The surrounding local community provided the public oversight necessary. Without resort to the state apparatus, local informal policing by the community affirmed that marriage was a well-defined public institution as well as a contract made by consent. Carrying out the standard obligations of the marriage bargain—cohabitation, husband's support, wife's service—seems to have been much more central to the approbation of local communities at this time than how or when the marriage took place, and whether one of the partners had been married elsewhere before. The informal public had expectations for behavior of spouses and typically would not brook adultery, or nonsupport, or desertion, or extreme cruelty or neglect. Testimony from lawsuits shows clearly that when marriages generated conflict, neighbors and extended kin were often willing to interfere between husband and wife, to give advice, urge better behavior, or defend a victimized spouse. And this form of community self-policing was generally effective.[32] Reputation was an important form of capital in local communities. One's behavior as a spouse composed a very significant part of it.

Local communities tolerated even such seeming aberrations as self-divorce and remarriage, if the situation seemed to warrant it. Self-divorce, accepted among slaves if a marriage was full of friction, and traditional practice among many native American groups, may have been more frequent and justified among white Christians than is usually assumed. The New York shipyard boss who hired Frank Harley as a ship carpenter around 1830, for example, said, "I don't want any binding indentures, and all that sort of thing. When I don't like you, or you don't like me, we'll quit and separate. Master and man, or man and wife had always better cut adrift when they get to quarreling."[33] In informal marriages, made only by the couple's reciprocal promises, self-divorce seemed especially reasonable.

Desertion was another name for self-divorce. Female petitioners for legal divorce often told this story: They were wives whose husbands had departed. Since their marriages had one-sidedly ended, law-abiding wives wanted to extricate themselves from their status as *femes coverts* in order to act independently economically and perhaps to remarry. The wide-open spaces of the United States made it easy for a deserter to re-marry in a new state or territory. Record-keeping was usually poor. The Reverend Nicholas Collin of the Old Swedes' Lutheran Church in Philadelphia, who married three thousand couples between 1789 and 1818, could have married even larger numbers except that he scrupled against marrying a person who already had a spouse elsewhere.

Collin's exactness about inquiries could not have been typical among clerics and justices of the peace, for bigamy in this form of serial monog-amy seems to have occurred all over the United States—most of it un-prosecuted, although bigamy was a crime in every state.[34] Because it was so difficult for women to travel alone safely and find a livelihood in a new place, husbands were the main deserters. Local communities seem often to have accepted the remarriage of a wandering husband if his first wife had also departed or the marriage had deteriorated to the point where the partners could not live together in peace. Men's acceptance of adventur-ism by their sex no doubt fed into this attitude. Where prosecutions for bigamy occurred, juries (composed of men) were lenient if the accused persuaded them that the first marriage had ended by mutual consent, or that the first spouse had grievously neglected marital obligations. Insofar as marriage was contractual, one partner's outrageous affront to the con-tract provided good reason to leave.

Bigamists in court, acting strategically, endorsed the ideal of mo-nogamous Christian-modeled marriage and found juries sympathetic, though that sympathy may have mainly expressed tolerance for male sex-ual prerogatives. Nearly 90 percent of those convicted of bigamy in New York City between 1800 and 1860 (almost all men) received no jail sen-tence.[35] But wives such as Rachel Donelson Robards Jackson could also enjoy this kind of tolerance: the Tennessee community viewed her first husband as having broken his side of the marital bargain, and vindicated her behavior, seeing that she and Jackson behaved appropriately as wife and husband.

Following the pragmatism of local communities, judges were disposed to accept informal marriages, established by local repute, as equivalent to ceremonialized ones. They even included marriages that had begun bigamously, once the first partner died or was officially divorced. They were utilitarian about it. Sounding like the Maryland minister half a century earlier, the Chief Justice of Pennsylvania estimated in 1833 that if legal requirements for valid marriage were strictly enforced, the "vast majority" of children born in the state over the past fifty years would be rendered illegitimate. No one wanted that outcome. A Texas judge thirty years later thought that courts must, "upon the highest considerations of public policy," see that a marriage was "sustained as valid, whenever the consent of the parties and the intention to enter into the state of matrimony, and to assume its duties and obligations, is clearly shown." Judges often said they were defending the honor of women by sustaining informal marriages, though states just as clearly wanted to obligate men to support of their dependents.[36]

Except in the few states that absolutely prohibited or nullified self-marriage by law, courts were generally satisfied when a couple's cohabitation looked like and was reputed in the community to be marriage, whether or not authorized ceremonies could be documented. The inconsistent record-keeping in the nineteenth century meant that circumstantial evidence oftentimes had to be used to prove solemnized marriages also. The maxim *semper praesumitur pro matrimonio* (the assumption is always in favor of matrimony) directed and summed up judges' thinking. In line with the principle that anyone accused should be presumed innocent of a crime unless proved guilty, a couple living together was presumed to be innocent of immorality unless proved otherwise.[37]

Judges' opinions along these lines, together with states' moves in the early nineteenth century to empower more diverse personnel to perform marriages and to eliminate difficulties or fees associated with banns or licenses, added up to a shared public policy facilitating monogamous marriage. Although state statutes could certainly regulate it, informal marriage was valid unless it was specifically prohibited. The U.S. Supreme Court confirmed in 1877 what it regarded as "the settled doctrine of the American courts," that marriage was "everywhere regarded as a civil contract" based on consent. Even state laws indicating how marriages were to be solemnized were to be seen as directory, not mandatory, "because marriage is a thing of common right, because it is the policy of the State to encourage it, and because . . . any other construction would compel holding illegitimate the offspring of many parents conscious of no violation of law." In another decision seven years later, Justice Stephen Field delivered a ringing affirmation of this view, saying that a couple's known consent to marry and general repute as married was sufficient, so long as there was "public recognition" of the marriage— meaning acknowledgement by the informal public.[38]

On its face, this public policy generously honored couples' own choices and emphasized the contractual aspect of marriage. Yet courts' recognition of informal marriage silently incorporated a particular definition of "matrimony" and its "duties and obligations." In accepting self-marriage, state authority did not retreat, but widened the ambit of its enforcement of marital duties. By crediting couples' private consent, the law drew them into a set of obligations set by state law.

Local control and flexibility did not mean—as Daniel Carroll and Laura Smoak learned—that there were no standards, or that the community would never invoke the punitive authority of the state. Open adultery was ordinarily an affront in all communities, as was nonsupport. The trespass most conspicuously mobilizing community resort to the law was marriage across the color line. Six of the thirteen original colonies had prohibited and penalized marriage between a white and a Negro or mulatto (as did a French decree in colonial Louisiana); three more punished extramarital sex between them. By 1860, when there were thirty-three states, twenty-three state or territorial legislatures had passed similar legislation. Three were northern, nine southern, seven midwestern, and four western. Seven more states jumped to do so during the Civil War years, 1861–1865. It may seem surprising that neither South Carolina nor Alabama nor Mississippi nor Georgia (which did have a colonial prohibition from 1750) passed a state law penalizing marriage between black and white in the antebellum years, while states such as Illinois, Iowa, Maine, Michigan, Nebraska and California did. These southern abstentions can be attributed to the sufficiency of slave codes in maintaining social inequality, not to special tolerance. After emancipation, many southern states (including these four) instituted new bans; several made these marriages felonies and prescribed extremely high penalties. In Mississippi the penalty was life imprisonment.[39]

It is important to retrieve the singularity of the racial basis for these laws. Ever since ancient Rome, class-stratified and estate-based societies had instituted laws against intermarriage between individuals of unequal social or civil status, with the aim of preserving the integrity of the ruling class. British imperial policy in Ireland in the fourteenth century included such a ban, and the Spanish crown in 1776 issued a similar decree. But the English colonies stand out as the first secular authorities to nullify and criminalize intermarriage on the basis of race or color designations.[40]

These laws did not concern all mixed marriages. They aimed to keep the white race unmixed—or more exactly, to keep the *legitimate* white race unmixed—and thus only addressed marriages in which one party was white.[41] Amidst rhetoric deeming marriage between colored and white "unnatural," mutual attraction between individuals continually surfaced. Intermarriage bans policed this attraction by announcing that blacks were not worthy to marry whites. Sex was something else. Ella Clanton Thomas, a member of the slaveholding elite of Augusta, Georgia, saw the greatest southern hypocrisy in slaveholders' enjoying sexual intimacy with black and mulatto slaves while finding marriage abhorrent. She wrote in her diary:

> A most striking illustration of general feeling on the subject is to be found in the case of George Eve, who carried on with him a woman to the North under the name of wife—She was a mulatto slave, and although it was well known that he lived constantly with her violating one of God's ten commandments yet nothing

was thought of it. There was no one without sin "to cast the first stone at him," but when *public opinion* was outraged by the report that the ceremony of marriage had been passed between them—then his father was terribly mortified and has since attempted to prove that he is a lunatic—with what success I do not know. He preferred having him living in a constant state of sin to having him pass the boundary of Caste.[42]

In the south, the white men who passed laws prohibiting marriages did not give up their own freedom to use African American women sexually outside of marriage. Twice as many states (forty-one) nullified marriage between whites and persons of color as criminalized sex or concubinage between them (twenty). The marriage bans were far more enforceable. Legal marriage usually required a license (which would be denied to a mixed-race couple), and the nullifying statutes also prescribed a fine or other punishment for the person who would perform such a marriage. Auguste Carlier, a mid-nineteenth-century French visitor who wrote a book called *Marriage in the United States*, remarked that "the force of prejudice" against marriage between black and white was such that "no one would dare to brave it. It is not the legal penalty which is feared, but a condemnation a thousand times more terrible."[43] His comment (even if oversimplified and exaggerated) pointed to the strong congruence between community sentiment and law on this issue. Criminal prosecutions of mixed couples testified to neighbors' support for the legislation, because only their surveillance would alert the law.

Laws criminalizing marriage between whites and persons of color meant that the generous consideration usually given to informal marriage did not extend to couples transgressing the race barrier. An 1841 civil suit in Kentucky, for example, rested on the question whether a white property-owner was the wife of the black man whom she had bought as a slave and with whom she cohabited. The court admitted that "in ordinary cases" a presumption of marriage would arise "from mere cohabitancy ostensibly in the conjugal relation." In this case, on the contrary, the existence of a legal penalty for marriage between a black and white person "repelled" that presumption. The decision emphasized that even if a marriage was intended or consummated it was "void as against the policy and implied prohibition of the local law."[44]

Flexibility in the making of typical marriages did not predict similar casualness in marriages across the color line. Indiana laws of the 1840s and 1850s, for example, allowed any form of marriage ceremony whatsoever, so long as the couple consented before an authorized official; even a fraudulent ceremony could serve if the couple believed it to be legitimate. Indiana also provided easier terms and more extensive grounds for divorce than any other state in the nation. Yet its 1840 law prohibiting marriage between a white and a person having as little as one-eighth "Negro blood" stipulated whopping punishments: fines of $1,000 to $5,000 for the offending parties along with ten to twenty years in prison; and a fine of $1,000 to $10,000 for the person officiating, who would also be removed from his job. At a time when a master artisan's home, workshops, and outbuildings might be worth $4,000 at most, these fines were stupendous, the equivalent of many millions of dollars today. This law resulted directly from neighbors' horror at a marriage that took place in Indianapolis. A family had moved from Boston, and the father died. The widow and two daughters then relied more on their male servant, a mulatto who looked more or less white; and before very long one of the daughters married him. The family was mobbed, the new wife convinced to seek a divorce. The legislature rushed into session and passed the 1840 law. Its extreme penalties were revised downward within a year, however, on the reasoning that juries would not convict otherwise.[45]

Community sentiment against whites marrying African Americans was not limited to the south in the antebellum decades. Intermarriage bans and penalties echoed each other from state to state, north and south, east and west, together composing an American system. Where legal exceptions existed (mostly in the mid-Atlantic states and New England), community sentiment against "amalgamation" was shown in extralegal actions. The most destructive mob actions against northern antislavery advocates, such as those in New York in 1834 and in Philadelphia in 1838, were set off by evidence that an interracial marriage had taken place, or by charges that the reformers were seeking to promote "amalgamation" between the races. Abraham Lincoln debated Stephen Douglas, the Democratic senator from his home state of Illinois, on this issue in 1858. Douglas geared his politics toward "preserving not only the purity of [white] blood but the purity of the government from any . . . amalgamation with inferior races." He accused his opponent of being a race-mixer. Lincoln redirected the accusation toward southern plantations, where mulatto children provided evidence that white slaveholders were the main practitioners of "amalgamation."[46] But the charge against Lincoln followed his party, the Republicans, into the Civil War and after it.

When marriage across the color line became a political issue, catapulted into legislative halls and discussed by male politicians, the marriages of black men to white women always held the spotlight. The very first criminal law on the subject, passed by the Maryland colonial assembly in 1664, had singled out for punishment "freeborn English women" who made "shamefull Matches" with "Negro slaves." That textual specificity disappeared but the idea remained as subtext, and not only in the south. Men assumed that their own sex took the marriage initiative and that women might be vulnerable, needy, frivolous, easily swayed. In the constitutional conventions that took place in state after state between 1820 and 1870, delegates could frequently be heard asking one another how they would feel if a black man asked for their daughter's hand. Black men's affinity for white women was taken for granted. Although the prohibitory laws were written without gender content, prosecutions were skewed. In thirteen of the seventeen interracial fornication prosecutions between 1840 and 1860 in backcountry North Carolina, for example, the man in the couple was African American. In the four cases where the man was white, he had done something unseemly, such as appearing with his darker partner at a public event as if she were his wife, treating her with the respect due to a white woman.[47]

Still, these laws, and even the community sentiment so much in tandem, were not endorsed by all or enforced for all. If the enthusiasm for punitive legislation was remarkable, so was its failure to accomplish its object fully. Just as neighbors could ignore state laws about marriage ceremony, bigamy, self-divorce, fornication, and adultery at times, they did not universally oppose marriage between black and white or wholly effectively prevent it. Consensual, long-lasting, informal if not legal marriages between black and white existed in many places throughout the south, where more than 90 percent of the African American population lived; temporary liaisons were even more frequent. Criminal court records revealed these relationships when couples living together were charged with fornication or (if one of the pair was already married) adultery. More frequently, civil suits over property transactions and inheritances showed marriage-like relationships between black and white that had *not* been prosecuted criminally.[48]

The historian Martha Hodes has contended that a mixed couple could more easily maintain a marriage-like relationship in the south during the slaveholding era than after the Civil War and emancipation. The argument has a counterintuitive logic: during the antebellum era the couple's exceptional relationship could survive, because it could not realistically challenge the ruling public order of racial slavery. But after emancipation, when independent manhood for African American men was a formal, legal fact, such a couple represented the looming reality of "social equality" between the races.[49] Unanimity did not exist: on this as on every marriage question, the laws implemented the consensus of a strong majority and constrained a minority. Beyond implementing majority views, the laws sustained, nourished, and reproduced those views. The laws kept the minority who would tolerate or engage in cross-racial marriage small, by exercising a moral as well as a literal force, by consistently repudiating the social equality represented by intermarriage. They confirmed the rightness of the social structure and state in subordinating blacks to whites and making intermarriage inappropriate.

White southerners' post-emancipation hysteria about African American men's threat to white women illustrated how far a man's freedom to marry and become head of a household defined his manhood, the quality that white slaveholders had denied and would continue to deny to their former male slaves. Emancipation lay far in the unimagined future, however, during the antebellum decades, when local communities oversaw marriages and evinced some flexibility even on the possibility of unlawful relationships between black and white. A striking case in point was the successful candidacy of Richard Mentor Johnson, a Democrat, for the vice presidency of the United States in 1836 (when Martin Van Buren was running for the presidency). Johnson, a bachelor, had a series of slave mistresses. One who commanded his devotion had become the mother of his two daughters, whom he educated and for whom he found white husbands. She died in 1833, but there was more attention to her during the campaign of 1835 than to his next mistress, who embarrassed him by attempting to escape to Canada. Political newspapers made much of his living with a "yellow concubine." His Whig opponents shrieked about the danger to public morality of his sexual license and his practice of "amalgamation." In Johnson's defense, the Democrats stressed that a man's private behavior should be kept separate from public questions. They charged that political opponents had violated the sanctuary of Johnson's family life (just as they had bedeviled his Democratic predecessors Thomas Jefferson and Andrew Jackson for committing intimate sins). Democrats also contended that if Johnson's local community in Kentucky still approved of and admired him— if he had not affronted their shared norms (which he apparently had not)—that was sufficient sanction, and others had no business criticizing him.[50]

Johnson likely would *not* have squeaked through a generation later. Where local traditions and self-policing had ruled, state legislatures were increasingly flexing their muscles. Law reform and rewriting of state constitutions were the order of the day. States supplanted the common law with their own law codes, aiming to modernize private and public affairs. The revision of marriage often generated a particular sort of tension between what had been and what legislatures would construct. Legislators' common sense told them that lifelong marriage on a Christian model came from natural law, and from God, and represented civilization—yet they also knew that they had the power to alter it. The standard treatise on domestic relations by Joel Prentiss Bishop defined marriage as "the civil status of one man and one woman united in law for life, under the obligation to discharge, to each other and the community, those duties which the community by its laws holds incumbent on persons whose association is founded on the distinction of sex." He was saying that marriage is a relationship conferred by the legislature. But Bishop endowed the institution with a more inspired genealogy by adding that "its source is the law of nature."[51] When state legislators went about altering marriage in response to social and economic pressures, they did so with some ambivalence, looking above and behind them as though a more powerful presence were watching.

In altering the terms of marriage, legislators saw themselves as not interrupting but polishing, refining, and perfecting an ongoing institution. This was so even when they provided more and more ways to *terminate* a relationship that had traditionally been conceived as lifelong. Divorce had first been legitimated by most states right after the American Revolution. New state legislators' willingness to allow divorce gave compelling evidence that the contractual ideology of the Declaration of Independence resonated through their thinking about spousal relations. The analogy between government and marriage as "sacred contracts" bore forcefully on their minds. How could consent in marriage (as in government) be considered fully voluntary, if it could not be withdrawn by an injured partner? Thomas Jefferson had reasoned that "no partnership" which showed "contradiction to its end and design" ought to have to be sustained. For "a long train of abuses," as the Declaration of Independence said, a marriage should be dissolvable also. Occasionally a divorce petitioner herself drew explicit analogy between governmental and marital tyranny. Petitioning a Connecticut court in 1788, Abigail Strong maintained that her husband's abuse had removed her obligation to obey him, since "even Kings may forfeit or discharge the allegiance of their subjects."[52]

Having justified rebellion against government tyranny, many state legislators were convinced that an innocent, ill-used spouse's escape from intimate tyranny should likewise be possible. This was not a complete innovation. Legislatures in a few of the Puritan-inspired American colonies had allowed divorce for adultery or desertion. The new states stipulated grounds for divorce much more systematically, however. Fearing a scene of sexual license if matrimony were no longer understood to be lifelong, legislators provided relief without taking too much risk. They selected a few, clear grounds for divorce, behaviors which clearly broke the contract that was understood as marriage: adultery, sexual incapacity, and an extended period of desertion were the most common. The U.S. Congress also included divorce in the Northwest Ordinance of 1783, which set up the basic law for that federal territory.

By instituting legal divorce, states mimicked the popular reasons for, and attempted to foreclose the practice of, *self*-divorce. Post-Revolutionary legislators wanted to reassert their authority over what (some) people had done under the aegis of local tolerance. The 1802 statute instituting divorce in Georgia declared frankly, "circumstances may require a dissolution of contracts founded on the most binding and sacred obligations . . . which dissolution ought not to be dependent on private will, but should require legislative interference; inasmuch as the republic is deeply interested in the private business of its citizens."[53] State provision of legal means of divorce put the appropriate "interference" back in. Self-divorce was objectionable from the state's point of view not only because it empowered the informal public but also because it disadvantaged wives. A husband had "many ways of rendering his domestic affairs agreeable, by Command or desertion," Thomas Jefferson had noted in 1771, while a wife remained "confined & subject." He saw this asymmetry as a reason to provide a legal way to end a marriage. More important from the state's point of view, self-divorce left support obligations hanging. Legal divorce would clarify obligations to provide and the transmission of property.[54]

Legal divorce in the nineteenth century was an adversarial procedure, far different from divorce today. It reflected the character of marriage as a unique contract in which husband and wife consented to terms set by a third party, the state. The plaintiff had to show that the defendant had broken the contract. Rather than aiming foremost at individuals' freedom, or intending to alter the concept that marriage was lifelong, early divorce statutes aimed to perfect marriage by weeding out the contracts that had been breached. If a spouse was divorceable, it was because he or she had committed a public wrong against the marriage as much as a private one against the partner; the public wrong justified the state's interposing its authority. Early divorce statutes typically allowed only the innocent petitioner to remarry, although it is unlikely that the spouse accused always refrained from remarrying.[55]

A plaintiff for divorce usually had to exhibit ideal spousal behavior in order to succeed. Courts paid attention to appropriate role behavior, in order to buttress the institution of marriage and to encourage husbands and wives to play their parts. A wife petitioning for divorce had to show how attentive, obedient, and long-suffering she had been (and of course sexually faithful) while she was being victimized. A husband's adequacy rested in economic support. If a husband provided passably for his dependents, he fulfilled the most important requirement of his manhood in marriage, as much as a wife showed her femininity by giving evidence of obedient service. Judges granted the divorce pleas of husbands who were not paragons of gentlemanly virtue if they had supported their wives and children. This was not only male privilege showing, but the cardinal principle that the husband had the role of provider. The intent to sustain standard economic roles in divorce had some unexpected consequences. Southern judges would award minimal alimony or property to a guilty wife in a divorce, in order to keep her from starving or going on poor relief—recognizing that as a result of coverture she would have no assets of her own to live on. These grants kept in place the assumption that wives were dependents with disabilities, husbands their supporters.[56]

Not long after 1800, almost every state legislature entertained petitions for divorce and a dozen states stipulated grounds for divorce suits to be brought in the courts.[57] The legislative petition method faded as judicial divorce spread almost everywhere and most states expanded the statutory grounds. In a number of states the two procedures were available simultaneously. The original southern states took slightly more time (to the early 1840s) to open their courts to divorce suits and South Carolina never did, but the new southwestern states had divorce grounds among the most permissive in the nation. Overall, during the antebellum period there was considerable and increasing legal provision for divorce. Not to deprive the unsuitably wed in the District of Columbia, the U.S. Congress in 1860 empowered the federal circuit court to grant them divorces.[58]

Between 1820 and 1860, as state legislatures generally boomed with activity, they repeatedly revised and enhanced their divorce statutes. First they made absolute divorce more readily available for infractions that formerly had warranted only "divorce from bed and board," or separation, as a remedy. Next, states added grounds such as extreme cruelty, fraudulent marriage contract, gross neglect of duty, and habitual drunkenness. Most of them shortened the period of desertion necessary (from five years to one or two). A few states gave the greatest leeway by writing what critics called "omnibus" clauses: in Connecticut, for example, the superior court could grant a divorce for "any such misconduct . . . as permanently destroys the happiness of the petitioner, and defeats the purpose of the marriage relation." Indiana added to seven statutory grounds "any other cause for which the Court shall deem it proper that a divorce should be granted." Illinois, North Carolina, and Iowa had similar clauses, as did the Utah territory by 1852.[59]

The more that legal means were stipulated, the more people ended their marriages. Rates of divorce before 1860, so far as is known, showed a consistent increase. In the south the climb was slower, which may have registered the persistence of informality in contracting and ending marriages among the poor as much as it suggested conservatism about family formation in the slaveholding elite. Nationwide, more wives than husbands sought legal divorce. The incidence was minuscule compared to the rate later in the century (to say nothing of twentieth-century rates), but it is always the direction of change that gives meaning, and by the 1850s, the frequency of divorce was producing shivers of alarm in newspapers and magazines. The first American novels in which divorce formed the main theme were published in that decade, with titles such as *The Deserted Wife, Iron Rule, or Tyranny in the Household,* and *The Hand*

But Not the Heart. Transcripts of juicy divorce trials, especially those involving elite parties, were rushed into publication. Local newspapers
pointed to shocking statistics elsewhere: the *New York Herald* noted the
hundreds of applications for divorce pending before the Maryland and
Pennsylvania state legislatures; the *Philadelphia Ledger* reported that the
Supreme Court of Vermont had during one session granted nine divorces
in a single small county; the *Baltimore Sun* attributed a rate of one hundred legislative divorces per year to Alabama. Local self-criticism also
flourished. Editorials and news reports peppered San Francisco newspapers in response to the area's judges' forgiving interpretations of California's already permissive divorce statute. A *San Francisco Chronicle*
writer sardonically commented in 1854 that "marriage among us seems
to be regarded as a pleasant farce—a sort of 'laughable afterpiece' to
courtship." He went on to predict (with some prescience if not exacti-
tude) that divorce rates in the city "will exceed in a tenfold ratio the number in any other part of the Union of equal population."[60]

By the mid-nineteenth century, European visitors saw the various
states' divorce laws as composing a uniquely American system more liberal than their own. The move among states was consistent. But it was
not identical, and variations among states caused what was later called
"migratory divorce"—a restless spouse's move from one state to another
to end a marriage legally. This phenomenon propelled Indiana into the
headlines in the 1850s as a reputed "divorce mill." The state had an omnibus clause, along with hardly any residency requirement. A plaintiff
had to be an Indiana resident only at the time of seeking a divorce and
could establish residence by personal affidavit alone. An unhappy spouse
from New York, for example (where divorce was allowed only for adultery), could move briefly to Indiana, sue for divorce with a persuasive
narrative of marital breakdown, publicize the suit solely in the newspapers *in Indiana,* and conceivably obtain the divorce. These possibilities
formed the eye of a storm of controversy inside as well as outside the
state. An editorial in the *Indianapolis Daily Journal* of 1858 complained
that that city was "overrun by a flock of ill-used, and ill-using, petulant,

libidinous, extravagant, ill-fitting husbands and wives as a sink is overrun with the foul water of the whole house." By 1859 the Indiana legislature had significantly tightened residency requirements.[61]

However much the multiplying grounds for divorce may have seemed to risk it, legislators were not intending to dilute the solemn institution of lifelong marriage. The political and judicial rhetoric of the time emphasized that states were acting to assure that the marital bargain continued to be rightly observed. Some petitions for divorce gave the impression of asking for the state's imprimatur on a couple's self-divorce. But the notion that a husband and wife could end their marriage themselves, and go their separate ways, perhaps each to find a new mate, was exactly what state legislators intended to cut short by providing legal termination.[62] State legislatures wanted to control the ending of marriages just as they set the requirements for beginning and keeping them.

By declaring what behavior broke the bargain of marriage, states were reiterating what composed it. They intended to keep the marriage bargain static: sexual fidelity was required; a man who deserted or cruelly abused his wife was not a "husband"; a wife who absconded or failed to serve a man's needs was not a "wife."[63] Rather than inviting husbands and wives to pursue marital freedom, the states in allowing divorce were perfecting the script for marriage, instructing spouses to enact the script more exactly.

State legislators' refinements of the grounds for divorce announced their own role in constructing marriage, as did their contemporaneous revisions of coverture. This very central expression of marital unity made a woman's property, labor, and earnings her husband's. Legislators' intent to alter coverture had less to do with concerns for women's rights than with worries about the economic relations between men and the property interests of male-headed families. Between the 1830s and the 1870s, state after state passed "married women's property" laws, declaring that wives owned the property they brought into or were deeded during marriage. Although from a modern point of view this sounds like the emancipation of the wife from coverture, and a rupture of marital unity, legislators were envisioning intact marriages as before, in which property in the wife's name would be safe from the husband's creditors. The laws aimed mainly to keep ordinary families solvent, at a time when most farmers operated in a dangerous cycle of borrowing and amassed dangerous levels of debt. Democratic-minded legislators also wanted to equalize the leverage of middle-class and richer families. Rich families had devised a way under the common law to separate a woman's property from her husband's upon marriage by creating a trust, with trustees in charge of the assets of the wife. Canny fathers had thus protected their daughters' wealth to be passed on to grandsons, in case the daughter had married a scoundrel. These moves by the rich were not necessarily against a husband's interest, however, and might well be undertaken with his approval and connivance. The new married women's property laws intended to extend to all wives this possible protection, and to enable debt-ridden families to preserve some assets in the wife's name.[64]

Like the provision of divorce, married women's property legislation bespoke state legislatures' power to redefine marriage and had radical potential to disrupt the institution—but was implemented conservatively. Legislators joined this move to breach the marital unity of a couple's property with some hesitation—not as readily as they provided grounds for divorce. The laws at first lay with minimal weight upon the legal tradition of wives' economic dependence. Most of the early married women's property acts simply declared that married women should hold their property as separate estates, without including any language enabling wives to *use* property by making contracts, buying, selling, and so on. This may have reflected state legislators' assumption that the laws would mainly aid husbands acting on behalf of and in concert with their wives.

In northern and midwestern states, women's rights advocates had begun to speak up by the 1850s, and legislatures pressed to improve on the first married women's property acts. Ernestine Rose and Elizabeth Cady Stanton and their friends lobbied and lectured in New York state for years after a married women's property act was passed in 1848. An improved law of 1860 added enabling language, and made the wife the owner of her earnings as well as her property. Most states passed married women's property acts first, and followed with a later round of statutes on wives' earnings. Legislators who passed the later laws were usually inspired by narratives of plucky working-class wives and mothers who supported themselves and their children by hard labor while their irresponsible husbands haunted saloons. Legislators were willing to redirect these long-suffering wives' earnings away from their shiftless husbands and toward the children's support.[65]

Still, the tradition of marital unity had such force that courts took a very conservative view of laws asserting a wife's right to her property and earnings. Coverture expressed the legal essence of marriage as reciprocal: a husband was bound to support his wife, and in exchange she gave over her property and labor. So long as the husband's legal responsibility continued, judges found it difficult to treat a wife like a single woman with respect to her earnings, especially if the earnings resulted from labor done at home. To do so would contravene the economic definition of marriage. Even in the face of declarative state laws, judges continued to interpret wives' housework as owned by their husbands.[66] So deeply rooted was the doctrine that it took more than a century to emancipate wives legally from marital service.

Coverture had literally expressed the union of the marital pair: it underlay the husband's prerogative as head of the household and his political representation of his wife. State legislators had to row hard against this current. Yet they did feel empowered to pass the new laws. They fractured the unified property regime of marriage just as they altered the dictum that marriage must last "till death do us part." Far from being an institution fixed by God, marriage was in the hands of the legislature. This legislative legerdemain of the antebellum decades taught the lesson that "rightful and formal" marriage was political, rather than simply natural or God-given. For decades state law had hovered in the background while the informal public of local communities had been conducting marriage sanctions. But state legislatures' flurry of activity in passing laws on divorce and married women's property showed their hand: marriage was their political creation.

Paradoxically, as state legislatures inserted their qualifications on marital conduct into every nook and cranny of the institution, individuals felt a gain of greater room to maneuver. Although a wife who tried to contest her husband's domestic authority would still be confined by conservative interpretation, the new regime of separate property and earnings allowed wives to act (and think of themselves) more individually. Married women's property laws effectively raised the proportion of wealth held by women as the nineteenth century went on.[67] Divorce, although a last-resort choice at the time, also conveyed a sense of greater freedom of action. The lifting of a "life sentence" in an impossible marriage had to have made the institution feel more equitable and more voluntary, more truly chosen. State legislators had reason to underline this point, that the voluntary nature of marriage was as essential in its political definition as were the fixed roles of husband and wife.

3

DOMESTIC RELATIONS ON THE

NATIONAL AGENDA

*I*n 1857 an Indiana judge confidently called marriage "a great public institution, giving character to our whole civil polity."[1] Yet by that date both marriage and the character of the civil polity of the United States had become hostages to sectional conflict between the slaveholding south and the free-labor north. As the south and the north contended for dominance, marriage definitions and practices became both means and ends, illustrations and purposes, in political debate. Nonconformists and critics of the institution further politicized it. Local control lent flexibility to couples in antebellum communities, but the point that state legislatures had made by manipulating divorce and coverture—that marriage was politically structured—was clear, and became more momentous when it reached the federal government and engaged questions of national sovereignty.

All the British colonies in America, north and south, had countenanced slavery, but by the mid-eighteenth century humanitarians, especially Quakers, were opposing all human bondage. The Revolutionary-era emphasis on "the rights of man" intensified these objections. Shortly after independence all the northern states (where slave labor did not contribute in a major way to the economy) eliminated it, by gradual or immediate methods. To bring opponents and supporters of slavery together in one nation, the Constitution of the United States supported the continuation of the institution but prohibited importation of slaves after 1808. In subsequent decades, however, democratic and liberal thinking gained force in the north, and the presence of masters and lifelong slaves affronted Americans who saw free labor to be as essential a characteristic of the nation as free choice of marital partner. Religious revivals after 1800, spilling into social criticism, deepened northern Protestants' moral disapproval of slavery. By 1830, insistent radical critics of slavery had begun to speak up, insisting on the immediate abolition of slavery with no compensation to be given to owners. These abolitionists were a tiny minority among critics of slavery, but they were loud, and sure of the superiority of their moral stance.

The contest between the differing labor systems and values of north and south sharpened as new states were being formed from western territories. Would slavery be legal in these new states? The Compromise of 1850, a series of laws intended by Congress to settle questions about the extension of slaveholding to new states, failed to do the trick. The compromise included the Fugitive Slave Act, which committed the federal government to help slaveowners recover slaves who escaped to nonslaveholding states. It also set forth the controversial principle of popular sovereignty (a plebiscite among the white men in the territory) to decide whether new states would be "slave" or "free." These provisions escalated rather than alleviated conflict. During the decade that followed, southern defenses of the "peculiar institution" of slavery became more aggressive, as did northern abolitionists' rhetoric and actions, culminating in John Brown's seizure of a federal arsenal at Harper's Ferry and his own martyrdom.

Marriage values and practices animated the rhetoric of both sides. Abolitionists, forcefully rejecting slavery for turning human beings into chattel, harped on the way it deformed marriage. They called the denial to slaves of legally recognized and binding marriages a human tragedy, and a crying affront to American pretensions to value the purity of family life. When abolitionists vituperated that slavery caused "a complete extinction of all the relations, endearments and obligations of mankind, and a presumptuous transgression of all the holy commandments," they were referring unmistakably to violations of Christian monogamy: the master's power to sever relationships between slave couples and families;

the inability of enslaved women to prevent unwelcome white masters, overseers, and sons from using their bodies sexually; and slave men's inability to act effectively as protectors or defenders. By respecting neither his slaves' marriages nor his own, the slaveholder "totally annihilates the marriage institution," one polemicist remonstrated; this was "the most appalling feature of our slave system," another contended in William Lloyd Garrison's abolitionist newspaper *The Liberator*. Slaveholders' grievous assault on slave marriage and kinship resounded through tracts, treatises, speeches, and fiction. To elaborate on *Uncle Tom's Cabin*, her renowned antislavery novel (published in 1852), Harriet Beecher Stowe wrote, "The worst abuse of the system of slavery is its outrage upon the family . . . one which is more notorious and undeniable than any other."[2]

The slaveholder's callous lust—his moral violence as well as his physical cruelty—gave abolitionists their most effective theme. Sexual abuse of female slaves by rape, incest, forced mating, and concubinage figured even more sensationally in abolitionist literature than the sale of slave family members. The abolitionists who described scenes such as the stripping and whipping of female slaves expected such portrayals to evoke moral revulsion in their listeners. "No part of the dark and hidden iniquities of slavery" deserved revelation more than its travesty of the "nuptial covenant" with "odious lusts," the abolitionist George Bourne intoned, referring to the master's unchecked freedom to use the bodies of his female slaves. Samuel Ward, a fugitive slave, observed of the other fugitives in Canada, "the slaveholders are publishing, as in so many legibly written volumes, in the faces of their mulatto offspring, the sad, sickening evidences of their abominable immoralities . . . What a religion must that be, which declares that the system, of which these deeds are part, is ordained, sanctioned, owned and blest, of God!"[3]

Slave women had no resort in the law. As a legal treatise of the 1850s stated, "the violation of the person of a female slave carries with it no other punishment than the damages which the master may recover for the trespass upon his property" (if another man took advantage of her and the master decided to prosecute).[4] Abolitionists found it especially repugnant that the slaveholder's sinful freedom to satiate his lust brought him additional valuable property, because any child born of a slave mother would be a slave. They thought that a system in which marriage had no sanctity, and fathers sold, prostituted, and committed incest with their own children (the daughters of their slave mistresses), travestied every proposition of Christian morals.[5] Not in public but in their private diaries and conversations, some elite women of the slaveholding class also condemned this regime, although they were more concerned with its effect on the white than on the black family. The most pungent was Mary Boykin Chesnut (herself married, but childless), who recorded just after her husband became a Confederate general: "God forgive us, but ours is a monstrous system, a wrong and an iniquity! Like the patriarchs of old, our men live all in one house with their wives and their concubines; and the mulattoes one sees in every family partly resemble the white children. Any lady is ready to tell you who is the father of all the mulatto children in everybody's household but her own. Those, she seems to think, drop from the clouds."[6]

To answer northern opponents who railed at the immorality of slavery, defenders of the southern social order had to be creative in justifying their way of life. One main avenue they took was to find slavery in the Bible. Southern evangelical Protestants led the way in citing chapter and verse to show that the institution of slavery was approved by God. More than half the proslavery tracts published were composed by ministers.[7] "We find masters exhorted [in the Bible] in the same connection with husbands, parents, magistrates; slaves exhorted in the same connection with wives, children and subjects," a religious leader attested. Or, similarly, "the Christian slave must be submissive, faithful and obedient for reasons of the same authority with those which oblige husbands, wives, fathers, mothers, brothers, sisters, to fulfill the duties of those relations." That God "included slavery as an organizing element in that family order which lies at the very foundation of Church and State," was a typical claim.[8]

Proslavery ideologues contended that Africans and African Americans benefited from constraint and dependence—that "the guardianship and control of the black race, by the white," was "an indispensable

Christian duty." Because social hierarchy was good for public order, they said, some classes had always been subordinated, and liberty should be granted only to those capable of using it wisely.[9] Yet when abolitionists stressed that slaveholders prevented binding marriages among slaves, encouraged promiscuous mating, and crossed the color line themselves illicitly, what legitimation or biblical corroboration could be found? The divine origins and lifelong character of marriage were supposed to be articles of faith in the Protestant churches of the southern elite. No southern defender could avoid being confronted with these contradictions, yet hardly anyone, even among ministers, addressed them. A transplanted northerner residing in New Orleans related a conversation with an elder in the local church that left her horrified and baffled: "he remarked on the 2d Chap [sic] of Genesis that we there saw clearly the sacredness of the marriage institution. I asked him, how, then, it could be violated by the laws of our state, and not the laws of God violated at the same time? O! he said, the blacks did not care about marrying, they were willing to take up with each other, they did respect it to some extent."[10] Benjamin Palmer, an influential Presbyterian minister of New Orleans, composed enough sermons on the topic of family duties to publish a book on the subject, but under headings such as "Subordination of the Wife," "Supremacy of the Husband," "Authority of Masters," and "Subjection of Servants," he wrote no word about about slaves' inability to marry legally.[11]

In response to abolitionists' attacks, southern defenders "domesticated" slavery, rather than treating it simply as a labor regime. They portrayed it as a benevolent practice in which the white master protected and spoke for "my family black and white." In this counterattack, proslavery spokesmen legitimated the inequalities of slavery by praising all the domestic relations of domination and subordination—master-servant, parent-child, and husband-wife—as one and by seeing the three types as indivisible. Major tracts from southern ideologues of the 1850s lambasted the northern wage-labor system for being exploitive and heartless, and portrayed the south's paternalistic social order as harmonious and stable, in contrast.[12]

The domestic emphasis remade slavery as a set of relationships intended to foster qualities desirable in family members. Parental wisdom, protection, support, and discipline were expected from masters and cheerful, childlike obedience from slaves. This vision of slavery as one among several accepted relations of dependence naturalized its imposed inequalities. By portraying slaves as children, southern masters also justified their own role of command as a benign and natural one. This emphasis on the head of the household as benevolent patriarch was calculated to gain the broadest possible group of adherents among white men, whether slaveholders or not (and the great majority were not). What white man would not endorse his own position of command over his dependents?[13]

There was a problem, however, with using the parent-child analogy to legitimize slavery: childhood was fleeting, whereas slavery was a permanent status. By the late 1830s southern defenders had supplemented the parental analogy with a marital analogy for the relation between master and slave. While abolitionists were decrying the way slavery warped legal and Christian monogamy, southern defenders nonetheless focused on the same institution, and turned the abolitionists' claim upside down.[14] The southern elite believed that God and nature intended women to be the subordinates in marriage. Individual competence did not matter. Working from that premise, proslavery spokesmen argued that God had ordained for slaves, as for wives, a position in the inevitable hierarchy of society, with particular rights and duties attached. Notions of universal or inherent rights faded in significance as southern spokesmen emphasized particular obligations in given roles. In the case of marriage, southern defenders specified that the position of the wife was suitable and noble, not to be misunderstood as demeaning her personally or labeling her inferior. Just as women were fitted by nature and God to conform to their place as wives, enslaved African Americans were suited for slavery; and slavery, like marriage, was a relationship of unequals benefiting both parties. Both women as a sex and blacks as a race flourished best where they were guided and protected, it was said. Both marriage and slavery were justified as protecting and guiding those who were (appropriately) dependent. If the subordination of wives was for their own best interests (as it was held to be), so was the subordination of blacks for their own best interests. Both scientific and political discourse at the time abounded with new details on the "natural" differences between women and men, and between blacks and whites.[15]

The Anglo-American legal tradition supported this approach because both slavery and marriage were called domestic relations in the law. Although slaveholding shaped the public order of the antebellum south, it was legally categorized as a private relation, emanating from the household. Slavery fell under the "master-servant" category in the law, which also included employer/employee relations. Master-servant and husband-wife relations were categorized together as domestic relations, because the authority vested in the household head determined them all. That did not make them identical: the most fundamental difference was that the wife's and the employee's relation to authority was based on consent but the slave's was not. Still, the pairings of master and slave, husband and wife shared similarities.[16] Each was conceived as a pairing of unequals, linking someone superior in power and capacity to someone inferior. The superior was independent, the inferior dependent. Because there was a disparity between them, their reciprocal relationship required different duties from each party. The superior, who was independent, was to provide basic support and protection to the dependent. The dependent, inferior in power, was to be obedient, to do as the superior directed. That was the price of dependence. The very term "dependent" brought along with it the expectation of submission to another's authority.

This is not to say that the experience of a wife, being married, was equivalent to the experience of a person in bondage, being a slave. It is to say that structurally, conceptually, and legally the relations of husband to wife, and master to slave, were parallel—with the very important differentiation that marriage was joined voluntarily, by consent, and slavery was an inherited condition. The most important commonality between the two institutions was the master-husband's power to command the dependent. Keeping the analogy between marriage and slavery vivid lent racial slavery a beneficent patina without changing its power relations.

This linkage brought marital relations to the defense of slavery, making the preservation of slavery appeal to the three quarters of white men in the south who owned no slaves. Justification of slavery in these analogical terms clothed all white men, slaveholders or not, with mastership over their households.[17] "Marriage is too much like slavery not to be involved in its fate," the southern polemicist George Fitzhugh warned. The "intimate connexion" and mutual interdependence between marriage and slavery meant that they stood or fell together, in his view.[18] Besides playing a role in encouraging nonslaveholding men to identify with the system, this doubled defense helped to keep white women in their place. Any attack on either slaveholding or the marriage relationship appeared to undermine both. Elite white women could hardly raise a complaint in public about their own positions vis-à-vis their husbands without appearing traitorous to the south.

As the diverging ideological visions of north and south confronted each other, marriage as a public institution figured centrally. On the one side, abolitionists lambasted slavery's warping of marriages both black and white. On the other, southern spokesmen advocated slavery's likeness to marriage as the system's strongest justification. Even if one found fault with the southerners' analogy, it was indisputable that marriage and slavery were both "domestic relations" in the law. Both marriage and slavery were systems of domination and subordination—or more favorably, of protection and dependence—based on assumptions about inequalities between the parties involved.

The analogy between slavery and marriage cut two ways, of course. If the two domestic relations were parallel, a person who found slavery repugnant might well criticize the power of the husband over the wife in marriage. Pathbreakers of the nascent women's rights movement perceived exactly this damning parallel. Unlike southern defenders, women's rights reformers who emerged from within the antislavery movement analogized the wife to the slave as a critical polemic. They contended that both institutions, slavery and marriage, harbored inequalities inconsistent with American principles of liberty and equality. A wife's enforced dependence on her husband had in the past been one of numerous unequal relationships in social life and politics, such as the subject's dependence on the ruler and the apprentice's dependence on the master. As social contract thinking and free-labor ideology made these other dependencies seem unjustifiable, the wife's position appeared more anomalous and objectionable. Free-labor ideology in the north, the inheritor of seventeenth-century liberal ideas, assumed self-ownership to be a basic natural right. John Locke had defined the individual as "proprietor of his own person," and had said that it was by applying his labor to nature's resources that an individual could create wealth and property for himself.[19] The southern slave lacked this essential right to own his person and labor—and in the newly opened eyes of women's rights activists, so did the wife under coverture. The self-possession denied to the slave was denied also to the wife, in their view. This was shown in her ceding her property, her free will, and her name to her husband.[20]

Women's rights advocacy bloomed after Elizabeth Cady Stanton and several Quaker friends called a meeting in Seneca Falls, New York, in July of 1848. Hundreds attended women's rights conventions in various towns of the northeast and the midwest during the 1850s, giving speeches and making resolutions, until the Civil War interrupted their momentum. Although women's demand to vote has been emphasized retrospectively, participants' resentment at wives' subordination within marriage sounded more often during these conventions. Thus the abolitionist Antoinette Brown objected in 1853, "The wife owes service and labor to her husband as much and as absolutely as the slave does to his master." Her friend Lucy Stone likewise protested: "Marriage is to woman a state of slavery. It takes from her the right to her own property, and makes her submissive in all things to her husband." Stone's keeping her own name after her 1855 marriage to Henry Blackwell symbolized the couple's intent to repudiate these and other attributes of conventional marriage. Ernestine Rose, a coworker with Elizabeth Cady Stanton in New York state, urged, "Let us first obtain *ourselves* . . . Give us ourselves and all that belongs to us will follow."[21]

It was hardly an innovation to compare the wife to a slave. Since the emergence in England of political theories based on natural rights, some writers had seen the paradox in women's consenting "freely" to give up their freedom, and had used the analogy to critical or ironic purpose. Mary Astell, a highly educated philosopher and polemicist who never married, wrote tersely in 1700 in "Some Reflections on Marriage": "If 'all men are born free,' how is it that all women are born slaves?" To the heroine of Daniel Defoe's 1740 novel *Roxana*, "the very nature of the marriage contract was . . . nothing but giving up liberty, estate, authority, and everything to the man, and the woman was indeed a mere woman ever after—that is to say, a slave."[22]

With the institution of slavery a prominent feature of Western society since the fifteenth century, the contrast between bondage and freedom was available as a metaphor for all sorts of references. The notion that a male suitor became his loved one's "slave" was of long standing, and was employed in the post-Revolutionary discourse on love and marriage, for example, in a poem called "Woman's Hard Fate."[23] Playing with the simile between tyranny and slavery, mastership and sovereignty, a woman's voice lamented the "slavish chains" wives had to don in moving from courtship to marriage:

> . . . the tyrant husband next appears,
>   with aweful and contracted brow;
> No more a lover's form he wears;
>   Her slave's become her sov'reign now.
> . . . Oh cruel power, since you've design'd
>   That man, vain man, should bear the sway,
> To slavish chains add slavish mind
>   That I may thus your will obey.[24]

The convergence of proslavery and antislavery rhetorics on marriage gave renewed prominence to the comparison between the wife and the slave. Women abolitionists mined this vein. Lydia Maria Child and Sarah Grimke each published books in the 1830s examining the history and condition of women worldwide, noting the many cultures in which wives were equated with property or slaves.[25] In the 1850s, women's rights conventions and publications voiced this parallel and advocated new laws on married women's property and earnings.[26] Even elite southern women could not resist using the analogy. One complained wryly to her husband about having to accept his frequent absences, "I belong to that degraded race called woman—who whether her lot be cast among Jew, or Turk, heathen or Christian is yet a *slave*."[27]

Underlying women's rights advocates' concern with self-ownership was something even more basic than property—the body itself. The abolitionist framework prepared the way here too. Abolitionists' most effective propaganda drew attention to the slave's abused body, portraying scenes of arbitrary whippings and mutilation.[28] Slaves could not effectively protect themselves from their masters' physical impositions. The middle-class reformers who composed the vanguard of women's rights activists saw the wife as inhabiting a similar if not so terrifying terrain, because she was unable to say no to her husband's sexual demands. He had the common-law right to command her; and Christianity, in saying that "the twain shall be as of one flesh," endorsed the same prerogative.

While appreciating that the wife's position began with consent, unlike the slave's, women's rights activists articulated, haltingly, their visceral feeling that a woman's agreement to marry should not constitute perpetual consent to every one of her husband's sexual initiatives, regardless of her desires. Lucy Stone objected repeatedly to the common-law doctrine of marriage for giving "the 'custody' of the wife's person to her husband, so that he has a right to her even against herself." To her good friend Antoinette Brown Blackwell she wrote that "the real question" for their movement, underlying all "little skirmishing for better laws" was, "has woman, as wife, a right to herself?" To Stone, property and voting meant "very little . . . if I may not keep my body, and its uses, in my absolute right. Not one wife in a thousand can do that now, & so long as she suffers this bondage, all other rights will not help her to her true position." When Stone agreed to marry Henry Blackwell, he not only renounced the attributes of coverture but also guaranteed her the right to decide "how often you shall become a mother."[29] This was the polite way nineteenth-century women and men referred to marital sex.

Even though the public language of middle-class women reformers was usually veiled, their use of words like "degradation" signaled their concern with this issue. Elizabeth Cady Stanton found her female audiences far more moved when she spoke about the wrongs of marriage than when she talked about the vote. "How the women flock to me with their sorrows," she reflected on her speeches about marriage. She wrote to Susan B. Anthony in 1853: "I feel as never before that this whole question of women's rights turns on the pivot of the marriage relation."[30] To women's rights advocates, the concept of bodily self-possession had quite literal meaning. They were arguing for marital sex to take place by consent and desire of *both* spouses, not on the husband's terms alone. With few sure means of birth control and a primitive state of medical knowledge, wives had practical and self-interested reasons to want to control marital sex: pregnancy and childbirth endangered the health and even the life of the mother, while producing another mouth to feed and a child to care for. Repeated pregnancies and childbirths meant tremendous wear and tear on a woman's body. For wives whose husbands had sex with prostitutes, marital intercourse risked venereal disease and its train of bodily ills for mother *and* child: paralysis, brain dysfunction, and blindness were outcomes of the tertiary stage of syphilis, and sexually transmitted diseases could infect the child in the womb. Sex was a double-edged invitation to women at this time. They had good reason to want to regulate their husbands' sexual rights. The slave analogy was forceful because the slave also had to respond on the master's terms.

The women's rights advocates of the 1850s (much like the abolitionists of the 1830s) had their most important impact as agitators who flung a wrench into the sentimental national conversation about the family and household. They gained mainly bad press, scorn, bathetic parody, and ridicule, rather than a large crowd of supporters. Nonetheless they succeeded in making unforgettable their objections to the power disparity between husbands and wives, often by deploying the analogy between the wife and the slave. They made their issues figure in social and political life. Putting these questions of women's rights on the national agenda, women's rights activists were putting the question of marriage there, as southern defenders and also abolitionists had, yet from a third perspective.

Yet even they were not the most shocking entrants on the scene. A small group of radicals called "free lovers" emerged in the 1850s as even more thoroughgoing critics of marriage. Although sexual heterodoxy had appeared earlier, the advocacy of free love did not crystallize until 1850. Its proponents were free-floating mavericks, some abolitionists, and some Spiritualists (heterodox Protestants who believed that the spirits of the dead could be summoned into communication with the living).[31] One free love community was founded in Berlin, Ohio, and another, called "Modern Times," outside New York City. The polemical pamphlet *Love vs. Marriage* ignited a following and a debate that filled the pages of the *New York Tribune* and drew in such eminent participants as the newspaper's editor, Horace Greeley, and Henry James, Sr. Thomas Low Nichols and Mary Gove Nichols published their 466-page diatribe, *Marriage: Its History, Character, and Results; Its Sanctities, and Its Profanities; Its Science and Its Facts*, in 1854; Hannah Brown opened the pages of her paper *The Agitator* to those who would abolish the institution. The *New York Daily Times* episodically published snide or scandalized reports on the establishments of free lovers; one writer contributed a long monitory article, "The Free Love System: Origins, Progress, and Position of the Anti-Marriage Movement," associating it with "Socialism, . . . universal Libertinism and Adultery."[32]

Although it was attacked as "Free Lust," "free love" did not mean an embrace of promiscuity, its adherents insisted. It meant a refusal to abide by the terms of lifelong Christian marriage as prescribed by the state and the church. The institution of marriage corrupted love, said free lovers; people were drawn into marriage by mercenary or other defective motives; people stayed in and suffered from loveless marriages because custom, religion, and law said they had to. Most free lovers gave at least lip service to woman's rights, and some were fierce partisans. At a meeting called the Free Convention held in Rutland, Vermont, in 1858, where the nature of government, free trade, slavery, woman's rights, marriage, maternity, land reform, immortality, and the Sabbath were all subjects of discussion, Julia Branch announced herself a free lover and proposed a controversial resolution "that the slavery and degradation of woman proceed from the institution of marriage: that by the marriage contract she loses control of her name, her property, her labor, her affections, her children, and her freedom."[33]

Although some free lovers dissected marriage and property relations, most simply argued that the love between a man and a woman would be purified and elevated by releasing it from marriage bonds. Free lovers took prevailing ideals about the spiritual values of romantic love to a logical extreme. Sexual relations outside formal marriage were not to be condemned if they were inspired by true love; and someone in a loveless marriage should be able to leave and seek another partner. In contrast to the free love they advocated, they called marriage slavery. "I am a *free* lover, and not a *slave* lover," wrote Edward Underhill, who had established a small community called the "Unitary Household," to the editor of the *New York Daily Times:* "I believe the institution of civilized marriage to be at variance with the instincts of human nature, which rebel against all systems of slavery . . . I believe that whatever is lovable to us we should love . . . without the impertinent interference of either state, Church, or public opinion."[34]

Not surprisingly, those who wanted to fend off the appeal of free love emphasized that marriage could not be equated with slavery because it was based on consent. An outraged review of the pseudonymous autobiographical novel written by the free lover Mary Gove Nichols conceded that marriage was not perfect, but insisted that it was sacred and "a *voluntary* relation—one assumed by the full and free consent of the parties to it, one which no compulsion or constraint can ever force upon them, if they see fit to resist."[35] More conservative woman's rights reformers such as Henry Blackwell feared (with reason) that free lovers would "thrust their immoralities before the public in the 'Womans Rights' disguise." It "would be an infinite shame & pity," he thought, "to allow the just claims of women to liberty of person, to rights of property, to industrial, social & political equality, to be associated with a conspiracy against purity & virtue & all the holiest relations of life."[36] A majority hostile to women's rights as well as to free love did, predictably, mix the one with the other in order to reject both.

Believers in free love, although usually highly individualistic, formed communities among the like-minded, participating in the remarkable efflorescence of intentional, alternative community-founding in the several decades preceding the Civil War. These experiments sprouted on the landscape like so many weeds in a carefully cultivated garden. Virtually every intentional community (except a few purely religious ones) sprang from a critique of the conventional arrangement of work and marriage. The communities drew on a vein of criticism first voiced in the 1790s by radical democrats such as William Godwin and Mary Wollstonecraft in England.[37] England, France, and Germany led the way by producing the social visionaries whose ideas Americans adopted or adapted. Robert Owen in Britain (and his son Robert Dale Owen, who migrated to the United States), Claude Saint-Simon and Charles Fourier in France, theorized modes of collective living to address and counter the inequalities of wealth and power they saw growing around them as commercial and industrial capitalism began to dictate the temper of life. Although political theory in the age of revolutions had seemed to move in a democratic direction, the market mechanisms and work relations of capitalist society increased economic stratification and inequality. Larger-scale commercial manufacturing began to replace artisanal crafts, and long-distance markets began to dominate local markets, making the process of work more regimented and occupations more segmented. Inequalities of wealth visibly increased. People without capital felt their economic destinies were no longer under their own control: they saw hard work bringing few rewards, while the few with command of capital amassed power over others very easily. The unpredictableness of the situation unmoored people. The late 1830s and early 1840s, when many alternative communities were founded, were especially rocky: a major financial "panic" began in 1837, bringing a depression that hung on for years. "Every thing is moving and changing. Persons in poverty, are rising to opulence, and persons of wealth, are sinking to poverty," the educator Catharine Beecher observed of the United States.[38]

The intentional communities inspired by Owen, Saint-Simon, and Fourier in the northeastern and midwestern United States—nearly seventy of them, ranging in population from a dozen people to several hundred—tried to be economically self-sufficient. "Socialist" was the term they used to describe their communitarian solutions, which intended to free the individual's experience of labor from oppression or alienation.[39] Most of them aimed to share the wealth and to value the work of each member equally, as part of a larger democratic aim of achieving equality and freedom. Though not identical in their solutions, all these efforts to institute equalitarian labor reform required rethinking marriage. To prevent disparities of wealth and also to prevent childbearing wives from being dependent on their husbands' earnings, most communitarians eliminated private property. The Owenites had an especially sophisticated analysis of the roots of inequality between the sexes. Fourier's plans, more frequently adopted in the United States than Owen's, centered on relieving workers' alienation and the injustice of differential compensation, but he likewise saw conventional marriage as part and parcel of industrial problems. Fourier envisioned a better life taking place in a planned, collectivized community to be called a Phalansterie (rendered in English as a "Phalanx"). There everyone would work according to his or her "passional attraction," meaning personal inclination, and receive the same reward. American community founders seriously adopted the French philosopher's aims and terminologies.[40]

The minority of Americans who founded and lived in Owenite or Fourierist communities were attempting to establish a new social environment, a veritable counterculture within but not of the dominant society. For their sexual and household arrangements contrary to legal monogamy, they were culturally shunned and often libeled. Polemics against collective households focused on the sexual arrangements more than on work: "passional attraction," for example, was assumed to mean something about free love, rather than about occupational leanings.[41] Alarmists tended to lump into one heap all those who criticized monogamy and call them free lovers—whether they were advocates of more liberal grounds for divorce, communitarians, socialists, women's rights reformers, or indeed avowed free lovers.

The communitarians were not prosecuted by state authorities for their flouting of legal monogamy, however. The tradition of local control that enabled communities to be pragmatic seemed to extend to these strayings too. Even the Oneida community in upstate New York, which announced itself in 1849 with a first annual report and a pamphlet called *Slavery and Marriage: A Dialogue,* was tolerated. This most long-lived experiment did away with the exclusive pairing of couples. Under John Humphrey Noyes's strong-arm leadership and supervision, the community instead encouraged love and sex between any and every man and woman, within a quite rigorous formal structure, including eugenic reproduction, called "stirpiculture." Initially using the designation "free love," the community members shifted to calling their unique regime "complex marriage." By the early 1850s, "Oneida" had become a code word for blasphemy against monogamy.[42]

Alarming as these communities were to close observers, they paled in comparison to the overtly polygamous community in Utah. The foundational political contrasts between polygamy and monogamy, despotism and republicanism, came into play as Americans reacted to the Latter-Day Saints. Joseph Smith, leader of the Church of the Latter-Day Saints, had received a revelation mandating "plural marriage" in 1843 when the group lived in Illinois, but it was kept secret. Hounded and persecuted by neighbors, their leader Smith murdered, the church migrated to the western territory of Utah, where in 1852 the elder Orson Pratt read the revelation aloud. A systematic alternative to Christian monogamy was being practiced in this federal territory, and members of the group aggressively attempted to recruit new adherents. The suspicions of those who had visited Salt Lake City mushroomed into public outrage.

Polygamy in Utah quickly evolved from a local scourge to a national embarrassment. This was not a small alternative community. The Mormons were a burgeoning population—the U.S. Census said 40,000 by 1860—inhabiting and ruling a territory bidding fair to become a state. If marriage molded the form of government, as the founders' political philosophy assumed, Utah presented more than a religious and social aberration. It was a political threat to the integrity of the United States. Popular novels published in the 1850s, with titles such as *Mormonism Unveiled* and *Female Life among the Mormons,* equated polygamy with political tyranny, moral infamy, lawlessness, and men's abuse of women; monogamy in contrast represented national morality and lawful authority.[43]

All the territories of the United States were already lightning rods for political attention, because of the fierce contest over whether the states to be made from them would allow slavery. The shadow of Utah hovered over the developing partisan controversy. As a territory in which both slavery and polygamy were practiced, Utah was an example of what could happen when residents of a territory determined their own "domestic institutions," free from congressional intervention. Like slavery, polygamy showed how the institution of marriage could be manipulated. Its heinous peculiarities were frequently invoked in Congress in the hot debate over the admission to the Union of Kansas and Nebraska in 1853–54. Some opponents contended that the admission of either of these as new slave states would imply inevitable acceptance of Utah's bid for statehood, "until the prevailing nationality of freedom and virtue shall be lost."[44] Antislavery politicians likened southern sexual practices to those of the Mormons, because slaveholders had harem-like privileges over their female slaves. The newly risen Republican Party condemned the "twin relics of barbarism—polygamy and slavery—" in its party platform of 1856, and asserted the sovereign power of Congress over the territories and its "right and duty to prohibit" both enormities there.[45] To confront the Mormon leader Brigham Young, the Democratic president elected in 1856, James Buchanan, took the drastic step of sending federal troops to Utah—in part to show that his party no less than the Republicans abhorred polygamy. This expensive venture kept Mormonism in the political limelight for quite some time, although it ended in ignominy with no result.[46]

When Mormon polygamy was discussed, slavery was never far from politicians' minds, and the reverse was also true. Congressmen were well aware of the language of the Republican platform linking slavery and polygamy when they debated a bill, introduced by Representative Justin Morrill of Vermont in the spring of 1860, intended to criminalize polygamy in the territories of the United States. Senator Charles Sumner gave a major address entitled "The Barbarism of Slavery," in which he stressed the system's "complete *abrogation of marriage*." "There are many disgusting elements in Slavery which are not present in Polygamy," Sumner declaimed, "while the single disgusting element of Polygamy is more than present in Slavery. By the license of Polygamy, one man may have many wives, all bound to him by the marriage tie, and in other respects protected by law. By the license of Slavery, a whole race is delivered over to prostitution and concubinage, without the protection of any law."[47]

Morrill's bill was premised on the power of Congress to regulate marriage in the federal territories, just as state legislatures did in the states. With a clear awareness that slavery as well as marriage was a "domestic institution," debate centered on whether the bill would establish a precedent for Congress to criminalize or prohibit slavery in the territories as well. "Every member from every section of the Union" was "ready to assert the odious criminality of polygamy," Representative Eli Thayer of Massachusetts eagerly pointed out.[48] Southerners were among the most vociferous in condemning the Mormons' aberration, calling it fulsome evidence of the risks inherent in northern liberalism.[49]

The bill put supporters of slavery between a rock and a hard place. The extent of support for it amazed Representative Emerson Etheridge of Tennessee, who had never expected to see proslavery and antislavery camps "harmonizing in relation to this controverted and vexed question of the legislative power of Congress over the domestic institutions of the people of the Territories." Etheridge warned that anyone who voted for the bill, understanding the power of Congress it involved, would "not be in a position hereafter to deny consistently that *Congress*, by 'unfriendly legislation,' . . . may cripple slavery in the Territories." Yet as an opponent of polygamy, Etheridge voted for the bill nonetheless.[50]

Representative Roger Pryor of Virginia found a way to support it too. Congress's right to regulate marriage in the territories was exactly analogous to the states' rights to do so for their own residents, and Pryor wanted to support that power. "Marriage has always been a subject of regulation by the State," he asserted. "Is marriage ever looked upon as only a private contract between the man and the woman, to be made whenever they alone think fit, to last only during the term they may agree upon, and to end at their own will? Is the State no party to such a contract? Has the State no voice in consenting that it shall be made, in regulating its conditions after it is made, and in determining when and how it may be dissolved? Away, then with this argument of the free-love school!"[51] Pryor's reference to free love was a sop to gain support—several congressmen referred snidely to "the practice of free-love principles" during this debate—but Pryor's concern showed slaveholding states' particular investment in their right to regulate marriage. Marriage was a signal domestic institution, as was slavery, and if the authority relations of one of these domestic institutions depended on the "law of the land" so did the authority relations of the other. Pryor supported the bill by arguing that bigamy or polygamy was a crime, which Congress surely had the power to suppress, while slavery was not.

These conundrums kept the House from acting promptly.[52] By the time the bill became law in 1862, the nation had ruptured in civil war, and Revolutionary-era tenets about the relation between marriage and the government took on renewed immediacy. Both slavery and polygamy had brought assumptions about marriage to the forefront of political consciousness and involved them in political controversies. Contemporaneous awareness of women's rights, marriage protests, the bogey of free love, communitarian alternatives, and state legislatures' provisions for divorce and married women's property rights strengthened the undertow tugging at the "great public institution." In northern Republicans' views, the southern states' denial of legal and binding marriage to slaves was the most systematic and wrongheaded of all the challenges. The form of slaves' marriages was now a matter of public policy that involved nothing less than the national character of the United States. Scorn for slave-holders' failure to honor slave marriages spread from radical polemics to the mainstream of political discourse in the Union.[53] Words such as "incest," "concubinage," "unbridled licentiousness," and "promiscuous prostitution" dotted Republican oratory to illustrate the way that slavery "necessarily abolishes the conjugal relation," as the south undertook a self-divorce and the Union dissolved.

4

TOWARD A

SINGLE STANDARD

$\mathcal{A}$t the level of political metaphor the Civil War—an agonizing fracture of the Union—foreboded ill for marriage. Abraham Lincoln drew on a venerable domestic metaphor when he warned, amidst sectional hostility between slavery and free labor, that "a house divided against itself cannot stand." In his message to Congress of 1862, he again showed that his point of reference for the Union was the marital couple when he said, "Physically speaking we cannot separate. We cannot remove our respective sections from each other nor build an impassable wall between them," and continued, "A husband and wife may be divorced and go out of the presence and beyond the reach of each other, but the different parts of our country cannot do this." Although Lincoln distinguished the two, the south's breaking of the original social contract by seceding was interpreted, predictably, as an unwarranted divorce. That reading could not help but refer to the contemporaneous increase in actual divorces and the marital transgressions manifest in free love, communitarian living, Mormon polygamy, and arguments for women's rights. A rhetorical relation had been set up between the institution of marriage and the success of the national compact so that what undermined one put the other at risk.[1]

Materially, the Civil War had an enormous impact on both existing marriages and future ones. Sometimes called the first total war because of the way it involved the entire population in its terrible work of death, it put a huge proportion of the population in uniform. About 2,000,000 white men (more than one third of those of military age) and almost 200,000 black men served in the Union forces, and about 900,000 whites (almost two thirds of those of suitable age) in the Confederate cause. Moralists worried that young soldiers, far from the controlling influence of their families and neighbors, would be exposed to brutality, drink, gambling, and prostitution. Would they adapt easily again to conventional morality and virtuous citizenship? By taking men away from home, the war put a huge weight of responsibility on women to sustain their families while also helping to supply the armies. Customary definitions of marriage presumed the domesticity and dependence of women, but the way they met the challenges of the war defied those definitions. The economic value and the aid to soldiers produced by wives unprecedentedly showed their capacities to "hold the fort" and to serve the nation. The experience proved their ability to operate in and outside the home without men.[2]

Whether wartime reversals would actually unseat conventional expectations of differences between the sexes remained uncertain. The horrors and deprivations of combat, the losses and separations, the maimings and loneliness created longings to return to prewar conventions and resume the familiar customs of home. Cruel wartime mortality prevented old arrangements from being resumed altogether, acting as an engine of change in gender roles, but also provoking nostalgia for the way things used to be. The Civil War killed more Americans than any other war the nation has ever entered: 618,222 men, an average of 182 deaths for every 10,000 people. (World War II, in comparison, caused 30 deaths per 10,000 in the United States.) More Union soldiers were killed than Confederates, but the Confederacy's population was so much smaller that its proportional loss was about three times as great.[3] On both sides husbands, fathers, sweethearts, and sons were dead, and huge numbers were temporarily or permanently disabled. A generation of women became widows early. Their chances of remarrying, like the chances of young women marrying at all, were significantly reduced because the pool of marriageable men was so much smaller than normal. In these demographic circumstances, the assumption that every woman would be a wife became questionable, perhaps untenable.

The elimination of slavery also cast a shadow on marriage. The two "domestic relations" shared structural and legal similarities. If one could be wiped out, was not the other at risk, especially if southern spokesmen had spoken a germ of truth when they saw an "intimate connexion" between the two? Although the north maintained that the Civil War was fought not to end slavery but to preserve the Union, the elimination of slavery came as a sure consequence—partially in the Emancipation Proclamation of 1863, which freed the slaves in territory held by the Confederacy, and then definitively with the thirteenth amendment to the U.S. Constitution, which banned slavery and involuntary servitude. On the floor of Congress, the Pennsylvania senator Henry Wilson triumphantly listed the steps: "By a series of legislative acts, by executive proclamations, by military orders, and by the adoption of the amendment to the Constitution by the people of the United States, the gigantic system of human slavery that darkened the land, controlled the policy and swayed the destinies of the Republic, has forever perished."[4]

Vast changes could be envisioned as the Union reconstituted itself politically—changes in marriage among them, given what state legislatures had done in previous decades to extend divorce grounds and modify coverture. The year that Congress passed the thirteenth amendment, no less than seventy amendments to the Constitution were proposed.[5] In this postwar environment of intentional political transformation, the parallel between the master's right over his slave and the husband's right over his wife still reigned. When the elimination of slavery by constitutional amendment was being discussed, a minority Democrat in the House of Representatives, who objected to the lack of compensation to slaveholders, insisted that the Constitution had to uphold local laws recognizing property rights. Reminding his male colleagues that their own prerogatives as heads of household, husbands, fathers, and employers rested on legal grounds similar to those underlying masters' ownership of slaves was the most forceful way he could find to drive his point home, and he emphasized, "A husband has a right of property in the service of his wife; he has the right to the management of his household affairs. The master has a right of property in the service of his apprentice. All these rights rest upon the same basis as a man's right of property in the service of slaves."[6]

Advocates of the thirteenth amendment found it important to clarify that it would *not* eliminate the other domestic relations. When language for an amendment was first introduced, with the war still going on, an early version began with the words, "All persons are equal before the law, so that no person can hold another as a slave." Senator Charles Sumner of Massachusetts, who was one of the most uncompromising abolitionists in the Senate, endorsed this language. But Senator Lazarus Powell, a minority Democrat from Kentucky (where slavery still existed), immediately protested that if a constitutional amendment could "regulate the relation of master and servant, it certainly can, on the same principle, make regulations concerning the relation of parent and child, husband and wife, and guardian and ward." Like his fellow Democrat in the House, he focused his alarm on the impact of such an amendment on the overall powers of male heads of household. The Republican senator Jacob Howard of Michigan pursued this line, inferring that such language would mean that "before the law a woman would be equal to a man, a woman would be as free as a man. A wife would be equal to her husband and as free as her husband before the law." Hearing this, Senator Sumner immediately dropped his support.[7] That phrasing was heard no more. The thirteenth amendment eventually read, "Neither slavery nor involuntary servitude . . . shall exist within the United States," without any general language stating everyone's equality before the law.

The senators and representatives who designed the amendment to eliminate slavery did not intend to revolutionize marriage law or customs—except in one respect, and that was to extend it to ex-slaves. It remained a very sore point in the north that no Confederate state honored "the relation of husband and wife among slaves, save only so far as the master may be pleased to regard it," in the phrasing of one congressman. Praising the thirteenth amendment being hammered out, a senator emphasized that it would not only make "the shackle . . . fall from the limbs of the hapless bondman," but also protect "the sacred rights of human nature, the hallowed family relations of husband and wife."[8] Just as emancipation meant the transformation of slavery into free labor to ruling Republicans, so it meant the transformation of mere coupling into marriage. Being freed from bondage, ex-slaves were also to be freed from their inability to consent and make contracts. Freedom to consent would enable them to be employed and to marry legally. The labor contract and the marriage contract—choice of work and choice of spouse— were parallel in many minds, both privileges and attributes of the free American.[9]

Union officials and northern missionaries and teachers, who flowed into the former Confederacy after the war to reconstruct the lives of ex-slaves, saw these freedoms to contract for work and marriage as complementary and mutually supportive. They intended to accustom the freedmen and freedwomen to labor for wages under contracts and to honor marriage, in order to suit them to be American citizens. A series of stories entitled *John Freeman*, written for the edification of the emancipated slaves and circulated by the American Tract Society even before the war was won, made this theme clear. It illustrated the work and family life of a model ex-slave family along with some not-so-model counterexamples. The responsibilities of marriage formed a central theme. In one story, young Hattie complained that she was looking for a new man because her husband, Prince, would not work hard but did spend her money. A teacher consoled her that Prince would behave better when he "learned more of the value of liberty." And Prince did improve, slightly and gradually, benefiting from the homily of a white Union officer who advised, "When a man has a wife and child to work for, he has a motive to industry and economy which others do not have. If he is good he will try very hard to make his family happy, and his home comfortable and pleasant, and will never want to spend money for his own selfish pleasure, which he can use for their enjoyment."[10]

The Republican Party's aims embraced this perspective, in which work and marriage complemented each other and the responsibilities of marriage were presumed to promote industrious work habits in men.

Representative William Kelley of Pennsylvania, for instance, was sure that African Americans would show themselves "hardy children of toil" once "the freedman [can] feel that he is a man with a home to call his own, and a family around him, a wife to protect, children to nurture and rear, wages to be earned and received, and a right to invest his savings in the land of the country."[11] Republicans intended the responsibility for supporting emancipated women and children to be delegated to the male heads of their households, and for husbands and fathers to be rewarded by the love and obedience shown by their dependents.

Reinforcing male responsibility for work and family through marriage seemed so important not only to secure economic support for the emancipated population, but also to turn ex-slaves into citizens. This was a fundamental political aim of the Republicans. It was freedmen whom they envisioned as future participatory citizens. Freedwomen who took active part in postwar community celebrations and local political questions considered themselves citizens (as they were, nominally), but to Union spokesmen, freed*men* were the citizens who mattered.[12] Members of Congress and Union agents in the south frequently spoke of and to the emancipated population as though they were all male, urging them, for example, to display "manly patience."[13] In doing so, these officials took it for granted that a man's consent to the responsibilities of formal marriage showed his manhood and gave him warrant for citizenship. Freedmen's responsibilities as husbands as well as their adherence to contracts for their labor were tied to their citizenship.

Even before President Lincoln read the Emancipation Proclamation on January 1, 1863, there were freed slaves in the south. Some had been liberated by the success of Union troops; others had fled behind Union lines. In the fall and winter of 1862–63 in a number of small towns in the deep south and the southwest, General Grant's army organized "contraband camps" where ex-slaves could be sheltered while Union superintendents began to assimilate them to their new lives of freedom; and on the liberated sea islands of South Carolina, a concerted experiment took place to see how well ex-slaves would labor for themselves on their own plots of land.

In these encampments during the war, the intentions of Union officers and chaplains prefigured the much larger program the victorious
Union would put in place when the war ended. Formal, legal marriage
was among the first priorities. Camp officials were directed to "lay the
foundations of society" among the ex-slaves by establishing public
schools, providing opportunities for religious worship, regulating trade,
and "enforcing the laws of marriage." Each camp director had to report
on the freedpeople's "marital notions & practices." One replied tersely,
"All wrong." Some officials noted that mutual consent and faithful attachment characterized slave unions, but usually the report (not always
rendered sympathetically) was that slaves "know what marriage is among
the whites but have yielded to the sad necessity of their case."[14]

By the spring of 1864, a Union military edict had authorized all the
clergy in the army to perform marriages among freedmen, and instructed them to issue marriage certificates and record the marriages.
The policy was implemented most systematically among the "colored
troops" of the Union Army. When the army required ex-slave soldiers to
be properly married if they had women partners, enlisted men responded with alacrity. "Weddings, just now, are very popular and abun-
dant among the colored people," a chaplain in Arkansas wrote to his
superior. Chaplain C. W. Buckley at Vicksburg instructed the soldiers "as
to the nature and binding obligations of the sacred rite," and judged after
only six months that "a deep and abiding foundation has been laid for
a vast change in moral sentiment." Another chaplain in Mississippi
thought he saw a "very decided improvement in the Social and domestic
feelings of those married by the authority and protection of Law. It
causes them to feel that they are beginning to be regarded and treated as
human beings."[15]

African American recruits welcomed the ability to marry as a civil
right long denied to them. Slaves knew the fragility of their marriages
was emblematic of their status. The escaped slave Henry Bibb had written in his 1850 narrative, "There are no class of people in the United
States who so highly appreciate the legality of marriage as those persons
who have been held and treated as property."[16] Also, marriage had the

potential to convey material benefits to the wives and children of soldiers. Wives could claim back pay, property, or "bounty" if they lost their soldier-husbands. Early in 1865, Congress passed a law freeing the (legal) wives and children of men who enlisted. This law was directed at the slaveholding border states that had not joined the Confederacy, and hence were not subject to the Emancipation Proclamation. When male slaves in Kentucky, for example, had run away to enlist in the Union Army, their wives still in bondage at home often suffered tremendous abuse from enraged owners or overseers. Congress intended the law to encourage more black recruits, which it succeeded in doing, but also meant it to acknowledge the integrity of slave families and to protect the family members of those new recruits.[17] Expedience and principle merged in the Union policy.

When Congress in the spring of 1865 authorized an utterly unprecedented federal agency to deal with the situation in the conquered south, the aim to reorient slaves' sexual and family behavior around legal marriage was already in place. Reformers, advocating a new federal bureau to take "paternal care" of the emancipated millions, saw postwar conditions as matters of "moral economy" as well as of "political economy." "The honor, the dignity, the moral and religious character of the nation is at stake," leaders of the Freedmen's Aid Society in major cities wrote the president.[18] Where "barbarism" and "unbridled licentiousness" had flourished, national honor, dignity and morality had to be restored, and could be so only through marriage.

The full name of the new agency was the Bureau of Refugees, Freedmen, and Abandoned Lands, though it quickly became known as the Freedmen's Bureau. It represented the first instance of the federal government's taking responsibility for the relief and sustenance of individual citizens.[19] The war had devastated the south. Thousands of refugees, white and black, driven from their homes and unable to return, needed charitable relief and employment. Congress felt obliged to superintend the freedmen's transition: the ex-slaves were illiterate, often homeless and without land or livelihood. Defeated Confederates were not expected to be kind to them. "Abandoned Lands" appeared in the title of the new bureau because Republican radicals planned for the victorious Union to claim farmland left by Confederates and allow refugees and freedmen to rent or buy it. Announced in July 1865 by O. O. Howard, the thirty-four-year-old head of the Freedmen's Bureau, that plan to enable ex-slaves to gain both dignity and livelihood was derailed by September, in the greatest travesty of Reconstruction. Lincoln's successor, President Andrew Johnson, had no desire to wrest ownership of land from defeated Confederates. Even the Republican-dominated Congress could not muster a majority for the plan. Thus ex-slaves did not get the small farms many had believed, during the summer of 1865, they would acquire, and they were reduced to working as hired laborers or sharecroppers on land owned by whites.[20]

The Freedmen's Bureau's main function became facilitating the transformation of ex-slaves into wage workers. The legislation establishing the bureau stipulated few details. Under an army-like bureaucracy, the agents—many of them former Union soldiers and officers, including chaplains—took up their work in every region and state of the former Confederacy. They provided relief for the exceptionally needy and the disabled. More generally, agents concentrated on familiarizing their charges with contracts and on urging them (indeed, requiring them) to make contracts for work under white landowners.[21] Since agents had a considerable stake in showing that a free-labor regime would be successful, they worked to improve labor relations and adjudicated wage disputes. They had to take on the great task of mitigating ex-Confederates' overt harassment and exploitation of ex-slaves while trying to assure ex-slaves access to neutral laws in the face of white southerners' hostility. Intending to remedy the general illiteracy the bureau men, with the assistance of northern volunteers, also set up schools, eagerly attended by adult freedmen and freedwomen as well as children.

Efforts to reform the sexual practices and family patterns of former slaves became central to the agents' and supervisors' work. For many years northern spokesmen had railed against the deformations of family life entailed by slavery; it was up to the Union to set things right.

Through the instrumentality of the Freedmen's Bureau, the federal government positively pushed legal marriage on ex-slaves and urged them to create or reconstitute male-headed nuclear families. "It was not a business with which the Federal Government had properly anything to do; but it was very properly taken up by the Freedmen's Bureau," the *New York Times* commented paradoxically.[22]

During the war, northern observers in occupied southern territory who were thinking about the future focused less on slaveholders' responsibility for warping African American family life than on the existing features of ex-slaves' marital morality. Speaking of the ex-slaves in the South Carolina sea island experiment, the educator Laura Towne said, "I think they have been systematically taught to disregard the marriage relation." The American Freedmen's Inquiry Commission (AFIC), a body set up by Congress to gather information preparatory to postwar policy-making, looked into the matter with seemingly prurient interest. "Colored women have a good deal of sexual passion, have they not—they all go with men?" was one of the leading questions asked of witnesses in 1863. The AFIC judged that "the disintegration of the family relation is one of the most striking and most melancholy indications of . . . barbarism" in the system.[23] A northerner who leased southern occupied territory during the war, using ex-slaves as free laborers, responded to questions rather typically, "Perhaps one of the most revolting effects slavery has produced upon the negro, is their almost utter want of chastity or modesty, hence the marriage relation is as yet but a loose bond, and in many cases the parties refuse to be married, preferring [*sic*] the system of concubinage brought out from slavery. It will take stringent laws rigidly enforced to break up the licentious habits of this generation, and a patient teaching of the young."[24]

The policy of the Freedmen's Bureau responded to this view that slavery had caused "moral degradation."[25] In the summer of 1865 the bureau issued "Marriage Rules," intended "to correct, as far as possible, one of the most cruel wrongs inflicted by slavery, and also to aid the freedmen in properly appreciating and religiously observing the sacred obligations of the marriage state." Where state legislatures had not yet reconstituted themselves, the bureau stipulated who was eligible to marry and to solemnize marriages; authorized causes and procedures for dissolving some marriages; and declared the end of merely consensual marital relations not legitimated by license or ceremony. "No Parties . . . will be allowed to live together as husband and wife until their marriage has been legally solemnized," the rules warned. Supervisors of black soldiers urged the troops to be "manly" in marital fidelity as they had been in other ways, to "set an example for their race," reminding them that "the enemies of the colored race who are opposed to their progress and freedom assert that there is no virtue among them."[26]

To give the lie to believers in the natural promiscuity of blacks and to vindicate their own efforts, missionaries, officers in command of black troops, and many ordinary agents expected ex-slaves to observe the "sacred obligation" of marriage when given the chance. The rhetoric of bureau personnel on this topic became more and more insistent as the year 1865 progressed. Publicizing his general approach, the assistant commissioner in Vicksburg counseled the freedpeople on their freedom, their claims for jobs and schools, and their need for patience, emphasizing also that in order to throw off the habits of slavery, "regular lawful marriage is a most important thing. No people can ever be good and great, nor even respectable, if the men and women 'take up together' without being married, and change from one to another and quarrel and part whenever the fancy takes them. Sin and shame of this class always destroys a people if not repented of . . . Let no woman consent to live with a man at all who will not at once marry her. Unfaithfulness to the marriage relation is such a sin and shame that it ought not to be heard of among free people." The Union general in charge in Alabama, Wager Swayne, tried to insist on a "general re-marriage" of those informally wed, under pain of prosecution and punishment.[27] While recognizing that emancipated slaves in Kentucky were facing "fiendish atrocity" from local whites, the assistant commissioner exhorted them to enter contracts, "work energetically and patiently," and form lawful homes. "'Taking up with each other' is an abominable practice, and must perish with the institution which gave it birth," he pronounced.[28]

Great numbers of former slaves responded with delight and appreciation to the long-denied opportunity to legitimate their unions. "This is a day of gratitude for the freedom of matrimony," exulted a leader of the African Methodist Episcopal Church, in a speech marking the third anniversary of the Emancipation Proclamation—no longer were his people "polygamists by virtue of our condition." Freedpersons came forward in droves to affirm marriage vows in every locality when the bureau made it possible, sometimes in mass weddings. They seized the opportunity to affirm their humanity and their civil rights, and bureau agents took these occasions as personal and policy successes.[29]

Scurrilous slanders, in the north as well as in the south, dogged their path. As the Republican-dominated Congress was considering legislation to assure civil rights for freedmen, the *New York World,* a Democratic newspaper, published a long article called "Negro Suffrage and Polygamy." Taking for granted that "the ungovernable propensity to miscellaneous sexual indulgence" was "inborn and hereditary" in Negroes, the author argued that if ex-slaves were enfranchised, Mormon missionaries would swarm over the south and provoke such toleration and "wide diffusion" of polygamy that within five years "polygamy will hold the balance of power in our politics." A New York Republican paper, the *Tribune,* rebutted briefly, conceding that enslaved and degraded peoples were "always lewd," but seeing the remedy in "freedom and equal rights." In a second and equally half-baked try, the *Tribune* cited evidence that Mormon missionaries had during three years in Jamaica made no headway among the black population.[30]

The irregular "connubial relations" that did continue horrified chaplains and overawed most agents. Bureau personnel probably exaggerated the extent of these digressions—since their aim was total compliance, something they would not have found had they looked at surrounding white communities—but it is impossible to say precisely. Alternatives and supplements to formal legal marriage did not disappear among the freedpeople. White clerics were most distressed by this, though some of them were also the most sympathetic about the reasons for it. Chaplain C. W. Buckley, who became the assistant superintendent of freedmen in Montgomery, Alabama, was "pained daily" by the situation: "Husbands & wifes [sic] are separating at a fearful rate and 'taking up' with other persons," he reported. "Not infrequently a man is living with two or three wifes. Though this has been the custom of the race and habit of the country for years, yet it cannot be looked upon in any light than a huge system of prostitution by sane persons."[31]

Within a year after the end of the war, southern state legislators had passed laws indicating how freedpeople could legally marry or register their existing relationships—often making cohabitation without legal marriage a misdemeanor punishable by a fine. Revived state authorities wanted to reassert their sovereignty and to collect the fees for marriage licenses or certificates. At this point the bureau relinquished its power to grant marriages but continued exhorting and assisting freedmen and women into compliance, in some cases arresting "adulterers" and bringing them before authorities. Coercion was effective: one woman, when asked why she had married her soldier-husband a second time after the war, said, "they were arresting people that did not have a ceremony between them."[32]

Not all white southerners believed in these policies, however. Local authorities and white ministers did not always implement legal marriage for former slaves, thwarting it by charging exorbitant prices, or refusing to grant marriage licenses, or failing to file certificates, or not allowing blacks to appear in court. According to a bureau agent's account, a former Confederate general said that the legalization of marriages of ex-slaves "stunk in the Nostrils of the people of Va. . . . [and that] the nigger was better off with as many wives as he chose."[33] Local courts in Kentucky did not cooperate, although the general assembly had approved an act making slave unions legal and authorizing African American ministers in good standing in recognized churches to solemnize new marriages. The Freedmen's Bureau filled in by performing ceremonies and by arresting freedpersons who did not conform to the law.[34]

In these instances of resistance, white southerners were recognizing the civil rights manifest in marriage by refusing to grant them. Freedpeople's embrace of marriage privileges recognized the same thing. "I praise God for this day! I have long been praying for it. The Marriage Covenant is at the foundation of all our rights. In slavery we could not have *legalized* marriage; *now* we have it," one Virginia member of the Colored Infantry rejoiced. A man wishing to marry wrote to the Freedman's Bureau to make sure that "we have the same right to make a marriage contract as a white couple would," as if it were too good to be true. A North Carolinian reported an instance where the community put pressure on a man who had failed to marry his partner, "trying to make their colored bretheren [sic] pay some respect to themselves and the laws of the country . . . and stop the slave style of living togather [sic] without being married."[35]

Still, noncooperation and resistance frustrated the hopes of bureau agents. The Virginia assistant commissioner reported "indifference and repugnance of the negro to registering in reference to marriage, for both men and women still have an aptitude for change of their marriage relations and their animal propensities are so strong that they heed not the consequences of the change."[36] These northern men had absorbed racial stereotypes, yet they rarely were as cynical as many white southerners about ex-slaves' capacity for conventional morality. An agent in Tennessee, reporting that ex-slaves were practicing "barbarian customs," wrote, "Do not understand me as intimating that the black race are by nature more depraved than the whites, for I believe the whole human family without regard to race or complexion are creatures of circumstance we are all more or less influenced by the surroundings. Abuses of matrimonial obligations by the blacks have not only been tolerated by the whites, but has been for ages encouraged and sanctioned by influencial [sic] legislative bodies. Therefore the wonder is that it is no worse."[37]

While slaves had formed lasting couples where possible, their owners' power to rupture their families had driven them to evolve a more diversified marital regime. More regularly than whites in many communities and regions, they undertook informal marriages, self-divorce, and serial monogamy. White men and women who lived in informal unions or left one marriage for another did so under the broad canopy of conventional Christian expectations that marriage normally meant a lifelong legal

bond; their informal unions were upheld by the law. Slave couples neither expected the same norms nor were protected by the same law. Their
marital practices had to include more departures from strict monogamy,
more marital breakups, and hence the likelihood of more partners for an
individual.[38] And slave couples could not enact the same economic bargain that free husbands and wives expected as part of a consensual union.

As the bureau men attempted to overlay and replace the ex-slaves'
marital regime with another, their aim proved more difficult to accomplish and more fraught with moral ambiguities than they had anticipated.
Urging a couple wed by custom to be wed by law was easy. But "owing to
the evils of slavery," as one agent put it, "the marriage relations of the
free people have been of a painfully complicated character; some men
having two or three wives, and women as often having several husbands."
This resulted in "much difficulty and trouble" requiring "delicate management."[39] Several southern states passed legislation simply recognizing
ex-slave couples living together at a certain date as legally married and le-
gitimating their children. The bureau in Virginia reported that ex-slaves
greeted such legislation "joyfully," but not all did in fact.[40] Many freedmen and women found themselves at the relevant date living with partners whom they preferred to leave, to seek lost loved ones and resume
earlier relationships that had been ended by force. For them such a law
posed a dilemma: by fiat the state had declared the more recent relationship sacred and lifelong. Addressing this problem, the Virginia state attorney decided that if the couple had earlier separated voluntarily, their
relation as husband and wife still existed and the new cohabitation was illegal; but if they had been forced to separate (by sale), the separation was
legal and the new cohabitation was a legal marriage.

This kind of sophistry came harder to the bureau agents, some of
whom agonized over settling competing claims, especially when a man
had more than one "wife." Confronted with a man who wanted to return
to his earlier partner after having been legally married to someone else
during the war, an agent in Arkansas arrested the bigamist; he then
brought the two women together, and they agreed that one would be the
wife and the other give up her claim in return for a certificate and $100,

which the husband paid. The agent also fined him $25, and felt the arrangement was "satisfactory to all parties," yet he was discomfited by his own intervention. If there were competing claims on a man between a wife with children and one without, bureau personnel resolved the dispute in favor of the first, so that the support of the children would be placed "as far as possible on the natural Guardian of the minor."[41]

Agents' discomfort with practices of "taking up," self-divorce, desertion, and nonsupport focused far more on husbands than on wives, whom they usually saw as passive and imposed upon. The commissioner's initial "Marriage Rules" contained a section called "Duties of husbands to former wives," and one called "Rights of wives and children," but none on husbands' rights or wives' duties.[42] One dismayed agent judged that the freedmen "cannot divest themselves of the belief that a Wife can be taken up and laid aside at will . . . for little trivial reasons." Another commented acerbically that "many Freedmen now take advantage of their freedom to get rid of their Old Wives, and allege as a reason that they were 'not married by the Book.'" He wished he could compel rather than only advise them to "support the women who have lived with them for years and borne them children." Still another criticized what he saw as "mormon practices without mormon laws to provide for the results of such practices," meaning that men had fathered children with several women, and then did not support them. An agent in Texas, dealing with a case in which a husband left his wife and took a false name to marry another, "ordered the husband to return to his first wife, . . . explaining to him the enormity of the crime." He feared there were "hundreds" of similar cases. A Virginia assistant superintendent observed with unintentional irony that many freedmen were not happy with marriage laws, "think[ing] their liberties very much curtailed by their freedom."[43]

Policing and reforming freed*men*, not freedwomen, was the bureau men's first concern. The bureau men understood their mission to be reestablishing the foundations of society, and they were accustomed to seeing social order based on male-headed nuclear families. They aimed to prevent a huge burden of orphans and relief funding, and just as significantly they assumed that freedmen, to *be* men, should be the providers and protectors for their families. The effort to keep husbands monogamous and industrious correlated with the hope to see them exercise political rights. If freedmen were to be envisioned as citizens, they had also to be responsible providers for their dependents. Marriage and work were the supportive bottom points of a triangle with citizenship at the top.

Preconceptions about the gender of citizenship joined the moral and economic reasons for the bureau to foster responsibly monogamous behavior among men. While the bureau disciplined husbands more closely than wives, it also gave them more power and economic resources. In the original plan for plots of land to be distributed to ex-slaves, men were to be the property-holders. General Howard's assistant commissioner General Rufus Saxton, a strong supporter of land distribution, wished to empower the freedman as family head: "I wish every colored man, every head of a family . . . to acquire a freehold, a little home that he can call his own," he said in May of 1865.[44] Although land was not forthcoming, the bureau was still intent on establishing husbandly supremacy. The labor contracts it promoted and enforced institutionalized coverture: the wife's wages were awarded to her husband, not to herself. White landowners expected to continue to use women's labor in the fields (although many freedwomen did not cooperate), and the bureau went along with this sense of entitlement. A directive from the New Orleans bureau that was sent with blank forms for labor contracts made clear that a "family wage" was the aim, so as to absolve the government of the need to provide relief for dependents: "As far as practicable," the circular said, "all the members of the same family should contract conjointly for their labor, so that the number of useful hands and the number of infirm who have to be supported may be regarded in fixing the rate of pay." When whole families of ex-slaves were employed on white landowners' acres, their labor contracts stipulated that the wages of the wife and children were to be paid to the husband and father.[45]

Bureau agents construed the freedman's command over the persons and labor of his wife and children as a reward of his free status and an evidence of his citizenship. Officials expected the freedmen/husbands to rise to the opportunity they were being given. A husband's traditional rights of ownership in his wife's labor—still potent even in states that passed married women's property laws—enhanced his manhood.[46] The rights of ownership over family labor to be acquired through the marriage contract became all the more important to freedmen when the initial plan for them to be landowners failed. When a man had no property but only his own labor power to indicate his independence and stake in society, he had greater interest in seeing his wife's labor as his "own."[47]

Republican congressmen, who were delineating the rights of ex-slaves as citizens, also equated a man's freedom with his rights and responsibilities as a husband and father. The slave, in contrast, "had no rights, nor nothing which he could call his own. He had not the right to become a husband or a father in the eye of the law," as one senator said.[48] Proponents of the bill that would become the Civil Rights Act of 1866 wanted to assure freedmen the basic rights to rule their households. The senators and representatives tended to accentuate what husbands deserved, in corollary to the emphasis of the Freedmen's Bureau on husbands' obligations. The "humblest" free man "may find some willing wife and lowly home," Representative Thomas D. Eliot of Massachusetts intoned. "No monarch upon his throne is more secure in the enjoyment of his rights than he . . . What he has is his own. His wife is his, . . . the sweet voices that call him father are the voices of his own."[49]

This was a sentimental appeal, intended to move congressional colleagues to identify with ex-slaves on the ground of common manhood.[50] "What are the attributes of a freeman according to the universal understanding of the American people?" Senator Jacob Howard of Michigan asked rhetorically. "Is a freeman to be deprived of the right of acquiring property, of the right of having a family, a wife, children, home?"[51] Representative John Kasson implied that personal liberty was coterminous with becoming a husband and father when he contended, "there are three great fundamental natural rights of human society which you cannot take away without striking a vital blow at the rights of white men as well as black. They are the rights of a husband to his wife—the marital relation; the rights of father to his child—the parental relation; and the right of a man to the personal liberty with which he was endowed by nature and by God."[52] In keeping with the common-law and biblical notions of man and wife as a unity, a man's right to his wife as "his own" was almost as self-evident as the integrity of his own body. Representative John Farnsworth of Illinois exclaimed, "What vested rights so high or so sacred as a man's right to himself, to his wife and children, to his liberty, and to the fruits of his own industry? Did not our fathers declare that those rights were inalienable?"[53]

While underlining the freedmen's entitlements as husbands and fathers, congressmen reinforced the earlier view that a wife was not self-governing because she did not control her own labor. Her husband had a right to it. Congressmen conserved a familiar understanding of the husband's marital rights as they revolutionized the status of men who had been slaves. Their rhetoric suggested that husbands' and wives' relative positions were rooted and fixed, although a legion of anxieties had assailed the subject of marriage since before the war. Congressmen knew that marriage was a creature of the law, vulnerable to political manipulation, no less than slavery itself. They came from states that had legislated new grounds for divorce and granted married women rights over their own property. They had lambasted southern states for denying marriage to slaves, and heard frequent reports on the Freedmen's Bureau's effort to establish new "moral foundations" among the emancipated population. They had passed a law making Salt Lake City's institution of "plural marriage" criminal. Although realistically congressmen could not be complacent about the immutability of marriage, they reaffirmed traditional understandings as they rebuilt the Union.

Congressmen's confirmation of marital hierarchy echoed through debates on citizenship and voting rights. When Republican postwar aims made the distinction between civil and political rights important, the position of wives as compared to husbands became a useful reference point. Republican leaders in Congress found themselves having to fend off the notion that freeing the slaves meant simultaneously endowing them with the powers to vote and to hold office. Because public opinion in the Union did not favor slaves being transformed immediately into voting citizens, advocates of emancipation stressed the limited meaning of citizenship, or civil rights, which centered on the contractual powers to manipulate property and on access to neutral laws and legal processes. Political rights went further and included voting, running for and holding office, and serving on a jury and in the military.[54] Lyman Trumbull of Illinois soothed Senate colleagues hostile to enfranchising freedmen by assuring them that "the granting of civil rights does not, and never did in this country, carry with it . . . political privileges."[55] The limited citizenship of white women handily illustrated this point. Half of the white adult population had basic civil rights without voting, holding office, serving on juries, or being called to the militia. "Women are citizens," Trumbull pointed out to his colleagues; "children are citizens; but they do not exercise the elective franchise by virtue of their citizenship." If being a citizen had to mean exercising political rights, John Bingham of Ohio contended in the House of Representatives, "your wives and mothers and daughters . . . are not to be considered as invested with the rights of citizenship."[56]

This example had unique force. It made the point that citizenship and political rights were not identical, and it also underscored the appropriateness of women's lack of political rights and the categorical distinction between husbands and wives in the eyes of the state. Congressmen tended to slip easily between statements about "women" and "wives" with regard to citizenship. The wife's enforced civic dependency influenced their views of all women, who were potential wives.[57]

Just at the time Republicans were referring to women's citizenship as a stable reference point, however, suffragists were staging a more vigorous challenge than ever before. Women activists in the United States emphasized the vote a generation earlier than their counterparts in Europe did, and although the American tradition of popular sovereignty influenced them, so did the contemporary importance of freedmen's rights. By 1866, Republicans who had initially been reluctant to say their goal was enfranchising the freedmen had changed their program for reforming the south. In expansive and eloquent language radical Republicans, the most advanced faction of the party, explained that exercising the right to vote was the basic freedom from which all other freedoms flowed. They revamped their definition of "fundamental" rights for the freedmen to include the right to vote, even calling it a natural right.[58] To woman suffragists, a tiny but determined group, this emphasis made their own case self-evident. The political outlook of the radical Republicans reenlivened woman suffragists' embrace of the ballot.

As soon as Republicans proposed the fourteenth amendment, Elizabeth Cady Stanton and Susan B. Anthony sent a petition to Congress asking for the vote for women. They found the new amendment insupportable in one sense: in stipulating a punishment (reduction of congressional representation) for states that kept some citizens from the ballot, the amendment used the word "male" to describe those whose right to vote must not be denied. In the original Constitution, no sex qualification—no qualifications at all for voters—appeared. The matter had been left to the states. "If the word 'male' be inserted," Elizabeth Cady Stanton fumed, "it will take us a century at least to get it out again."[59]

Congress was unsympathetic. Even congressmen who said they supported women's rights and could envision enfranchising women in the future refused to diverge from their focus on the freedmen. Senator Howard baldly explained that women and children were "not regarded as the equals of men," and pinned this on the "law of nature." Others found a political principle: Senator Timothy Howe said that women, unlike freedmen, could be deprived of the ballot because "they exercise it by proxy, as we all know. Females send their votes to the ballot box by their husbands or other male friends." Senator Ben Wade likewise was satisfied that women were "in high fellowship with those that do govern"; they had others to "act as their agents." Being wives, women *were* represented in the political process, by their husbands.[60]

Congressional unresponsiveness to Stanton and Anthony, and the fourteenth amendment's protection of men's voting rights, reflected the same substructure of beliefs about husbands and wives' citizenship that underlay the Freedmen's Bureau's insistence on formal marriage. Wives' dependence on their husbands for representation, along with their presumed economic dependence, formed intrinsic elements of men's

citizenship. In revising the Constitution, could Congress seriously enter-
tain the reality of women becoming independent voters, when marital hierarchy informed men's civic rights, when wives' dependency supported
their husbands' participation in the polity? The fourteenth amendment,
at the time of its formulation, said no. (A century later, however, reinter-
pretation of the amendment's guarantees of due process and equal protection would dismantle laws based on sex discrimination.)

Where Republicans championed a vital relation between freedmen's
citizenship, enfranchisement, and manhood, southern Democrats (ex-
Confederates) deplored it. White southerners saw not only political but
sexual empowerment in African American men's votes. They inferred the
connection from the political tradition in which a man's participatory citizenship built on his marriage and headship of a household. Civil rights
meant freedom of marital choice as well as potential admission to the
ballot, and both bothered white southern opponents of black equality.
When a North Carolina member of the Ku Klux Klan—the postwar
white vigilante organization that specialized in terrorizing blacks—was
asked his purpose by congressional investigators, he answered that it was
to keep the "colored" from "mixing" with whites. Asked to clarify, he
said, "To keep them from marrying, and to keep them from voting," as
though he found the connecting link self-evident.[61]

Freedom to marry included freedom to choose white women. During
the war, the question of sexual relations between black and white hovered
behind congressional discussion of the future of the emancipated slaves,
but laws about intermarriage were rarely mentioned. Instead, accusations
were regularly traded back and forth between the Democrats in Congress
and the abolitionist Republicans as to whether slaveholders' lust or the
process of turning slaves into citizens was more to blame for fostering
"amalgamation."[62] In 1863 enemies of the Republican Party coined the
word "miscegenation," meaning mixing of species, to brand the practice.
The word built on a theory of "polygenesis" offered by American eth-
nologists. According to the theory, the black and white races were created
separately and unequally, each with distinctive physical and mental char-

acteristics; mixing them would produce weak, probably sterile offspring and degrade both races.[63]

After emancipation, white women's accessibility to African American men became a demon of the white southern imagination—far more than it was during the centuries of enslavement. As a result of white fears and projections, which were not limited to the south although were more virulent there, states rushed to pass or solidify legislation criminalizing marriage across the color line. More laws of this sort were passed during the Civil War and Reconstruction than in any comparably short period. Ten states created new bans; eight others reiterated or refined theirs; others kept previous laws in place.[64]

These laws were in the minds and on the lips of senators and congressmen designing the Civil Rights Act of 1866 and the fourteenth amendment. In an early draft, the civil rights bill prohibited states from denying to blacks "any of the civil rights or immunities belonging to white persons," on pain of federal punishment. It seemed self-evident that freedom to marry was a civil right, because it was so often invoked as the emblem of the free man. But that identification was problematic, because marriage regulation was a prerogative of individual state sovereignty, off limits for federal legislation. If the right to marry was a civil right, then the conclusion followed that the civil rights bill overreached itself, interposing federal power where state sovereignty should be supreme. State laws banning marriage across the color line seemed likely to be vulnerable to civil rights prosecution. Did not a law preventing a black man from marrying a white woman deny him his full exercise of civil rights?

For states' rights defenders who opposed the civil rights bill, laws against mixed marriage became the bedrock of federalism. These representatives and senators, mostly white Democrats, were hostile to federal power for many reasons, and they made state power over marriage a favorite and effective means to raise the alarm. "Are not the several States sovereign enough to determine upon this question of miscegenation? Are they not as sovereign to determine upon it as they are upon the question of polygamy, the question of incest, or any other question which it is believed and is thought would materially affect the interests of the community constituting the State?" one senator typically demanded.[65] When President Andrew Johnson vetoed the Civil Rights Act, he cited the vulnerability of mixed-marriage bans as a principal example of the bill's unconstitutional assertion of federal power over "the internal police and economy of the respective States."[66]

This approach did not prevent the Civil Rights Act from passing—since the Republicans in favor had such a decisive majority that they overrode President Johnson's veto—but it did succeed in insulating marriage legislation from the act's reach. Only a rare civil rights supporter aimed to undo the many laws, northern and southern, on this subject. Although the Republicans wanted to guarantee freedmen equal rights before the law in most respects, they did not have in mind guaranteeing them the right to marry white women. Debate showed the limits of Republican politicians' feelings on the question; they twisted and turned to argue that the bill would not have the impact feared. Senator Lyman Trumbull of Illinois made light of laws against intermarriage as unnecessary "where there is no disposition for this amalgamation."[67] A more common approach was to say that the choice of marriage partner in itself was not a civil right: it was "a simple matter of taste, of contract, of arrangement between the parties," as one congressman contended.[68] Most often, supporters argued that the federal civil rights legislation would not touch antimiscegenation laws because the laws constrained whites and blacks equally. A black person could not marry a white; but neither could a white marry a black.[69] This was also the approach the U.S. Supreme Court took fifteen years later, when it considered the constitutionality of an Alabama statute that penalized marriage, adultery, or fornication between a white and "any negro, or the descendant of any negro to the third generation," with hard labor for up to seven years. Intraracial adultery or fornication in Alabama carried only a $100 fine. On the theory that the law punished both races equally for the same crime, the Supreme Court did not see a denial of equal protection in its provisions.

Since the case revolved around a fornication charge, however, it was not definitive on the marriage question.[70]

The Civil Rights Act and the fourteenth amendment did embolden couples to challenge racial restrictions on marriage. The U.S. Constitution had declared that no state was allowed to pass any "Law impairing the Obligation of Contracts" (Art. 1, Sec. 10), and the Civil Rights Act of 1866, with the freedmen's protection in mind, reiterated federal protection of citizens' contractual rights. Contracts formed by free consent were supposed to be private matters; they gave lifeblood to a private property system, and states were not to interfere in them.[71] The fourteenth amendment, ratified in 1868, added federal guarantees to the requirement for states to extend the "equal protection of the laws" to everyone. Inspired to claim that marriage was a contractual right which state laws could not constitutionally abridge, interracial couples contested antimiscegenation laws in numerous states over the next twenty-five years. They did not succeed. Fifteen cases reached state supreme courts (in nine states), where, with the exception of a very brief interlude in Alabama and a longer one in Louisiana before reversal, they were definitively turned down.[72]

The fact that marriage had a public as well as a private character undergirded these results. Marriage was not simply a contract, the appellate judges who heard these cases insisted, but also a status and an institution. These two sides, the contract and the status side, were the legal equivalents of marriage as private arrangement and public institution. The Supreme Court of North Carolina was especially clear and succinct in 1869, in explaining why federal protection of equal rights did not unseat antimiscegenation law. Marriage, though formed by contractual consent, was "more than a civil contract," the court declared: "it is a *relation*, an *institution* . . . And every State has always assumed to regulate it." Marriage had "never been left to the discretion of individuals." The court also saw "no discrimination in favor of one race against the other," in preventing whites and blacks from intermarrying, since the law "operates upon both races alike; neither can marry the other." Besides, the federal

Civil Rights Act of 1866 had "no application to the social relations . . . but only [to] civil and political rights."[73] Members of Congress had voiced both these points during the debate on that act. The undefined terrain of "social rights" was where battles would rage for a century over the meaningful acceptance and incorporation of freed slaves and their descendants into American life. Here, the North Carolina court signaled how central marriage law would become to the claim that social equality could not be legislated.

North Carolina's emphasis was echoed in other states, becoming the means to preserve laws banning marriage across the color line. The legal understanding of marriage as a civil contract still stood; acceptance of informal marriage and the provision of divorce causes both relied on it. The power of government to prescribe and regulate marriage was equally clear nonetheless, making marriage a peculiar hybrid. This was not new. Joseph Story, a U.S. Supreme Court justice before 1850, and an influential legal thinker, had treated marriage as a contract but called it "something more than a mere contract. It is rather to be deemed an institution of society, founded upon consent and contract of the parties." The institutional or status aspect of marriage became more useful to deflect challenges to the institution after the Civil War. As if to hold back individuals' impulse to redefine marriage, courts emphasized that the marital bargain, although entered by consent, could not be changed, modified, or ended thereby: its "rights, duties, and obligations" were "of law, not of contract," "the creation of the law itself," the Supreme Court of Maine held. Marriage had to be "more than a contract" commented the Indiana Supreme Court; it was the result of "public ordination" as much as private agreement.[74]

The U.S. Supreme Court endorsed this view when a plaintiff claimed that the Oregon territorial legislature had unconstitutionally impaired a contract of marriage by granting a divorce. The high court had just recently affirmed that marriage was "everywhere regarded as a civil contract" in order to validate informal marriage, but in this 1888 case Justice Stephen Field clarified that marriage was not simply a contract. Marriage was "an institution, in the maintenance of which *in its purity* the public is deeply interested." Although the case was not about racial limitations, Justice Field's stance and his references to civilization, morals, and purity nodded positively toward the laws criminalizing marriage between whites and blacks. "Marriage, as creating the most important relation in life, as having more to do with the morals and civilization of a people than any other institution, has always been subject to the control of the legislature," he wrote.[75]

Courts' justifications of state impositions on marriage implied that more uniform standards of control were desirable. A tremendous increase in the use of judicial review after 1860 moved the appellate judiciary into a much stronger position as makers of public policy.[76] Now that the south's divergence on slave marriages had been eliminated, a national standard of formal and legal monogamy could conceivably move from rhetoric to practice. The power of the nation-state was newly prized in the wake of the Union victory. Elite organs such as *The Nation* magazine and the *New York Times* even mentioned that federal control of marriage standards might be a good idea. *The Nation*'s editor linked the issue of "deciding on what terms men and women shall live together in wedlock" with "framing the organic law of political societies."[77]

During the Civil War, the Congress had taken a big step toward establishing a national marital and family policy by authorizing soldiers' pensions as an incentive to men to enlist. Endlessly renewed by Congress, pensions for disabled men and for soldiers' widows and aged parents became a major federal expenditure, taking 40 percent of the federal government's budget in 1893.[78] With these pensions, the government stepped in to take the dead soldier's place for hundreds of thousands of widows and children. General O. O. Howard's later judgment that the Freedmen's Bureau had begun a new identity for "the Nation, as something to love and cherish and to give forth sympathy and aid to the destitute" might have more aptly been applied to the Civil War pension system.[79]

The pension system, reaching far into the ranks of the very poor, Indians, African Americans, and recent immigrants from among whom soldiers had been recruited, reinforced the standard that the husband and father was the provider and family members his dependents. So many of the claimants had *not* been ceremonially wed that the program gave credit to informal marriages. This liberality in policy was balanced by government wariness of fraud, which led pension administrators to snoop into claimants' domestic situations to look for unacknowledged male partners or other evidence of irregularity. Thus through surveillance of pensioners' qualifications, the federal government enforced a uniform standard of faithful monogamy.[80]

Enacting a new benevolence of the nation toward its citizens, the pension policy ordained an integrative moral standard among them and aimed to instill a common conscience, as the Freedmen's Bureau also did.[81] Both of these war-born policies took an unprecedented step in bypassing the mediation of state governments; they were the first form of federal "welfare" policies. Both gave evidence of a new deployment of national sovereignty, standing above the general rule that states managed the regulation of marriage. State sovereignty over marriage was not necessarily at odds with a national standard, however. Although the variation among divorce provisions rattled reformers, in fact state legislatures looked over one another's shoulders and in judge-made law, where contested issues about marriage were most often resolved, national convergence was predictable.

At the time, the apparatus to enforce a national standard of marriage was minimal, but perhaps having the apparatus was less important than having the ideal. The reframing of American political society after the Civil War incorporated a preferred model for American marriage, which renewed emphasis on the spouses' being of the same race, highlighted the state's role in the marriage, and continued, as of old, to see the whole inspired by Christian principles, including the consent and unity of the couple, with the husband representing his wife. The unified nation had newly expressed stakes in every union's being freely chosen, monogamous, and legal. Intraracial Christian monogamous marriage could begin to be seen as a positive instrument of national policy—as the crushing of Mormon polygamy would show.

5

MONOGAMY AS THE LAW
OF SOCIAL LIFE

*T*raditional monogamy appeared to need bolstering after the Civil War. Communitarian and free love alternatives had bedeviled the institution in the 1850s; then wartime disasters threatened known ways of life. Publicity about the Freedmen's Bureau's efforts to regularize the informal and multiple marriages among ex-slaves, and the spread of innovations on married women's property and divorce, furthered the general awareness that the laws of matrimony were susceptible to alteration. Women reformers were in the halls of the Capitol demanding independent rights for wives. And the Mormons in Utah were more numerous and vociferous than ever. Brigham Young felt confident enough to declare in a nationally publicized conversation that he would defy the Morrill Act's prohibition of "plural marriage." He bragged that his people were 70,000 strong and would soon be 300,000, at which point it would be impossible not to admit Utah as a state. When that happened, he said, with an assertiveness that uncomfortably echoed Confederate pronouncements, the state would "have an equal right to make laws protecting polygamy."[1] But he did not foresee the consolidated Union that had been forged in postwar reconstruction, nor the way federal authorities would bring the marital behavior of nonconforming groups into line.

Postwar reaction to turbulence in the institution of marriage burst out in negative attention to divorce. When the self-styled philosopher Henry James, Sr., had the temerity to ask, in an unsentimental *Atlantic* essay of 1870, "Is Marriage Holy?" the editor of *The Nation* promptly took him to task. A new weekly that dedicated itself to national sovereignty, *The Nation* had already expressed concern about marriage with editorials inquiring "Why Is Single Life Becoming More General?" and probing "The Future of the Family."[2] James defined marriage as a "civic tie" that gave a husband certain "civic rights, such as the right to found a family," but also exposed him to the "civic pains" of divorce if he proved unworthy.[3] His allusion to state-authorized divorce as a virtual corollary of state-authorized marriage touched a nerve.

Secular commentators were led by clerics' alarm. The manipulations of Christian-model monogamy in evidence by the 1850s had assaulted its reign in common sense, so that religious leaders felt more obliged than before to reiterate God's law. The Reverend Theodore Woolsey, president of Yale College, led the charge in several essays published in 1867 and 1868 examining "Divorce and Divorce Legislation" in the United States. His essays, widely reprinted and collected in a book by 1869, surveyed the most common grounds for divorce: adultery, desertion, imprisonment for a crime, failure to provide for a wife's maintenance, habitual drunkenness, and extreme cruelty. More than half a dozen states had an omnibus clause besides, which gave great latitude to judges. Woolsey lamented the uneven and unwarranted expansion of divorce grounds. He expressed his fears for marriage and hence for society, and made the case that the only divinely approved (and therefore truly legitimate) reason for divorce was adultery.[4] And only the innocent spouse in a divorce due to adultery should be free to remarry, not the guilty sinner. This was the position of most Protestant churchmen, who along with their Catholic counterparts responded to Woolsey's prompting by putting their own perturbations into print. Diverse magazines and newspapers followed the lead of Woolsey's findings: the *New York Times*, for example, had an article every few months in 1868 and 1869 called "Marriage and Divorce" or (disapprovingly) "Divorce Made Easy." Religious essays with titles such as "Marriage and Divorce," "The Divine Law of Divorce," and (in the *Catholic World*) "The Indissolubility of Christian Marriage" became common and continued to multiply.[5] Although the frequency of divorce was minuscule (not even two divorces per thousand marriages, in 1870) compared to the divorce rate in the late twentieth century, at the time it was noticeably higher in the United States than anywhere in Europe—and the seemingly relentless upward trend caused panic. By 1900 there were four divorces per thousand marriages.[6]

More than divorce itself was at issue. Divorce was the leading edge, the visible incarnation of many menacing possibilities. Divorce as a last resort for a long-suffering spouse, an escape hatch for an abused partner, complemented the conception of marriage as a just contract for lifelong union. But the availability of divorce could be seen as a different proposition, an open incentive for a husband or wife to become dissatisfied and seek another partner. Such a vision of divorce suggested far less predictability in marriage than the law had previously allowed. It stimulated the vagaries of desire, which Christian-model monogamy had meant to foreclose. It allowed the possibility of more than one sexual partner in a lifetime, rather like polygamy. If married men's sexual adventures outside of marriage had often been tacitly accepted, married women's had not—yet divorce was available to both, and more women than men sought and gained divorces. When anyone from ordinary concerned citizens to political conservatives or agitated ministers deplored the phenomenon of divorce, their imaginations might be seeing free love, polygamy, or a world in which husbands no longer controlled their wives, household dependents, and property.

The scandal and trial of Daniel McFarland, who murdered Albert Richardson, added fuel to this fire. In New York City, a small-time aspirant to an acting career named Abigail McFarland had reacted to her husband's abuse by moving from their home to a boarding house in the fall of 1867. There she began seeing a newspaperman named Albert Richardson. When her husband, Daniel, found out about this, he began a legal action against Richardson. Late in 1868 Abby moved to Indiana to take advantage of its liberal divorce laws. When she moved back to New York about a year later (having divorced her husband), and it became clear that she and Richardson were involved in a relationship—perhaps were even living together—and intended to marry, Daniel McFarland walked into the office of the *New York Tribune,* where Richardson worked, and shot him, point-blank.

That was in December 1869. Albert Richardson married Abby McFarland in a deathbed ceremony performed by the famous minister Henry Ward Beecher, and expired not long after. The trial of McFarland for murder took place in the spring of 1870, becoming a cause célèbre, followed in daily papers all across the country. Because Richardson was a public figure as a journalist and had friends and acquaintances in high places, the story amounted to a national media event. McFarland's defense counsel portrayed him as driven insane by Richardson's wily seduction of his wife.[7] In public discussion, the "seduction," divorce, and murder formed the centerpiece, but the lovers' nonconformist circle of writers and entertainers and, even more, Abby's boldness in getting a divorce, gaining custody of one of her two children, and thinking of herself as a would-be career woman all mattered. Some of the facts of the relationship were disputed and all, of course, had more than one interpretation, making national commentary elaborate and kaleidoscopic. Nonetheless, when the all-male jury announced acquittal, the great majority of journalists condoned McFarland's murderous act.

In commenting on McFarland's trial, many journalists endorsed husbands' property rights in their wives as firmly as the Republican Party had in its policy toward the freedmen—embracing husbandly superiority and lifelong fidelity as crucial to marriage. The *New York Herald* summed up common opinions after the jury had spoken. Not stopping to recount the well-known facts of the twenty-four-day-long trial of which "the public was never tired," the editorial said it was less the defendant than "the principles, the morality and social questions involved" that proved so riveting. "The whole community" saw "dangerous doctrines . . . which tend to undermine the social fabric and the sacred ties of marriage" as being on trial—namely, those ideas of "free lovers" that had encouraged Abby McFarland and Albert Richardson to think that a one-sided separation and divorce warranted the betrayal of a husband.[8]

The *Herald,* being a rival of Richardson's employer the *Tribune,* had something to gain in accusing the other paper's circle of being "weak sentimentalists and pretended philosophers" who caused the tragedy. Nonetheless its analysis of public reaction seemed on the mark. Far more elite organs such as the *New York Times* and *The Nation* also condemned Richardson's supporters for suggesting that "a man does no wrong in tempting a wife away from her husband." More conservative and religious voices held that "a man and a woman, who have sinned against the law of marriage, [should] be kept by law from marrying one another." *The Nation* saw a categorical difference between a marital separation and the freedom of one of the parties to engage in a subsequent love relationship. The former was fine (so long as children were provided for)—but the latter meant "free love—by which we mean simply that the tie between man and woman known in civilized communities as matrimony, would rest simply on inclination."[9] Many commentators labeled Albert Richardson's attentions to Abby McFarland and her subsequent divorce "free love" practices, thereby expressing their consternation at all the challenges to monogamous marriage of the past several decades.

Fearing that traditional marriage was an endangered species, a new crop of marriage reformers sprang up among ministers, educators, and publicists. They were sure that divorce was rampant. Believing that marriages were being formed hastily, and also feeling that ceremonial marriage induced greater respect for the institution and fidelity to its purposes, these reformers wanted to see all the states require ceremonies, invalidate informal or "common-law" marriage, and minimize grounds for divorce. They thought that informal marriage led to the frequency of divorce, because, being created by the couple's consent, informal marriage logically implied that a couple should be able to end their marriage by mutual consent too. The reformers wanted no one to go where that logic led.

Gaining force in the 1870s and 1880s, reformers pressed state legislatures with some success. Analogies between the breakup of marriages and the dissolution of the national political compact were still fresh: A minister active in the Divorce Reform League condemned the simply contractual orientation of informal marriage by likening it to the Confederacy's defective understanding of the national union. The federal emphasis on ex-slaves' marrying formally also had an impact. Several states passed laws to invalidate informal marriage. Occasionally judges agreed explicitly with reformers who saw conformity to the law as helpful in conditioning individuals' long-term marital behavior. The Maine Supreme Court, invalidating informal marriage, commented that if people understood that they could marry "only in compliance" with statutory requirements, they would stop attempting to marry in any other way and would be "led to regard the contract as a sacred one, . . . in which society has an interest, and to which the state is a party."[10]

Several states, chastened, tried (unsuccessfully) to reduce divorce by retracting their omnibus clauses in the 1870s. What many alarmists mourned was a disenchantment with or secularization of marriage—a loss of its sacred quality—but the only remedies reformers proposed were more civic, legislated actions. Many states put stricter controls on marrying, "guarding the altar," as one historian has called it, using the public power of the state to raise the age of consent and to instigate hygiene-based or "eugenic" requirements, supposed to safeguard the next generation by refusing to license people with venereal disease or mental incapacities to have children.[11]

The suggestion to federalize marriage law came up, too. The differences among states' grounds for divorce seemed to reformers an unhealthy provocation to migrate in order to shed a spouse. A uniform (national) legal code for marriage and divorce would fix that, and also cure the lack of unanimity among states on the validation of informal marriage. This proposal became a favorite of reformers of many different stripes, brought time and again before Congress, but the individual states too jealously guarded their "domestic institutions" for it to become a reality.[12] The U.S. Congress responded to another of the reformers' pleas, however, by authorizing a survey of the nation's marital behavior. (At the time a new word, "statistics" meant information arrayed for government uses.) The head of the U.S. Department of Labor, the statistician Carroll Wright, produced an overview of marriages and divorces in the two decades after 1867. Showing significant regional and state differences, and confirming the increasing frequency of divorce, the survey and its successor did not exactly calm fears, but did announce that marriage and divorce should be seen as national concerns.[13]

On several counts, the Utah territory made reformers long for a national standard of legal monogamy. Divorce was more common there than elsewhere, for Utah allowed a judge to grant a divorce whenever he found it appropriate. A petitioner did not even have to be a resident but merely had to express the intention to become one. Fears that this leniency would affect the rest of the nation intensified when the transcontinental railroad was completed in 1869. It was rumored that lawyers in Utah used divorce forms preprinted with a notice of intention to take up residency and the claim of irreparable marital breakdown, so that only names and the date need be added.[14]

The Mormons' liberality with divorce exacerbated the errors of their defiant polygamy, which seemed all the more heinous after slavery was eliminated. No matter that only a small proportion of the Latter-Day Saints, mainly among the top hierarchy, could afford to indulge—they posed a threat to the political and moral character of the nation.[15] The continued practice of any polygamy in the west (now completely in the jurisdiction of the United States, which had not been the case in the early 1850s) evoked a huge and protracted federal opposition. The "zeal and concentration" of the federal firepower aimed at polygamy was, in the words of one legal historian, "unequalled in the annals of federal law enforcement."[16]

President Ulysses S. Grant, who owed his election to his prestige as a Union commander, wanted to appear as forceful against the Mormons as he had been against the Confederacy. He appointed as governor of Utah a general who had been instrumental in the occupation of the defeated southern states, and appointed as chief justice for Utah's Supreme Court James McKean, who made clear the political challenge ahead. The Latter-Day Saints had established, McKean said, an intolerable "*imperium in imperio*"; the contest was "Federal Authority against Polygamic Theocracy." The territory's control of marital practice denoted incipient state-building, which had also been evident in a fleeting plan of 1850 to print money and have its own "national" bank. Grant's successors as president—Hayes, Garfield, and Arthur—all referred to the Mormon question in their annual messages; all were willing to use federal power to eliminate polygamy.[17]

The Morrill Bill of 1862, which made bigamy a federal crime punishable by up to five years in prison, proved unenforceable. Because Utah did not register marriages, a person indicted for bigamy could simply deny a second or third marriage. More important, Mormon juries were uncooperative and would not convict. In the Senate, Shelby Cullom of Illinois took a more forceful approach. He introduced a comprehensive antipolygamy bill with forty-one sections that would suspend one attribute of Mormon men's citizenship after another, from jury trial to the ballot. Congress was also presented with an alternative approach: rather than disfranchising Utah's men, enfranchising the women. That idea, inspired by woman suffragists' agitation in response to the fourteenth and fifteenth amendments, was championed by the few congressmen who could swallow the idea of women voting. Antipolygamists were sure that plural wives were degraded and oppressed, their possibility of free consent to marriage suppressed. Perhaps Mormon women with the ballot would vote polygamy out of existence.[18]

This assumption shattered Humpty-Dumpty–like when Mormon women in Salt Lake City staged public demonstrations against the Cullom bill early in 1870. At several mass meetings, Mormon women endorsed plural marriage and protested the way Congress was proposing to treat their fathers, sons, brothers, and husbands. A representative spokeswoman, Harriet Cook Young, counted on their assemblages to "give the lie to the popular clamour that the women of Utah are oppressed and held in bondage. Let the world know that the women of Utah prefer virtue to vice, and the home of an honorable wife to the gilded pageantry of fashionable temples of sin." Turning the tables, she accused her accusers: "Wherever monogamy reigns, adultery, prostitution, free-love and foeticide [abortion], directly or indirectly, are its concomitants . . . The women of Utah comprehend this and they see in the principle of a plurality of wives, the only safeguard against adultery, prostitution, free-love and the reckless waste of pre-natal life."[19]

In response to this highly publicized meeting, antipolygamists, including Republicans in Congress, emphasized that Mormon women could not be seen as acting for themselves. A congressman from Indiana even proposed that plural wives should be protected by the Freedmen's Bureau, since they were so much like slaves. Politicians called plural wives "concubines voluntarily," "bound slaves," or "Indian squaws." The sponsor of the Morrill Act, Justin Morrill, labeled the whole system "Mohammedan barbarism."[20] Perhaps to thank Mormon women for their demonstrations and certainly to show the error in congressional attitudes, the Utah territorial legislature itself took up the idea of allowing women to vote. The U.S. Congress quickly dropped the idea. In 1870 Utah became the second territory to enfranchise its women, Wyoming having led the way the previous year.[21]

Congress failed to pass the Cullom bill but then found a more specific legislative weapon. The Poland Act of 1874 allowed federal courts in the Utah territory to try federal crimes (including bigamy cases under the Morrill Act), and it gave these courts authority to empanel juries on which at least half the members would be non-Mormons. As a result, polygamists began to be indicted and tried, and a test case came forward on the question whether plural marriage, being a religious duty in Mormon eyes, was protected by the first amendment's guarantee of religious freedom.

The U.S. Supreme Court gave a decisive negative when presented with the case, *Reynolds v. the United States*, on appeal. Chief Justice Morrison Waite emphasized that Congress had the power to prohibit and criminalize bigamy in the territory. Religious claims exempted no one, because constitutional guarantees of religious freedom had to do with *beliefs* only, and did not protect "actions in violation of social duties or subversive of good order." Polygamy was a criminal action, regardless of religious belief. Making the point unmistakable, the court asked rhetorically whether anyone would contend that a religious ritual involving human sacrifice could claim exemption from prosecution under the first amendment. To exempt plural marriage from criminality under the guise of religious freedom was to make religion "superior to the law of the land" and every citizen "in effect . . . a law unto himself," said Waite. To allow polygamy was to invite anarchy and reduce government to existing "in name only."

The Chief Justice's discussion of the defects of polygamy picked up threads woven through American political thinking. Waite had no doubt that it was legitimate for "every civil government to determine whether polygamy or monogamy shall be the law of social life under its dominion." In Montesquiean fashion, he declared that "according as monogamous or polygamous marriages are allowed, do we find the principles on which the government of the people, to a greater or less extent, rests." Polygamy was intolerable in the United States because it led "to the patriarchal principle . . . which . . . fetters the people in stationary despotism." Like congressmen who called Mormon women "squaws" or "Mohammedans," Waite racialized polygamy, calling it the preserve of "Asiatic and of African people," "always . . . odious" to northern and western Europeans.[22] On this point he cited Francis Lieber, an 1827 immigrant from Germany who became a pathbreaker in American political ethics, forerunner to the field of political science. Lieber's major works, the *Manual of Political Ethics* (1838–39) and *On Civil Liberty and Self-Government* (1853), became college texts. Relied on by jurists and politicians, he was consulted by Lincoln's administration during the Civil War, and his work was regarded as authoritative well into the 1870s and 1880s. The Chief Justice found Lieber's thoughts on polygamy quoted and paraphrased in Chancellor James Kent's *Commentaries on American Law*, a treatise of the 1820s used by generations of American law students, lawyers, and judges.[23]

Because Lieber had so much influence on nineteenth-century statesmen and lawyers, his strong convictions about monogamy and polygamy, which nested in his political philosophy from the outset, deserve to be noted.[24] When Utah first petitioned for statehood—a possibility Lieber strenuously opposed—he published in a widely read magazine an (unsigned) article that included this outburst:

Monogamy does not only go with the western Caucasian race, the Europeans and their descendants, beyond Christianity, it goes beyond Common Law. It is one of the primordial elements out of which all law proceeds, or which the law steps in to recognize and to protect. Wedlock . . . stands in this respect on a level with property . . . Wedlock, or monogamic marriage, is one of the "categories" of our social thoughts and conceptions, and therefore, of our social existence. It is one of the elementary distinctions—historical and actual—between European and Asiatic humanity . . . It is one of the pre-existing conditions of our existence as civilized white men . . . Strike it out, and you destroy our very being; and when we say *our* we mean our race—a race which has its great and broad destiny, a solemn aim in the great career of civilization.[25]

In light of such passionate conviction on the part of the foremost expositor of political ethics, the intensity of the federal campaign against Mormon polygamy—and even "the undercurrent of hysteria" that one legal historian sees in congressional debate on the Mormon problem—becomes more explicable.[26] The determinative capacities of both monogamy and polygamy, and the corresponding contrast between western and eastern cultures, became foundational categories of political thought in Lieber's essay. (Montesquieu had used the contrast more simply to show the superiority of moderation and the rule of law in government.) The racial content in Lieber's understanding of these categories must have owed something to his southern exposure. He lived in South Carolina for two decades, while writing most of his best-known treatises. He owned slaves, though his antislavery opinions gained strength and motivated him to leave the south in 1857 for a position in New York City. Lieber, and Chief Justice Waite in turn, allied the polygamy of Asia with Africa and with blackness. He worried that Utah might prove to be the first "*bona fide* Africanized" state of the United States.[27]

The association of whiteness, Europe, and monogamy visible in Lieber's thought infused the postwar discourse of Christian civilization, begun earlier by Christian missionaries. Protestant evangelicals had circulated their conversion efforts around the globe by the early nineteenth century. They began to ply listeners at home with firsthand descriptions of "heathen" society in places such as India, China, or Hawaii, as a contrast to their own, blessed with Christian values. Partly because missionaries often solicited female audiences for support, this contrast specialized in images of gender and family. "Heathen" women were routinely portrayed as ignorant, degraded, beasts of burden, overworked slaves to men, servicers of male lust. They stood in stark contrast to women in the United States, who enjoyed respect from men, monogamous domesticity, and the dignity of being credited with immortal souls, all thanks to the reign of Christianity.

By the late nineteenth century the foreign mission movement had swelled enormously, and more than half of American missionaries themselves were female by 1893. Nearly a million American women, organized through their Protestant denominations, raised money and followed missionary efforts, studying topics such as "Social Life among African Women," "Girl Life in the Orient," and "High-Caste Women in India." They thus absorbed and purveyed a formulaic vocabulary of "wrongs against women" or "characteristic atrocities" in non-Christian cultures: seraglio, concubinage, polygamy, child marriage, female infanticide, bride sale, foot-binding, and suttee. All of these signaled female degradation. Christianity was portrayed as emancipatory in contrast, and the high position women enjoyed as the hallmark of Christian civilization in the United States.[28]

The missionary vision overlapped with a secular understanding of the inevitable march of civilization. An Enlightenment conception of human progress existed before Darwin wrote about evolution. In educated Euro-American thinking, human societies and cultures were assumed to be originally savage, then to undergo stages of violent barbarism, and gradually to develop the religious, intellectual, social, civil, and political accomplishments and attributes that constituted civilization. Nourished by missionary doctrine, given raison d'être by extensive European imperialism and colonialism, and refurbished with the scientific impress of evolutionary ideas, belief in "the progress of civilization" came to have a powerful ideological life in the nineteenth century. Had that not been the case, abolitionists and Republicans in the 1850s would not have been able to condemn slavery and polygamy so effectively by associating them with barbarism. During and after Reconstruction the words "savagery," "barbarism," and "civilization" peppered common parlance, to praise and to condemn. The author of an *Atlantic* essay on the history of "the marriage celebration," for example, criticized the preeminently contractual emphasis of American informal marriage as no better than "the law of nature as it exists among savage tribes, and as it was in the Middle Ages, the darkest period of modern times." He reproached the states that failed to incorporate parental consent into marriage licensing for policy "inferior not only to that of leading civilized nations, but to that even of our savage Indian tribes."[29]

Neither the Christian nor the Enlightenment understanding of civilization excluded any people or culture from progressing along the scale. All humankind were imagined to have the possibility to see the light, to be converted or acculturated; all could look to the same promising destiny. Certainly missionaries claimed Christianity was a universal faith. But because it operated by ranking peoples along a linear and chronological development—a scale of predetermined progress from savagery to barbarism to civilization, with white Europeans and Americans at the front—the discourse of civilization profoundly separated the more civilized from the less, disparaging the latter. The intensification of racial categorization along with evolutionism in the last third of the century deepened this distinction, couching gradations of civilization in terms of race or color. The popularity of Lamarckian evolutionary thinking, which posited that acquired characteristics could be inherited, strengthened the notion that civilization itself was a racial trait, achieved and now passed down by birthright among whites (especially Anglo-Saxons).[30]

Being indebted to this framework, antipolygamy rhetoric in the United States in the 1870s and 1880s in effect made the Mormons over into nonwhites. It was common for Americans who addressed Mormon polygamy not only to call it a "monstrous evil" or a "deadly menace to free government," but also to link it to the "Incas of Peru," "Turkey," "Mohammedan countries," or "the Barbary states"—savage and slavish places of colored peoples. Even an author critical of extremism among antipolygamists could not forbear identifying the Mormon priesthood with "the King of Dahomey."[31] The Supreme Court's opinion declaring polygamy unprotected by the first amendment incorporated this discourse about civilization and elevated it to the level of constitutional interpretation. Since *Reynolds v. U.S.* was the first major decision on religious freedom, its influence rippled through subsequent constitutional interpretation.

Yet the Supreme Court's pronouncement did not accomplish the desired aim in Utah, because it was very difficult for a prosecutor to prove plural marriage. Congress made two new moves in the Edmunds Act of 1882. It criminalized bigamous "unlawful cohabitation"—that is, marriage-*like* relationships with more than one partner at a time—and also deprived anyone who practiced it of the right to vote and to hold public office. A man was required to swear that he was not a polygamist and a woman to swear that she was not the wife of a polygamist before either could cast a ballot. The move to incapacitate Mormons politically for their aberrant marital practice bore some resemblance to the disfranchisement of Confederate officials after the Civil War for their treason. Severe antipolygamist pronouncements of the 1880s commonly likened the Mormons' political threat to the peril posed by the Confederacy, and even suggested that another civil war might be necessary.[32]

A number of Mormons who were denied the vote in the 1882 election because they would not take the required oath sued the registrar of ballots. Their case made its way to the U.S. Supreme Court, where the justices unanimously turned it down, finding it appropriate for Congress to make marital status "a condition of the elective franchise." The court commented that a sovereign power could legitimately "declare that no one but a married person shall be entitled to vote." Since monogamy was "wholesome and necessary" to a "free, self-governing commonwealth," Congress could suitably take political power away from those who appeared hostile to monogamy.[33]

The Utah problem did not go away, although about a thousand men were jailed for unlawful cohabitation during the 1880s.[34] A federally appointed Utah Commission (under the aegis of the Department of the Interior) reported dolefully on enforcement of the Edmunds Act: Mormons publicly and privately declared "their right and religious duty to continue in violation of the law their polygamous relation; and they deny the authority of Congress to regulate and interpose any restriction as to the marital relation." The Forty-ninth Congress of 1885–86 seriously entertained a proposal for a constitutional amendment to prohibit polygamy in the United States (something Francis Lieber had suggested twenty years earlier).[35]

No amendment resulted, but Congress in 1887 exerted even more muscle, with the Edmunds-Tucker Act. This legislation repealed the act of incorporation of the Church of Jesus Christ of the Latter-Day Saints, which had been in force since 1851, and set in motion legal procedures for seizing the church's property. It also asserted significant new federal powers over the institution of marriage by assigning jurisdiction over the crimes of adultery, incest, and fornication to federal courts in Utah, and by allowing (plural) wives to testify against their husbands, something traditionally impermissible under coverture. With some congressmen comparing plural wives' voting in Utah to women's committing suttee in India—both slavish practices that had to be stopped—the Congress disfranchised Mormon women outright. Nowhere but in Utah were women granted the vote by a local legislature only to have Congress take it away.[36]

Mormons resisted the provisions of the Edmunds-Tucker Act by legal suit. They were turned back again, definitively, by the Supreme Court. In order to answer the central question whether Congress had the power to dissolve and expropriate the corporation of the saints, against the church's claim to be a protected religious and charitable body, Justice Joseph Bradley felt it necessary to assess polygamy. He summarized, for the court, that polygamy was "a blot on our civilization . . . in a measure, a return to barbarism. . . . contrary to the spirit of Christianity and of the civilization which Christianity has produced in the Western world." He intended moral condemnation as well as political rejection. In full cognizance of the constitutional separation of church and state, the court assumed that the United States was a Christian nation.[37] The opinion said, in essence, that polygamy was so abhorrent that it could not be considered a religious tenet; the group practicing it could not be a church; consequently there was no constitutional bar to the government's dissolving the corporation.[38] At this point the saints saw the light. In September of 1890, the church issued a manifesto acceding to the federal prohibition of polygamy and advising its members "to refrain from contracting any marriage forbidden by the law of the land." Plural marriages continued to take place secretly for a decade, but in public the Mormons realigned themselves with the rest of the nation, paving the way for Utah's statehood in 1896.[39]

Extraordinary in its intensity and in its explicit defense of monogamy, the anti-Mormon campaign was emblematic of the era in its merger of political and outspokenly moral aims. While Congress was trying to eliminate Mormon polygamy, it was also taking further steps to bring native Americans into "civilized life" so that they too could join the nation. The government's reservation policy, instituted in 1867, dispossessed native Americans in the west of all land except for two major areas—in the Dakota and the Oklahoma territories—to which they were expected to migrate. By instituting this reservation policy and enforcing it militarily, the federal government destroyed tribal unity and the power of the chiefs.[40] The destructiveness of these policies elicited passionate criticism in the 1870s and 1880s from humanitarian reformers, who feared that the nation was committing genocide. These reformers proposed that native Americans were assimilable to American life and that they should be saved, civilized, and incorporated. Through the Bureau of Indian Affairs, the federal government took an increasingly active role in this program of "civilization," one part of which was establishing special boarding schools where Indian girls as well as boys would educated and acculturated. Most white reformers thought they were improving the position of native American women—whom they saw as beasts of burden, items of exchange, sex objects, or slaves—just as supporters of foreign missions hoped to end the "characteristic atrocities" against non-Christian women around the globe.

"Civilizing" meant instituting faithful monogamous households, turning Indian men into farmers motivated by the work ethic, and urging Indian women toward norms of modesty and domesticity. The federal government's concern with monogamy became more insistent by the 1880s. As the secretary of the interior, who oversaw Indian affairs, perceived it, "the Indian race has reached a crisis in its history," because American civilization had so successfully reduced natives' numbers and "surrounded them." In his view, "the Indians can no longer exist in this country in a savage or semi-civilized state, nor can they [any] longer recede before the advancing march of civilization." Numbering a little over a quarter of million (by his estimate), Indians were no longer a danger to the security of the United States, and keeping them on reservations tended by the Indian Bureau cost the federal government six or seven million dollars a year.[41]

Instead of segregating native Americans, both the secretary and humanitarian reformers thought the better approach was to civilize them more fully so that they could become citizens. If Indians were viewed as potential citizens, however, the extent of polygamy and self-divorce among them became as reprehensible as it was among Mormons. The bureau in the mid-1880s exerted more pressure on Indian men to abjure "plural wives" and stop being "lax" in husbandly responsibilities. Henry Teller, who resigned his Senate seat from Colorado to become secretary of the interior in 1883, acknowledged that "while the Indians were in a state of at least semi-independence, there did not seem to be any great necessity for interference"—nor was there great promise that interference would be efficacious—but now that they were living on government reservations, "the marriage relation" had to become a priority. "The Indian having taken to himself a wife should be compelled to continue that relation with her, unless dissolved by some recognized tribunal," Teller advised all Indian agents, "instructed that he is under obligations to care for and support" his wife and his children, and told that he would be punished for "failure . . . to continue as the head of such family".[42]

If native Americans were potential citizens, then they had to be responsible husbands: the Indian Bureau echoed the Freedmen's Bureau in this approach. The presumed conjunction of marriage, property-owning, household headship, and male citizenship, so deep rooted in American political thinking, blossomed further in the Dawes Severalty Act of 1887 (also known as the Allotment Act). Many humanitarian reformers saw a remedy to the devastation of native Americans in securing land to them—not reservations occupied by Indian groups as collectivities, but freeholds allotted, in "severalty," to individuals as property-owners. For decades, successive treaties between the United States and different Indian groups had included offers of land and citizenship to those heads of household who were willing to leave native culture. The 1887 act, named after Senator Henry Dawes of Massachusetts, made this approach general. Senator Dawes argued on the floor of Congress that Indians who showed their willingness to join the polity were at least as suitable citizens as freed African Americans, or as the hundreds of thousands of European immigrants flowing through American portals. The act dissolved the collective ownership of most tribal lands, broke up Indian Territory, arranged for individual plots to be granted to each native family, and established procedures for conferring U.S. citizenship upon the household heads who accepted the allotments.[43]

Congress enacted this policy on the principle that "a home of his own" for "each head of a family" was "the way to start a people in the direction of civilization," in one senator's words. Patronymic family surnames were assigned to Indians (against native cultural tradition) to keep identification and property succession clear.[44] Implicitly following Lieber's conviction that property and marriage formed the essential basis for the state, the government meant to prepare Indian males for citizenship by making them heads of households, legal husbands, and property-owners, just as the precedent of the Freedmen's Bureau indicated. And federal agents of Indian Affairs sounded the same tone as agents of the Freedmen's Bureau had when native Americans were casual about sex outside of marriage, or failed to observe monogamy consistently, or to marry or divorce legally and properly. They expressed consternation in their reports, and found means to "correct the evil," as an agent at Round Hill Reservation in California wrote, and to "compel those who can legally do so to get married." Indian courts (under federal aegis) in the 1880s and 1890s penalized polygamous marriages with fines, deprivation of rations, or hard labor. So-called squaw men—white men who came onto reservations "in the character of husbands to Indian women" and were considered to be disreputable cranks by government officials—were required to marry their Indian partners legally in order to stay on the reservation.[45]

The Dawes Act, hailed by its proponents as a tremendous benefit to native Americans, also had the anticipated consequence of releasing un-allotted native land for white settlement. It hastened the destruction of the Indians' communal way of life by securing individual property-ownership, and further subverted native American women's roles as agriculturists by presuming the Indian male should be the landowner and farmer. At the same time, it laid the groundwork for the United States to grant citizenship to native Americans of both sexes four decades later, in 1924.

Like ex-slaves and ex-polygamists, Indians were required by the federal government to adopt monogamy as "the law of social life" to become citizens. In the moral scheme of the national polity, formal monogamy was the approved channel for sexual desire. New federal regulation of obscenity in the 1870s taught the same lesson. Although economic regulation by the federal government was hotly contested in this era, moral regulation by Congress was not. Congress took barely three weeks from the introduction of a bill banning "trade in and circulation of obscene literature and articles of immoral use" to its final passage. Hardly a word of debate was recorded.[46]

Suppression of obscenity was an indirect way for so-called purity reformers to defend Christian-model monogamy. Even as federal official-dom pursued a single standard, challenges were multiplying. Earnest radicals pressed forward with alternative moralities, and commercialized sex boomed in towns and cities. Purity reformers intended not only to prevent circulation of raunchy pictures but to stamp out extramarital sexual relations and to make sure that sex stayed linked to monogamous marriage and childbearing, as fundamental Christian morality required.

They assumed that obscene items stimulated unwarranted sexual appetites and fostered prostitution. Birth control information was "obscene" because it separated sex from pregnancy. The two had to remain united not only to keep *extra*marital sex risky, but to secure conventional responsibilities *within* marriage—to stabilize the linkage of sexual adulthood to the roles of spouse and parent. Sexual relations should not only be enclosed by the wedding band but should mean motherhood for wives and the burden of providing for husbands.

The reformer Anthony Comstock, a fundamentalist Protestant who had been engaged in antiprostitution efforts in New York, was the prime force in raising obscenity regulation to the federal level. He shrewdly engineered the drafting of the law and had himself appointed a special agent of the post office in order to mastermind a national purity campaign.[47] The ability of Congress to control trade in "obscene" materials was limited, because such regulations conventionally belonged to the states. Therefore the federal law cleverly focused on circulation of information through the mail, implementing suppression by and through the U.S. Postal Service, still nearly the most active and certainly the most widely dispersed agent of the federal government. The 1873 law known as the Comstock Act banned and criminalized the use of the mails to circulate "obscene, lewd or lascivious" materials, and articles intended "for any indecent or immoral use." In federal territories and the District of Columbia, where Congress did have the police power, the statute additionally criminalized selling, giving, or possessing such materials, specifically including contraceptives and abortifacients.

In Congress this policy evoked easy assent, with no objection to the aims or the extent of federal oversight and no debate over what qualified as "immoral." Congressmen's consensus followed their implicit agreement on the character of Christian civilization. In a Supreme Court case three years later involving the mails but not obscenity, Justice Stephen Field seized the opportunity to quote the whole text of the Comstock law, to affirm the government's right "to refuse its facilities for the distribution of matter deemed injurious to the public morals." The court said this was no infringement of freedom of the press.[48]

Even before he pushed through the federal law that took his name, Comstock had fomented national publicity by having Victoria Woodhull arrested in New York City for circulating obscenity in the reform weekly she published. Woodhull, a free lover and woman's rights advocate already notorious for her maverick professional life and radical politics (among other things, she had run for president in 1872), had told the public that the most famous and popular preacher in the land, Henry Ward Beecher, was really a free lover. In her weekly, Woodhull accused Beecher of being a hypocrite because he abjured the principles of free love but carried on a secret love affair with one of his parishioners, Elizabeth Tilton, while both were married to others. Woodhull's accusations and Beecher's denials spiraled into trials in church and court in 1874 and 1875. The national publicity rivaled, perhaps even surpassed, the sensationalism of the McFarland-Richardson revelations, and the fact that Henry Ward Beecher had performed the last-minute marriage of Albert Richardson and Abby McFarland linked the two episodes. Despite hearing titillating testimony, the jury was unable to decide unanimously whether the Reverend Mr. Beecher had committed adultery with Theodore Tilton's wife. The liberal minister emerged chastened but still aloft on righteous assumptions, while Victoria Woodhull suffered obloquy.[49]

Like the trial of Daniel McFarland, the Beecher-Tilton scandal had conservative cultural consequences, reinforcing public maintenance of marital propriety. Comstock's application of federal power acted rather more directly, harassing and prosecuting the small number of free lovers who were publishing books or journals to circulate their ideas about marriage, sexuality, and birth control. One of his repeated targets was Ezra Heywood, author of *Cupid's Yokes, or the Binding Forces of Conjugal Life*. A sex radical from Kansas who, like other late-nineteenth-century critics, called marriage a slavish institution and likened it to prostitution because the wife exchanged sex for monetary support, Heywood had the temerity to name as "twin relics of barbarism" not slavery and polygamy, but the capitalist profit system and marriage.[50]

Comstock went after Heywood and other authors who were free lovers not only for publishing "obscene" ideas but also for providing information about birth control. Abortionists and sellers of abortifa-cients and contraceptive methods had been advertising extensively, if subtly, for decades, their main clients being married women. The distress of many doctors and eventually of legislators over the frequency of abor-tion led states between the 1830s and the 1870s to make abortion a crime, which it had not been previously. Both abortion and the market for con-traceptive aids such as condoms, pessaries, and douches gave unmistak-able signs that men and women, married and not, wanted to limit pregnancies. Comstock intended the federal law to hamper the advertis-ing and marketing of all methods of birth control and abortion, and it did. Where the federal government could only restrict the use of the mails, the states had legislative power to criminalize possession or sale of items considered dangerous to public morals. About half the states, fol-lowing the federal lead, passed "little Comstock laws" that made contra-ceptive devices illegal. Despite the laws, stalwart free lovers did not give up their ideas or practices (unless they were jailed), and not all means of birth control disappeared from advertising or from sale. Shrewd manu-facturers and retailers sold many contraceptive items, including con-doms, under the name of hygienic aids. Still, obscenity laws hedged such activities with real risk, and severely limited publicity about and develop-ment of birth control methods.[51]

The national government's initiatives to regularize and standardize monogamous morality as seen in the Comstock law, as well as in the Freedmen's Bureau, the anti-Mormon campaign, and Indian policy, had an ideological impact at the state and local level, where they crimped ear-lier flexibility toward marital practices. In New York City, where juries and judges had hardly sentenced men for bigamy earlier, the picture changed decisively in the war and postwar years. Only 11 percent of men found guilty of bigamy suffered any sentence before 1860 and those who did received minimal jail terms. The same kind of offense, committed by the same sort of working-class and often immigrant perpetrator, who used the same justifications for his behavior, aroused judges in the fol-lowing twenty years to punish 73 percent of those convicted, often with far longer sentences.[52] The community pragmatism that had allowed leeway for individuals' waywardness (while respecting formal marriage) seemed to be crumbling.

Another telling case was the prosecution of Lillian Harman and E. C. Walker in Kansas. Harman was the daughter of an outspoken free love advocate, Moses Harman, editor of *Lucifer, the Light Bearer*, a freethought and anarchist newspaper. When she married her father's journalist colleague Edwin Walker in 1887, they called their ceremony an "autonomistic marriage." Both her father and the groom made speeches asserting the absolutely private nature of the compact between them, "deny[ing] the right of society, in the form of church and state, to regulate it." Walker explicitly "abdicate[d] in advance all the so-called 'marital rights,'" and Harman kept her own name and would "make no promises that it may become impossible or immoral for me to fulfill, but retain the right to act always as my conscience and best judgment shall dictate." They did not obtain a marriage license or have the ceremony performed by a judge or justice of the peace or licensed minister, as Kansas law said a couple must to be wed. The day after their ceremony they were arrested for failing to do so. They were convicted in a jury trial and sentenced to jail (Walker for seventy-five and Harman for forty-five days).

The prosecution and imprisonment of Harman and Walker expressed the tenor of the times. In the 1850s, state law enforcement officials did not indict couples and groups who radically altered the terms of conventional marriage, as Lucy Stone and Henry Blackwell or communitarians and utopians did. In the postwar era, however, state authorities took up the banner the national government had been waving on behalf of legal monogamy. When Harman and Walker argued on appeal that their liberty of conscience was infringed by the Kansas marriage statute, the state Supreme Court sustained the trial court's judgment, saying the state could legitimately punish them for failing to observe the requirement of license and ceremony.

The Kansas court's decision appropriately focused on procedure, but the larger question hovered, whether their marriage—so explicitly disavowing legal definitions and customary obligations—was one in fact.

The court was "not prepared to say that the contract between the defendants *is* a common-law marriage." That hung in the balance. Two concurring judges could not so easily contain themselves from commenting on the wrongs committed by the couple. One took offense at their denunciation of the marriage statute as a "monstrosity," and spelled out how liberal Kansas was in recognizing the rights of a married woman, who could keep her property and earnings, shared equal prerogative with her husband over their children, could even take part in city elections, and was not her husband's "servant nor his slave." Replicating missionary discourse, he said that in Kansas, "the tyranny which degrades and crushes the wives and mothers in other countries, no longer exists." A second judge expostulated that "the union between E. C. Walker and Lillian Harman was no marriage and they deserve all the punishment which has been inflicted upon them." He refused to see their union as a common-law marriage because they overtly "repudiated nearly everything essential to a valid marriage" and "had no intention of creating that relation or status known and defined by law and by the customs and usages of all civilized society as marriage."[53]

Harman and Walker's crime lay in putting the whole weight of their relationship on its private contractual side and abjuring the public definition of the institution. Beyond Kansas, judges were rethinking the extent of flexibility to be granted to a couple to say they were married, questioning whether the state should always put its imprimatur on the consent and commitment a man and a woman made to each other, as if the institution of marriage had to be insulated or salvaged from misuse by irresponsible, unsuited, or defiant couples. The national government's insistence upon legal monogamy for ex-slaves, its war on polygamous alternatives, and its prevention of the mailing of obscenity and contraceptive information created an atmosphere of moral belligerence about Christian monogamous marriage as the national standard. The Oneida community too became a casualty. In existence since 1850, John Humphrey Noyes's unique social experiment in communism and "complex marriage" (in which no exclusive pairings were allowed, and sexual relations between any man and any woman could be contemplated) had prospered. Its residents were economically successful and had achieved a local reputation for industriousness and honesty, despite their sexual blasphemy and the women's pantaloons. But the Comstock law signaled a change for the community. Being circumspect, Noyes withdrew from the mails the community's publications about sex and birth control, which were now conceivably illegal. Noyes also recognized the decision in *Reynolds v. U.S.* denying religious protection to Mormon polygamy as a possible warning, since "whenever there was a stir-up about the Mormons there was usually one soon after" about Oneida.[54]

The *Reynolds* decision was announced in January of 1879, and gave local opponents of Oneida a green light. Shortly afterward, an orthodox Protestant minister named John Mears, who taught at nearby Hamilton College, took the lead in mobilizing fellow clerics and neighbors to extirpate the Oneidans' sexual communism. The bishop of the diocese of central New York, to whom the *Reynolds* decision "gave heart," the *New York Times* reported, likewise called on all the clergy in the area to "eradicate" the heterodox sexual regime. Mears seemed to take personal offense at both the Mormons' and the Oneidans' self-justifying religiosity. Citing the *Reynolds* decision in a published essay, he blasted the Oneidans' "systematic concubinage," classing it with polygamy as "a great evil and immorality" veiled and sheltered under the claim of religious liberty. He called upon the New York legislature to suppress the "immoral features" of Oneida just as the national government had refused to countenance polygamy in Utah. New York's representatives and senators in Congress were hypocrites to be opposing Mormon plural marriage in the nation's capital, he wrote, while tolerating the Oneidans' complex marriage in their home state.[55]

Mears created so much local rumor that legal action was pending against Oneida that Noyes fled secretly to Canada, in June 1879. From there, he sent a long missive back to his community, proposing a "Modification of our Social Platform." The core of it was giving up complex marriage. Noyes proposed to continue communistic property-holding and housekeeping arrangements while newly approving only conventional marriage or celibacy in sexual life, thus gaining peace by giving up what were labeled the community's "immoral features."[56] The Oneidans adopted this proposal and reverted to conventional marriage. Not long after, they abandoned the communistic property system as well, converting Oneida's assets into a joint-stock company.

Oneida's radical utopianism died by assault from outside, but it was also crumbling from within. Noyes's charismatic hold over his communicants had waned as he grew older. Dissension arose over who would be his successor as leader, especially when he anointed his own ill-suited son. Most important, many members of the younger generation, who had been born in the community through the program of stirpiculture, or controlled reproduction, longed for romantic love and conventional monogamy, seeing these as emancipatory compared with the authorized system of complex marriage.

It would be plausible to conclude that the younger generation in the community chose to revert to monogamous practice, rather than being hounded into it by religious condemnation and legal threat. Yet community members, who were not cordoned off altogether from their neighbors or nation, could not "choose" in grand isolation. The public prescriptions standardizing marriage behavior informed their outlook. Their choosing to abandon complex marriage was not unmediated, any more than the Mormons' decision to abandon polygamy was. Public authority in the form of legislation, court decisions, political discourse, and bureaucratic practices inevitably shapes people's sense of what is desirable in marriage. The Comstock law, the *Reynolds* decision, and the national sentiment behind them influenced what the upcoming generation of Oneidans wanted.

More generally, the laws, the moral tenor they maintained, and their judicial vindication helped to minimize the size and influence of the minorities who might seek alternatives to normative marriage forms. The post–Civil War federal actions in favor of standard monogamy exerted a force for moral regulation. Implementing the views of the majority, but at the same time nourishing and reproducing that majority, they shaped individuals' beliefs and outlooks.[57] Public policy that claimed to align itself with "Christian civilization" could be doubly efficacious in setting normative bounds. A refurbished alliance between national authority and Christian monogamous morality settled firmly in place, prepared to badger nonconforming citizens if not to make them disappear—and to weed out marital nonconformists among the foreigners thronging the gates.

6

CONSENT,

THE AMERICAN WAY

*A*lmost eighteen million prospective immigrants entered the United States between 1890 and 1920, putting new pressure on the relation between marriage and the polity. The vast inflow caused the nation to develop and change its immigration policy dramatically. Restrictions were instituted where none had been before, causing an avalanche of unprecedented federal activities, setting requirements for entry, monitoring ports, and implementing and overseeing the new apparatus legally and bureaucratically. Both the exercise and the apparatus of restriction manifested national power and sovereignty.[1] A post–Civil War generation of leaders intended to consolidate the United States and make it a power on the world stage, and that required knowing who belonged to the nation and who was welcome to join. Restriction asserted national authority to constitute the sovereign people.

Immigration and marriage questions were interrelated in several ways. Immigration promised—or risked—the creation of new citizens. The positive and hopeful view held that "the newcomer will soon be one of us," which meant not only taking employment but also marrying and having children.[2] Marriage bore on the shape of the body politic just as immigration policy did. Together the two had dynamic potential to create new kinds of citizens for the United States, because children born on American soil would be U.S. citizens regardless of their immigrant parents' own capacity for naturalization. The fourteenth amendment had announced that anyone born within the jurisdiction of the United States was a citizen, and in 1898 the U.S Supreme Court confirmed this, in the case of a child born of Chinese parents on American soil.[3] Besides being the legal avenue to reproduction of citizens, marriage affected the citizenship roles of men and women. The Union's treatment of emancipated slaves and native Americans implied that marriage suited a man for full citizenship by placing him at the head of a household. It made him the political representative of his wife and minor dependents, and correspondingly rendered her a less than fully empowered citizen. Marriage would have the same potential for immigrants.

The earliest federal legislation directly linking the citizenship of immigrants to marriage required very little debate, although it reversed a long-standing tradition. It was an act of Congress of 1855, declaring that a woman of any origin or nationality became a citizen of the United States upon marrying an American man, so long as she met naturalization requirements. That meant she had to be a "free white person," in accord with the naturalization statute of 1790. The same law specified that the child of an American male citizen, whether born on U.S. soil or abroad, was a U.S. citizen. Both of these privileges were specific to gender. They followed from Congress's view of a male citizen's headship of his family. Congressmen wanted to encourage the formation of families to settle the continent, and it made sense to them that an American citizen's wife and children should also be Americans. This stance expressed marital unity at the national level and signified the male citizen's prerogative of representation, which came along with his support responsibilities. In declaring this policy in 1855, Congress abandoned the foregoing common-law doctrine (articulated in 1830 by the U.S. Supreme Court) that nationality of either wife or husband was regarded as indelible and marriage alone could not change it, because the government had to be positively involved for nationality to change.[4]

The making of both marriages and citizens became pressing as immigration swelled. Just as consent was essential to entering marriage, it had always been considered essential to forming citizenship. Not every American colonial became an American citizen, only those who shifted their allegiance voluntarily from the British empire to the new republic. The Revolutionary nation welcomed newcomers who came by choice to embrace the political and ethical values of the American republic (who would, it was assumed, be "white," for only "free white persons" could gain citizenship through naturalization). The elimination of slavery further consecrated the value of free consent, as the only way to legitimize a bargain for labor. In the national imagination, the morality of the wage bargain depended on the freedom to make the contract. After the Civil War, the ideology of "liberty of contract" reigned supreme in economic life.[5] Freedom of choice in national allegiance, marriage, and work mirrored one another, forming a united whole in American national values in the late nineteenth century. Those who were unfree, who were bound as slaves, or who did not understand the value of the work contract or the marriage contract, did not fully belong.

Restriction of immigration began in an era when the qualifications for citizens were often expressed in terms of capacities for freedom, consent, and morality, but always engaged considerations of "race" as well. The late-nineteenth-century concept of "race" was protean, mixing physiognomy, color, nationality, culture, and religion. It was biologistic—frequently expressed in terms of "blood"—yet cultural, often used to mean nationality or national derivation. Categorizations of "races" were evanescent. Although his words sound very peculiar today, a congressman of New York thought he was "saying nothing new or strange" when he stated "the fact that human kind is divided into three great families, the Aryan, the Mongolian, and the Turanian. The Aryan family is comprised of those five great branches of the human race—the Grecian, the Italian, the Germanic, the Slavic, and the Celtic." The traits of races (like those of individuals) were imagined not as fixed in perpetuity but rather as capable of being altered by environmental influences, with absorbed traits then passed on to subsequent generations.[6]

The notion that acquired traits were inheritable held out a mixed promise. It could encourage emissaries of Christian civilization, but it also foreboded the dangerous possibility that the white race was not immune to degradation. Alarmists believed that when "lower" races intermingled with "higher" ones, the tendency of the whole was to "degenerate" to the lower type.[7] In some respects, "race" had taken on the power to wield either good or evil influence earlier attributed to "manners," a translation borne out by the occasional use of either term as a synonym for national character. Seventeen thousand "laboring men" in California who petitioned the U.S. Congress to prevent Chinese immigration predicted fearfully that the "vitiating influence" of the Chinese would "arrest the advancement of our civilization," although they foreswore any "illiberal feeling inimical to the less advanced races." Race also operated more literally through genealogy. A congressman responsive on the Chinese question warned, "No matter how high a moral standard a community may attain, the introduction in that community of any considerable number of persons of a lower moral tone will cause a general moral deterioration just as sure as night follows day. The intermarriage of a lower with a higher type certainly does not improve the latter any more than does the breeding of cattle by blooded and common stock improve the blooded stock generally." Thinking about race always also turned attention to marriage, as his comment showed.[8]

These mixed concerns about race, morality, and the importance of consent to the American republic pervaded the rhetoric of restrictions placed on Chinese immigration—the first and most severe restrictions by country of origin or "race" in all of U.S. history. Opponents of Chinese entry argued that vast and insuperable differences between the two societies—between the two "races"—made the Chinese an "indigestible mass in the community," unassimilable to American political values of freedom of choice and self-representation.[9] Chinese peasants had first immigrated to the United States to try their luck in the California gold rush. By the 1850s they were in demand by American capitalists in mining and railroad-building, as manual laborers who would subsist on low wages and require few amenities. Anti-Chinese feeling burst forth after the completion of the transcontinental railroad in 1869. White workingmen feared competition from cheap labor, and believed Chinese "coolies" were satisfied with substandard wage rates and habits of living. Organized white workers raised the banner of an "American standard of living," which linked a certain level of household consumption to the pay enabling it.[10]

In the views of opponents, Chinese immigrants were not voluntary emigrants, but bound, brought as "contract laborers" to an employer or work site in the United States by prearrangement. This was anathema, an un-American form of coercion, expressive of the centuries of despotism that had oppressed the Chinese, accustoming them to bondage and unsuiting them to understand American values. Actually, Chinese men usually arrived by purchasing tickets on credit and paying the cost back through their wages, not through a "coolie trade."[11] Men outnumbered women among Chinese immigrants by at least ten to one, and the men themselves numbered barely 100,000 by 1882. Yet when Congress took the first federal step in U.S. history to restrict immigration, in the Page Act of 1875, the law was aimed at women. It prohibited and criminalized the entry or importation of all prostitutes, required the U.S. consul to make sure that any immigrant debarking from an Asian country was not under contract for "lewd and immoral purposes," and placed penalties on Americans' involvement in transactions for contract labor. It also made the entry of convicted felons unlawful (unless they were political prisoners).[12]

Passed in the wake of the Comstock Act, the Page Act shared its aim to support monogamous morality, and took heart from U.S. Supreme Court Justice Stephen Field's recent approbation of legislation that would suppress "all lewdness, especially when it takes the form of prostitution." The provocation for the Page Act was Chinese women immigrants, who were all typed as prostitutes, but Congress took the opportunity to exclude all "immoral" women.[13] Prostitutes defied the moral regulation that the Comstock law propelled. The "lewdness" of prostitution contravened monogamous morality; and in the view of politicians, it therefore had to be opposed. Prostitution and marriage were opposites: where marriage implied mutual love and consent, legality and formality, willing bonds for a good bargain, prostitution signified sordid monetary exchange and desperation or coercion on the part of the woman involved.[14]

Congressmen typically used the language of coercion to describe not only Chinese prostitution but the whole trade, and from the Page Act forward always targeted for penalty the pimps and traffickers who brought in prostitutes, not the women themselves, who were assumed to be victims. This perspective built on their Victorian presumption that women felt only minimal sexual desire, and would engage in sex willingly only for love or the prospect of maternity. It also reflected their conviction that love and sexual relations, if "true" and voluntary, could not be conjoined with economic considerations. Their rhetoric of coercion highlighted the association of marriage with true love and consent. If marriage was consensual, its opposite, prostitution, must be coercive, and the more that prostitution could be shown to be coercive, the more that marriage could be assumed not to be.[15]

The Page Act was sparked less by the scale of Chinese prostitution, which was small, than by what it banefully represented. The trade run by Chinese secret societies was notorious for bringing in women ignorant of their fate and kept against their will. "Chinese women in California are bought and sold for prostitution, and are treated worse than dogs; they are held in a most revolting condition of slavery," a government inquiry reported.[16] Prostitutes echoed the evil pinned on Chinese contract laborers: their presence in the United States signified coercion, more akin to the slavery tabooed a decade earlier than to the voluntary choice of welcomed migrants. In the eyes of opponents, both prostitutes and "coolies" inhabited a slavelike status, evidence of Chinese acceptance of authoritative hierarchy and deference. Neither was considered capable of the free consent and voluntarism requisite for American political allegiance. If immigrants were expected to arrive freely in pursuit of healthy wages, monogamous marriage, household formation, and the achievement of an American standard of living, the prostitute and the coolie undermined and assaulted this vision. They were not Christians; their inherited culture accepted polygamy; their livelihoods showed them to be enemies of the civilization embraced by the American nation. The Chinese prostitute, standing outside of and boding no good for Christian-model monogamy, signified the threat to American values in

Chinese immigration even more intensely than did the coolie, because she threatened to reproduce alien citizens on American soil. Her very being implied the "coolie" as her client while her evil presence also alluded to white workingmen's resort to commercialized sex.

Once it was put into place, the Page Act virtually ended Chinese women's entry into American ports. In California the population of Chinese women stayed at about 3,800 from 1870 to 1880 and the number of prostitutes (who were pursued by local authorities as well) dropped from over 2,000 to about 750.[17] Congress proceeded to prohibit the entry of all Chinese laborers. The Chinese Exclusion Act of 1882 reduced immigration from China to a trickle of specific categories of merchants, ministers, sojourners, and students. The Foran Act followed in 1885, excluding all contract laborers.[18]

A clarion call of racial exclusivity, the 1882 act, no less than the Page Act, was presented as a regulation on behalf of morality. "Race" itself had moral dimensions, which sprang from the inability of the group to understand consent. "The American race is progressive and in favor of a responsible representative government. The Mongolian race seems to have no desire for progress and to have no conception of representative and free institutions," reported the first House and Senate committee inquiry into Chinese immigration. Citizens on the Pacific coast apprehended the "influx of Chinese" as "a standing menace to republican institutions" and to "the existence there of Christian civilization." Still working on the premise that a republic required a virtuous and homogeneous population to succeed, congressmen weighed how much diversity the American republic could tolerate before collapsing. The committee acknowledged that some California employers found cheap labor convenient, but itself took the longer view that a people "with the servile disposition inherited from ages of benumbing despotism" were undesirable.[19]

White Americans' prejudices against Chinese immigrants had surfaced in Congress as early as 1870, when Senator Charles Sumner proposed, in the spirit of radical Reconstruction, to revise the 1790 provision that only "free white persons" could be naturalized. His attempt to eliminate the word "white" was stymied by senators from western states, who protested that Asian immigrants could then become citizens. The naturalization statute passed was a compromise, adding to "white" persons those of African descent, thus intentionally leaving out Asians.[20] The Chinese Exclusion Act of 1882 reiterated that no court could allow a Chinese immigrant to become a citizen via naturalization. Three more times over the next two decades, Congress reaffirmed and extended the exclusion of Chinese laborers and their ineligibility for naturalized citizenship.

Congress revamped immigration procedures in 1891, fully establishing federal regulatory control and the means to enforce it. New restrictions were added: polygamists were excluded (a legacy of the campaign against Mormon polygamy), along with paupers, the insane, felons, and those with a loathsome or dangerous disease.[21] After anarchists were also prohibited from immigrating (as a result of the assassination of President McKinley by a reputed anarchist), polygamists and anarchists always appeared in sequence as excludable, deportable, and ineligible for citizenship, as if disloyalty to monogamy were equivalent to overthrowing the government.

An extension of the exclusion from actual polygamists to "persons who admit their belief in the practice of polygamy" in 1907 caused a diplomatic fracas between the United States and the Ottoman Empire. The new clause raised the question whether all Moslems had to be excluded, because their religion tolerated polygamy. The Turkish government protested that the United States was discriminating against its Moslem subjects by excluding them because of their belief in polygamy. To avoid quarreling with the Ottomans, the commissioner-general of immigration and the Department of State found a thin reed of compromise, averring a "well defined distinction between belief in a religion which tolerates a practice and belief in the practice itself." The polygamy exclusion was hardly an empty threat, however: between July of 1908 and February of 1910 alone, 131 would-be immigrants from countries as varied as India, England, Holland, Syria, and Russia, as well as Turkey, were denied entry because they were polygamists.[22]

From the 1890s through the 1920s there was hardly a session of Congress that did not debate restriction of immigration, still interweaving racial, economic, moral, and political themes, as in the initial restrictive law of 1875. An almost continuous dialogue went on between those who championed mass immigration and those who wanted to clamp the flow. Large business interests generally opposed restriction in order to assure a ready supply of needy workers, while the skilled craftsmen of organized labor generally favored it, saying they wanted to preserve labor standards.[23] With prostitutes, the Chinese, coerced laborers, and polygamists excluded, concern focused on the increasing numbers of people arriving from southern Italy, Greece, Russia, Poland, and elsewhere in eastern Europe. Most of these "new immigrants" were Catholics, Greek Orthodox, or Jews.

Restrictionists such as the white Protestant men who founded the Immigration Restriction League in Massachusetts found these ethnic groups unassimilable to the American republic, as Californians had argued with respect to Chinese.[24] Representative Elijah Adams Morse, for example, stressed that "under our free republican form of government" the "character and stability" of the government depended upon "the character of the citizen" and warned that the country could not continue safely "incorporating into its body politic the ignorant, criminal, dangerous and hostile elements that are now being emptied upon these shores." Woodrow Wilson, a scholar at Princeton two decades away from becoming president of the United States, accepted the connection between "blood" and polity, writing, "our own temperate blood, schooled to self-possession and the measured conduct of self-government, is receiving a constant infusion and yearly experiencing a partial corruption of foreign blood . . . We are unquestionably facing an ever-increasing difficulty of self-command with ever deteriorating materials, possibly with degenerating fibre."[25]

Although restrictionists often gave blood or "race" as the motive for their opposition to a given group, racial classifications were not written into law. The main instrument proposed between the 1890s and the 1910s to discriminate among immigrants was a literacy test. Illiteracy was much higher in southern and eastern Europe and Russia than in northern European countries and in Britain. A leader such as Senator Henry Cabot Lodge of Massachusetts, a principal spokesman for the Immigration Restriction League, thought that a requirement to bar immigrants unable to read and write (in a language of their choice) would keep out those he found objectionable. As Lodge explained in 1896, introducing his bill, "the illiteracy test will bear most heavily upon the Italians, Russians, Poles, Hungarians, Greeks, and Asiatics, and very lightly, or not at all, upon English-speaking emigrants and Germans, Scandinavians, and French. In other words, the races most affected by the illiteracy test are those . . . with which the English-speaking people have never hitherto assimilated, and who are the most alien to the great body of the people of the United States."[26] Literacy itself would take on the task of limiting certain national or "racial" groups.

When the literacy requirement was first introduced in 1896, the two houses of Congress offered different versions, causing a debate that brought out congressmen's underlying assumptions about marriage as well as about race. The Senate version introduced by Lodge would have required literacy of every immigrant above the age of fourteen. The House bill required literacy only of males, aged sixteen to sixty, because its authors imagined female immigrants mainly as domestic servants whose literacy was immaterial. Discussion focused on the male immigrant. He was the determining character; *his* capacity for labor, *his* capacity for citizenship mattered most. These qualities were linked to his potential to be a husband and father, the head of a household bound by ties to dependents whom he supported.

Because congressmen understood the immigration of potential citizens in these terms, the Lodge version foundered. A literacy test applied to both men and women would prevent a literate male immigrant from being accompanied by his illiterate wife. If he had come alone, it would prevent him from later bringing in his illiterate wife. Senators and representatives vigorously objected, assuming that a man's prerogative in America included having his wife and children with him whether or not they were literate. Representative Wayne Parker expostulated, "If we wish to say that no man shall come here who can not read and write, let us say so; but let us not say that no man shall come here who has a wife who can not read and write, unless he leave her behind . . . We want members of families. We do not believe that it is better to admit a man, no matter how well educated, to be separated from his family and to live here by himself. It is better neither for the country nor for him."[27]

The compromise passed by Congress, although not enacted until 1917, achieved the exclusion of illiterate workers of both sexes while preserving men's family rights, thus answering the aims of both houses' original versions. It required all immigrants over the age of sixteen to be literate, but exempted the members of a male immigrant's (or male resident alien's) immediate family—his wife, children, and aged parents.[28] Even congressional restrictionists did not wish to turn back a literate husband and father because his illiterate wife could not enter the country, nor did they wish to see him stay without her. Indicating the same priorities, a congressional committee in 1911, having produced an immense multivolume study in the interests of reducing immigration, recommended excluding unskilled workers who were unaccompanied by families, or increasing the head tax for each immigrant except for men who came with their families.[29] Animus focused on male sojourners (dubbed "birds of passage") who earned good wages in the United States and then returned home. The welcome new citizen was a literate man who was married, who brought his wife and family with him, and who took on the responsibility to support them.

In the literacy exemption for family members, congressmen installed the understanding that a man's role and rights as husband and father were part of his citizenship. "The first essential for a man's being a good citizen is his possession of the home virtues," declared Theodore Roosevelt, who became president at the turn of the century. He associated the capacities for good citizenship and good government with "the qualities that make men and women eager lovers, faithful, duty-performing, hardworking husbands and wives, and wise and devoted fathers and mothers."[30] Cultivating the "home virtues" among male immigrants and citizens, seeing these as complements to civic duties, fostered moral regulation no less than exclusion of polygamists and prostitutes did. As the United States entered the world stage in the Spanish-American war at the turn of the century, political leaders implicitly viewed the nation acting as protector of smaller, weaker territories as the male citizen-husband-father writ large—exercising husbandly protectiveness or paternal benevolence in taking over Spain's former colonies. Pro-imperialists such as Roosevelt, Lodge, and Albert Beveridge believed that men of character were those stout-hearted enough to take care of others. "It has been races of marrying men that have made the heroic epochs in human history," wrote Beveridge, the young and influential senator from Indiana, in a homily to young men. "If your arm is not strong enough to protect a wife . . . you are not really worthwhile."[31]

The prejudice in favor of the husband and father as potential citizen implied that the female immigrant was also desirable, but in her role as a dependent rather than as a full citizen. Congress's clearest statement that a husband's citizenship rights trumped his wife's came in the 1907 immigration law, which included the provision "that any American woman who marries a foreigner shall take the nationality of her husband." Since 1855, the foreign-born wife of an American man had been deemed a citizen herself, but that law left unclear the nationality of American women who married foreigners. The court decisions on this question in the late nineteenth century were mixed: some judged that an American woman lost her citizenship by marrying an outsider, and some did not. Nonetheless, congressmen formulating the 1907 statute had no hesitation in declaring that all wives should assume their husbands' national allegiance, even though the provision would make aliens of their countrywomen who married foreigners. Most European nations had adopted this principle by the late nineteenth century, influencing American policy-makers.[32]

The new law intended administrative rationality as much as anything else: it was more convenient for the bureaucracy if members of families had the same nationality. This was at a time when about a million foreigners were entering the United States every year. For immigrant couples, the law meant that the husband's naturalization made his wife a citizen too; but an immigrant wife could not become a citizen herself if her husband did not choose to. So accustomed were advocates of the 1907 provision to giving priority to the male citizen that they did not see it as a slight or a threat to American women, whose citizenship was assumed to be relatively unimportant because they did not have political rights anyway.

The movement for women's political rights was flourishing by 1907, however. Women could vote in four states, and eight years later when the U.S. Supreme Court reviewed the policy on wives' citizenship, woman suffragists' gains had advanced further. In California, where women got the ballot in 1911, Ethel Mackenzie was prevented from registering because she was married to an Englishman. Mackenzie took the issue to court, contending that it was unconstitutional for Congress to deprive her of her rights as a citizen because of her marriage.

No court sympathized with Mackenzie, not the trial court, nor California's high court, nor the highest in the land. The U.S. Supreme Court, unanimously endorsing the 1907 provision, embraced the "ancient principle" of "the identity of husband and wife." Justice Joseph McKenna's opinion conceded that there had been "much relaxation" of the doctrine of marital unity, but explained that it could not be abandoned. A married couple's "intimate relation and unity of interests" made it "of public concern in many instances to merge their identity and give dominance to the husband." McKenna emphasized, as the California high court also had, that Ethel Mackenzie's marriage was a voluntary act. Since the law warned her of the consequences of choosing a foreigner, her willingness to marry was "as voluntary and distinctive as expatriation."[33]

This decision affirmed that both marriage and citizenship were voluntary bonds, but allowed a very different political outcome of marital consent for a husband and a wife. The policy treatment of the male citizen who married a foreigner could not have been more different from the treatment of a female citizen who did the same thing. The man's wife immediately belonged to the nation (if she fit the racial requirement for naturalization) and so did his children. The woman and her future children were ejected from the national community for her foreign marriage, and could rejoin only if her husband decided to be naturalized.

The impact of husbands' prerogatives in the civic realm also showed in the 1907 diplomatic arrangement with Japan called the Gentlemen's Agreement. Japanese immigration had been minimal and no cause for remark when anti-Chinese sentiment crested. After 1885, however, the Japanese government opened its doors and more Japanese laborers emigrated to the United States. Although the numbers were tiny compared to European immigrants—130,000 Japanese came in between 1900 and 1910, when 2 million from Austria and 1.5 million from Russia entered—the Japanese presence stirred protest.[34] The state of California passed several discriminatory laws. Demands for Japanese exclusion arose, but the military power of Japan made U.S. leaders reluctant to treat it like China with regard to immigration. President Theodore Roosevelt did not want to cause direct offense by excluding Japanese immigrants, and Japan did not want to lose face through exclusion. When the San Francisco school board's decision in 1905 to segregate Japanese children in the "Oriental School" provoked the government of Japan to protest, President Roosevelt stepped in.

The Gentlemen's Agreement, made in private at the highest level of both governments, substituted for a Japanese exclusion law. San Francisco would allow Japanese students (who numbered only ninety-three) to attend the public schools; the government of Japan would itself restrict laborers' emigration to the United States; and the United States would allow in *some* Japanese immigrants. Those admitted would be the wives and children of Japanese men already in the country.[35] Useful in many ways, the agreement responded to exclusionist sentiment in the United States by stanching the flow of Japanese laborers, while it enabled Japanese men already residing in the United States to have Japanese brides rather than resorting to prostitutes or paying court to white women. (Eight states by 1913 had laws against whites marrying Japanese or Chinese.)[36] It pacified the government of Japan by circumventing the congressional will to act even more harshly. It also held out an olive branch to Japanese male residents, applying to them deeply held assumptions about male citizens' domestic rights and rewards. Although Japanese men could not become naturalized citizens, the Gentlemen's Agreement encouraged them to *look* like citizens by forming appropriate domestic units via marriages within their own racial/national group.[37]

As the crisis with Japan was resolved, immigration numbers were booming. Alarms about contagion in the body politic fueled dozens of proposals to strengthen restrictions, including the exclusion of prostitutes. A national hysteria over the international "traffic in women" was in the making. Amidst rapid change in urban life, in sexual mores, and in occupations, vice reformers envisioned a huge international conspiracy to infiltrate the nation with "white slaves," inveigled into a life of shame by predatory procurers.[38] The United States joined a dozen European nations in an agreement to suppress the trade by sharing information, but this did little to reduce the panic.

Congressmen expended fulsome prose on the "soul-harrowing horrors" of the traffic, calling it "the meanest, the blackest crime that was ever instilled into the human heart," and deeming white slavery "a thousand times worse and more degrading" than any other kind.[39] The 1907 immigration law strengthened the language barring and deporting alien prostitutes and punishing the traffickers. Three years later, Congress enacted a statute called the White-Slave Traffic Act, which penalized the transportation of girls or women for immoral purposes (and the inducement, persuasion, compulsion, and so on, to transport them) *within* the country, through interstate or foreign commerce. It became known subsequently as the Mann Act, after its sponsor, Representative James R. Mann of Chicago.[40]

This legislation built on the many reports of Marcus Braun. A onetime private detective, he was hired by the federal government as a special undercover agent and dispatched on several long investigative trips to Europe, Mexico, and Canada between 1905 and 1909. Braun embraced his mission wholeheartedly. He aimed to eradicate a trade that he believed involved 10,000 pimps and procurers and 50,000 foreign-born prostitutes in the United States, "a crying shame upon our much boasted 20th Century Christian Civilization."[41] In country after country, Braun found that large numbers of prostitutes were emigrating, but he also found that most were not coerced to come to the United States. They arrived either "by their own enterprise" or in a man's company, knowing "precisely for what purposes they are taken." Braun attributed the scores arriving on "almost every steamer" to Jewish procurers in Russia, Galicia, and Romania (who were, indeed, active in the international traffic) and believed that only in "very rare" instances were the women deceived about their destination.[42]

Immigration officials and the Congress heard Braun's results in detail, repeatedly, yet found it hard to budge from the assumption that prostitutes were coerced, just as antipolygamists believed that Mormon wives were victims of tyranny. Even if an international conspiracy had not brought the foreign-born prostitutes, Commissioner-General of Immigration Daniel Keefe continued to assume that they were subjected to "brutal treatment" and kept in a "condition of virtual slavery."[43] Trying to be vigilant, agents of the Immigration Bureau worked city streets as well as ports of entry, for the bureau had the power to deport foreign-born prostitutes found within three years of their entry. To officials' dismay, prostitutes and the men around them proved to be "intimately acquainted with the provisions of the immigration law" and creative in showing that their residence exceeded three years.[44]

Foreign-born prostitutes also took unforeseen advantage of the American principle of male headship of the family: they evaded deportation by marrying American citizens. Because of the 1855 law awarding citizenship to an American citizen's wife, any male procurer or pimp with American citizenship could take a foreign-born (though not Asian) prostitute out of the reach of immigration laws by marrying her. And they did. Prostitutes married citizens hastily, instrumentally, clearly to avoid the net of immigration inspectors, as soon as warrant proceedings against them were instigated.[45]

This boomerang of the marital unity principle in citizenship tripped up immigration officials trying to pluck prostitutes out of their habitats. The commissioner-general's response reflected something more than frustration with the practical difficulty presented. He saw prostitutes and the men who protected or exploited them as callously employing both marriage and citizenship for their own immoral and illegal ends. He wanted to insist that a marriage "entered without genuine intention to be bound as man and wife and with the collateral purpose of escaping the operation of the immigration law" could not really make an alien woman into a citizen. The bureau pressed so hard on the attorney general of the United States to agree that he conceded that a marriage joined "merely for the purpose of evading the immigration laws" might be invalid. Perhaps deportation of the woman claiming to be a wife was warranted. "To hold otherwise," he came to see, "would be to say that the mere observance of the forms of marriage, no valid marriage subsisting, would operate to confer the rights and privileges of citizenship upon one who had shown, in the most unequivocal manner, her absolute unfitness therefor, and permit fraud of the grossest nature to act as a bar to the operation of the immigration laws."[46]

The intertwined meanings and obligations of marriage and citizenship and male headship of the family were all deformed and devalued by prostitutes' marriages to citizens, in the eyes of bureau officials. In such a marriage, consent was abnormally merged with fraud and force, and this made the citizenship associated with it suspect. Fraud and force were supposed to characterize white slavery, not marriage. Marcus Braun wanted to strip away the American citizenship of any man who "stoops to be willing to marry a Prostitute" because he was "unworthy." A man's choosing so wrongly, and a couple's marrying so opportunistically, lay outside the pale of patriotic expectations. The bureau seriously considered Braun's proposal.[47] Its alarm about the situation far exceeded the evidence, which showed barely a handful of cases of alien prostitutes marrying Americans (usually their pimps) in order to escape deportation.[48] Nonetheless, in 1914 the new Department of Labor (where the Bureau of Immigration was relocated) testified that the single greatest mode of circumventing the ban on entry of "alien immoral women" was their marriages to citizens. The department recommended that American citizenship via marriage be denied to them, and the Immigration Act of 1917 added this exception to the law of 1855.[49]

The bureau's hyperbole reflected the size of its concern for free choice and voluntary allegiance as emblems of virtue. Fraudulent marriage claims at ports of entry became an ongoing concern of immigration officials. Often, a man came to the United States, resided long enough to become a naturalized citizen, and then had his wife or prearranged bride follow him. Marcus Braun stressed that "one of the principal subterfuges adopted by the procurers of prostitutes" was to say that "they are American citizens and that the women accompanying them (who are, in fact, prostitutes) are their lawful wives, thus securing the admission of the women practically without examination." He thought the "immense number of alien prostitutes" in the Seattle area and in California, "whether French, Canadian, Russian or Polish Jews, or Japanese," had possibly entered that way and far from being lawful wives might be "held . . . in a kind of slavery." As a result, the Bureau of Immigration significantly tightened its operations, with more searching inspections, new methods for expediting warrants, and boards of special inquiry set up at large ports.[50]

Braun suspected all Jews at entry ports; only Asians drew more fire. Looking for violations of the Gentlemen's Agreement and of the Chinese exclusion laws at ports of entry, Bureau of Immigration agents were suspicious of Japanese and Chinese women immigrants claimed as wives and ready to believe that nine tenths were being brought in as prostitutes under cover.[51] Asians and Jews were indeed conspicuous as pimps and procurers, but so were men of other nationalities and ethnic groups. Jews and Asians were more easily accused of masking prostitution as marriage because of American officials' willingness to believe that "racially" different and non-Christian groups were likely to commit such grotesquery. In this thinking about "race," differences in marriage beliefs and practices mattered. Both Asians and Jews—the latter via the Old Testament—were tainted by association with polygamy. (Mormon polygamists claimed Old Testament patriarchs as their model.) Also, both Jews and Asians in their home cultures used arranged marriages, in which overt economic bargaining and kinship networks beyond the marrying pair played acknowledged parts. In Russia and Poland, Jewish extended families took the major initiative in assessing the suitability of the bride and groom, often employing matchmakers. The young man and woman went along with varying levels of participation. Chinese and Japanese parents regularly took the decisive part in arranging marriages for their children, often well in advance of the marriage date. These traditions did not ignore considerations of affection and sexual satisfaction, but considered them alongside economic and familial suitability.

In contrast, Americans were very much committed to marriage founded on love. Victorian-era courtship had not lacked romantic intensity, despite the often formal aspects of respectable marriage, with its distinctively defined roles of husband and wife. In what could be called a willful mystification, American rhetoric and popular culture had for some time put love and money on opposite sides of the street. Mercenary or cold-blooded motives for marrying were labeled crass, unethical, and destined for disastrous fate. "True love," the crucial requisite, was ever more ardently highlighted as new psychologies around the turn of the century instigated public discussion of sexual attraction. New media such as movies and graphic advertising infused the notion of consent in marriage with awareness of the magnetizing power of sex. True love was envisioned as springing up of its own accord, neither obeying rational discipline nor answering family considerations or monetary concerns. When the sociologists Robert and Helen Lynd explored a midwestern town as dispassionately as if it were an exotic village, they found that belief in "romantic love as the only valid basis for marriage" had persisted rock-solid from the 1890s through the 1920s. Only through some "mysterious attraction" that "just happens" were two young people supposed to find each other, they reported; the townfolk seemed "to regard romance in marriage as something which, like their religion, must be believed in to hold society together."[52]

The contrast between arranged marriage and the "love match" was very present in the minds of social workers, settlement house residents, reformers, and government officials who addressed themselves to immigrants' social adjustment and assimilation to American life. In "Americanization" efforts, immigrants' achievements in marriage and domesticity were taken to measure their moral adaptation. Virtually all "Americanizers" of the early 1900s, no matter how much they appreciated diversity among cultures, disapproved of familially arranged marriage. Not putting love first, arranged marriage appeared to bear only a debased likeness to the real thing—akin to contract labor's travesty of consent. The whiff of compulsion of the couple by extended family members, the possible instrumentalism of the marriage choice, and the importance of monetary considerations all ran against the American grain. An arranged marriage represented coercion—whether brokered by a Jewish matchmaker or by a Japanese go-between, it seemed as un-American as Mormon polygamy. European immigrants themselves, when they came to write memoirs and fiction, often used the contrast between arranged marriage and the love match to stand for the difference between the Old World and the New, between outdated tradition and modernity, between falsity and truth, tyranny and freedom.[53]

Only marriage based on a love match paralleled the voluntary allegiance that would make a nation of immigrants great. Distrusting arranged marriage, immigration officials imagined that Jewish and Asian couples were capable of nefarious deceptions. Suspicion especially focused on Japanese immigrants for "proxy marriage," or "picture brides." In Japan, it was not uncommon for a friend or relative to act as go-between for two families who had marriageable progeny. The go-between sent the man's picture to the bride and her parents, describing him and what he offered. If interested, the bride's family sent her picture to the go-between, to be conveyed to the proposed groom, to see whether an agreement could be struck. Japanese bachelors who had immigrated to the United States made use of this system at long distance. Usually the marriage would be performed in Japan without the groom present—a "proxy" standing in for him—so that the woman who arrived in the United States would already be his wife, by Japanese reckoning. Korean immigrants (fewer in number) also used this system.[54]

As officials and inspectors at ports dealt with picture brides, they were defending their understanding of marriage as a bargain based on consent. Hawaii, where most picture brides landed, inaugurated "searching investigation of the character of the alleged husband" before permitting the bride to land, and if no reason for rejection was found, required that proxy brides remarry their "alleged husbands" right away, in an American ceremony at the port.[55] The San Francisco and Seattle commissioners followed suit. The man in charge at Angel Island (the west coast immigration arrival port, corollary to Ellis Island on the east) assumed that "proxy marriage itself raised a doubt as to admissibility." Denying that proxy marriages were real ones, U.S. officials were countering the venerable legal doctrine that a marriage, if valid where it was contracted, should be deemed valid everywhere. The U.S. district attorney would not accept the validity of a Japanese proxy marriage on the reasoning that only one of the parties to the marriage was under Japanese jurisdiction when it took place. The United States's refusal to recognize polygamous marriages contracted elsewhere was sometimes cited as a precedent.[56]

The commissioner-general of immigration in Washington directed "every possible caution . . . to prevent the perpetration of imposition and fraud." Justifying the requirement of a remarriage "in accordance with American custom" before the brides could be allowed into their grooms' "custody," the commissioner-general insisted that conformity in "so important a social relation as marriage" was necessary. He had the economic function uppermost in mind. The fact of marriage had to be validated because the woman was allowed to land "on the theory that she is provided for because joined by marriage to a man who under our laws and customs will be responsible thereafter for her support." The Japanese groom was "the head and responsible unit of the newly constituted family."[57]

After 1912, Japanese civic associations in the United States began to object to the remarriage policy as cumbersome and expensive. At the same time, anti-Japanese voices in California and Washington agitated against proxy wives' entering at all. The San Francisco Labor Council, representing over 50,000 organized male and female workers, petitioned President Woodrow Wilson to exclude picture brides, protesting that they were not simply wives but "in fact laborers," working as horticulturists with their husbands, thus displacing white farmers. The petition also warned that Japanese couples reproduced faster than whites did, so that picture-bride entry contained "the germ and growth of a new race question which in time, if unchecked, will become as great and vexatious, well-nigh impossible of solution, as the negro question."[58] The numbers were far smaller than the severity of the alarm indicated, as in the case of alien prostitutes who married citizens. Pressured by the Japan Association of America, the Bureau of Immigration conceded that only 865 proxy brides landed in San Francisco during the year from June 1914 to June 1915. The California population at the time numbered nearly 3 million. Still, on the floor of Congress, Senator James D. Phelan of California objected to "picture brides" in no uncertain terms. "The marriage that is contracted on the other side—the parties are separated by an ocean and merely exchange photographs—is no marriage at all."[59]

On May 1, 1917, the literacy requirement went into effect, unexpectedly causing a transformation of the treatment of picture brides. All illiterate women entering as wives, Japanese women among them, now had to show proof of marriage, to claim the exemption. This brought to the surface a contradiction in the foregoing policy. Picture brides' entry presupposed that they were married to their grooms, for only as wives of resident Japanese men could they enter under the Gentlemen's Agreement. Yet proxy-wed couples were compelled to marry again in the United States on the argument that no (valid) marriage had taken place. Could a couple both *be* married sufficiently to enable the woman's entry, and not be married? If picture brides were not really married, then they could not qualify for the wifely exemption under the literacy test.

Japanese objections to discriminatory treatment came to a head at this point and the Department of Labor, in collaboration with the State Department, changed its policy, under pressure from the Japanese embassy. The fact that the United States had entered the Great War, with Japan an "associated Power" of the Allies, must have been influential.[60] The secretary of labor, newly in charge of the Bureau of Immigration, believed that proxy marriage was fully valid in Japan. As of mid-1917, if a picture bride brought copies of the Japanese records of her marriage with her to the United States, she would be considered no less than a "wife." Proxy marriages would now be "in no sense distinguishable from marriages generally."[61]

The admission of picture brides became all the more important and contested a loophole because the 1917 Immigration Act established an "Asiatic barred zone," which subjected virtually all Asians to exclusion.[62] Anti-Japanese sentiment ballooned in California and parts of Washington. As the world war ended, the front page of the *Seattle Star* screamed out in large black and red letters, "Japanese Picture Brides Are Swarming Here." By late in 1919—with both nativist and racist outbursts rising in the United States—the Japanese consul-general and the Japan Association of America seem to have concluded that the battle for proxy wives was not worth fighting. The Japanese government offered to take the initiative itself to prohibit picture brides from emigrating to the continental United States, because it placed "supreme importance" on good relations between the two nations.[63] As in the Gentlemen's Agreement, the Japanese government held back its emigrants rather than face exclusion.

The Department of Labor's nominal acceptance of picture brides did not last. By 1922, the department had declared that any marriage performed when one of the parties was in the United States and the other in a foreign country was invalid for immigration purposes. In the Immigration Act of 1924, Congress wrote that "the terms 'wife' and 'husband' do not include a wife or husband by reason of a proxy, or picture marriage."[64] Thus repudiating a form of marriage at odds with the American love match, the 1924 law (which would rule until the era of World War II) also rejected those who practiced it, deeming all Asians inadmissible to the United States.[65] Nothing else in the 1924 law equaled the fiat of Asian inadmissibility, but its establishment of "national origins" quotas—intended to duplicate the ethnic composition of the United States in 1890—also shrank admissions from eastern Europe and Russia, the homelands of most Jewish immigrants.

Many causes and voices figured in narrowing the gates between between 1875 and 1924. "Racial nationalism," meaning a commitment to retain numerical domination of the body politic by whites of English and northern European descent, probably works as well as any to indicate the main impetus.[66] Rejection of certain nationalities as too foreign to belong to America highlighted economic, political, and moral reasons and marriage practices helped to compose those reasons. While marriage was rarely the cardinal issue in contestation over immigration, insistence on a given model of monogamy was implicit in concerns about the virtue and character of the people. Nonconforming marriages represented all that was "racially" unassimilable in a given group. In excluding prostitutes first, in structuring the literacy requirement to incorporate male citizens' privileges and obligations as heads of household, in rejecting the Chinese and Japanese for defective morality and suspecting their marriages as subterfuges, immigration policy merged moral with political considerations and weighted marriage heavily in the balance.

Congress had long been glad to bolster the citizenship of men through marriage. Immigration policy reiterated that commitment in the literacy requirement and in the forced dependency of married women's nationality, yet it also put those men who were seen to have abused their prerogative (by choosing the wrong wives or marrying them in the wrong way) outside the circle of entitlement. Marriages suspected of being compelled or fraudulent would not be credited easily. American men who married prostitutes would not be able to hand citizenship to their brides with the wedding ring after 1917—thus Congress as well as the Department of Labor proved willing to tread on citizens as husbands if they misunderstood their domestic role and rights. The choice and consent embodied in approved marital union, its legality, its monogamous (Christian) morality—all these could be corrupted, compromising civic participation and governance, as the Mormons had shown. If marriages produced the polity, then wrongfully joined marriages could be fatal. The presence of such marriages and their perpetrators might infect the whole body politic. Immigrants inclined toward desirable patterns of love and marriage, on the other hand, were seen as voluntarily choosing and contributing to what it meant to be free Americans.

7

THE MODERN ARCHITECTURE
OF MARRIAGE

When Orville and Wilbur Wright sent a heavier-than-air machine into the sky over Kitty Hawk, North Carolina, to fly like a bird in December 1903, the flight was rightly seen as an augury of the new century. Many technologies that would make twentieth-century life distinctive, including telephones, electric power, the automobile, the movies, and the radio, came into being around the turn of the century. So did characteristics of the economy such as the consolidated national corporation, the moving assembly line, national brands, brand-name advertising, mass merchandising of consumer goods, and the white-collar and management occupations these created. Technological innovations such as electric lights and electrified urban transportation quickened the pace of life. Not only new immigrants but country folks were drawn toward towns and cities, so that the relative weight of the rural population diminished. New forms of civic life in local and national nonpartisan organizations grouped people together to pursue shared purposes; new forms of commercialized leisure such as vaudeville theaters, movies, window-shopping at department stores, public dance halls, and amusement parks beckoned wage-earners to entertainment and relaxation outside their homes.

Amidst wrenching changes in industry, technology, and the very composition of the American people—amidst what also seemed like sky-high openings to progress—public understandings of marriage were recreated. A twentieth-century shape for the institution began to come into focus. New possibilities for women outside wifehood and the home were perceived as the driving force, more than alterations in men's lives; but new patterns in women's lives were not simple or unidirectional and neither were signals about the institution of marriage. One shift was clear: government authorities eased up on political and moral strictures about marriage and concentrated more on enforcing its economic usefulness. In the twentieth century the public framework of marriage would be preeminently economic, preserving the husband's role as primary provider and the wife as his dependent—despite the growing presence of women in the labor force.

Public policy had always viewed the economic substructure of marriage as essential, but earlier, when the character of the American polity was still at risk, the relation of marriage to political citizenship and to the moral virtue of the citizenry was more important to articulate. The nation originally had few technologies of governance to monitor and control a people strewn unevenly over a huge expanse of land. Monogamous marriages that distinguished citizen-heads of households had enormous instrumental value for governance, because orderly families, able to accumulate and transmit private property and to sustain an American people, descended from them. As the polity itself and national solidarity became firmly established between the Civil War and World War I, however, the serviceability of marriage as a form of direct political governance lessened. And as the post-Victorian generation enjoyed what they considered a sexual revolution, they gave up their parents' exaggerated public emphasis on linking monogamous morality to political virtue. The marital model in which the individuality and citizenship of the wife disappeared into her husband's legal persona had to go, logically, once women gained the vote in 1920.

Yet marital unity was rewritten economically in the provider/dependent model, a pairing in which the husband carried more weight. This public policy emphasis emerged, ironically, while the doctrine of coverture was being unseated in social thought and substantially defeated in the law. Blanche Crozier, an exceptional feminist legal commentator, wrote acerbically that "public policy" had taken the place of common law, becoming "the new explanation, the new basis of justification," for marital inequality.[1] When she wrote in 1935, the economic bargain between a husband-provider and a wife-dependent had become the most important public stake in marriage. Twentieth-century public policy would not need to articulate the relation between marriage and political citizenship as before if it incorporated the expected marital roles economically. This economic emphasis was less directly coercive than coverture had been. It operated more through incentives than through ultimatums. Yet because the economic figuration of marriage blurred lines between public policy, law, economy, and society, it was inescapable.

When the federal government was called upon during the Depression to include social entitlements in the definition of citizenship, this marital patterning became central. The New Deal announced a qualitative change in the powers of the nation-state. Following many nations in Europe, the federal government in the United States sought to support and reshape economic life more directly. Enacting its aims involved defining social categories—such as earner and dependent—and the social relations between them. In the process of broadening meanings of citizenship, New Deal policy innovations lent new support to the old economic underpinning of marital roles. This policy orientation had been set as far back as the Freedmen's Bureau: if the federal government stepped into the social and economic lives of needy citizens with work or relief, the institution of marriage would serve as a template within which the aid was inscribed. The federal government would offer social provision while bolstering the basic structure of male providership and affirming the male citizen's domestic rights. It would retain within the innovation of government-granted entitlements the norm of private provision by a male citizen/head of household for his wife and children—a norm central to the system of private business enterprise as well as to the conception of the male citizen.

This evolution in government's stake in marriage was far less visible or remarkable to Americans living in the early twentieth century than the revolutions going on in the world and around them. A single extraordinary decade of political and cultural rupture after 1910 produced World War I, the Bolshevik Revolution, Cubist and Futurist art, and Einstein's theory of special relativity. In American cities, standards of behavior were cleaving the generations, as work and leisure habits and sexual mores were being transformed. Women's behavior especially attracted commentary. Sex became political—that is, it was emblematic of changing power dynamics between women and men. In expressing some sexual initiatives, women were seizing a prerogative seen as men's, just as they were treading on "male" terrain in the labor force and reform politics. Armies of immigrant women took factory jobs; and there was a huge jump in high school attendance as girls prepared themselves to staff the growing white-collar ranks. Even though women and men were slotted by sex into different jobs, their daily presence in factories, shops, and offices brought them into the same public world outside the home. In response, the woman's suffrage movement burst its nineteenth-century seams, broadening out to involve wage-earning women as well as middle-class matrons, black women as well as white, southern as well as northern and western. Hundreds of thousands all over the country paraded in vigils and interjected their voices continually in political debate. The very presence of women on the streets in state and national capitals registered women's willingness to use their bodies in new ways.

The moral superiority usually attributed to respectable, white, middle-class women in the nineteenth century had presupposed very different sexual regimes for the two sexes. A woman was to observe virginity before marriage, and fidelity after, while a man might sow his wild oats and even define manhood around a certain level of sexual aggressiveness. As a new frankness about sex took over urban discourse in the early twentieth century (percolating from the working class into the middle class), moral superiority seemed less desirable—and far less attainable. Young people socialized at public entertainments, unchaperoned. The erotic female "vamp" star batted her eyes in silent movies; on the dance floor the "bunny hug" was popular. The equation of sex outside marriage with something shameful came under severe question. The most advanced feminists spoke of "the liberation of a sex." Even the staid *Nation* conceded in 1912 that "as for the right of women to a frank enjoyment of the sensuous side of the sex-relation . . . no sensible person now disputes that right, but only, as in the case of men, the right to make it a subject of common conversation."[2]

By the 1920s, femininity was associated more with sex appeal than with sexual modesty, as it had been earlier. The privacy offered to young couples by the automobile, mass produced at reasonable prices, worried a lot of older observers, as did the movies they watched, such as *The Daring Years, Sinners in Silk, Flaming Youth, The Price She Paid, Name the Man,* and *The Queen of Sin.* A spate of books appeared with titles such as *Our Changing Morality* (1924), *Why We Misbehave* (1928), *Sex and Youth* (1929), *Sex in Civilization* (1929), and *The Bankruptcy of Marriage* (1928). Sexual experimentation before marriage by couples in love moved out of the shadows; some exploratory premarital heterosexual activity was granted to be normal. To the horror of conservative commentators, this meant greater easing of what had been seen as absolute interdiction of sex before marriage, although "going all the way"—especially with more than one partner, or without the motivation of true love—was still stigmatized and could be fatal for a woman's reputation. Belief in "true love" continued hand in hand with the new sexual frankness, since the ultimate destination (and vindication) of sexual desire was assumed to be the love match leading to marriage.[3]

Nonetheless, sexual liberalization was very controversial. Its threat to strict monogamous morality caused contests in many arenas, including the Supreme Court and the state legislatures. The Supreme Court had to decide three cases, in 1904, 1908, and 1911, all of which dealt, conceptually, with wives' challenges to the sexual and intimate aspects of marital governance. In all of these cases the court proved a bastion of conservatism, even of reaction—trying to erect a seawall against the incoming tide of women's sexual self-assertions. The court did so by reaffirming the very core of marital unity, the husband's private control of his wife's body. The first case involved a wife's consenting adultery, and her husband's rights to gain damages from the lover. In deciding it, the court defined a husband's right to exclusive sexual intercourse as "a right of the highest kind, upon . . . which the whole social order rests" and called the wife's consent to the love affair irrelevant, because she was "in law incapable of giving any consent to affect the husband's rights."[4] The second case justified use of Congress's ban on bringing women into the United States for prostitution or "other immoral purpose" to keep out a man who sought to enter with his mistress. The court here refused to distinguish among lovers, mistresses, prostitutes, and concubines, putting them all in the same "immoral" category. All these transgressive women were "hurtful to the cause of sound private and public morality," Justice John Harlan declared, because they displayed a common "hostility" to "the union for life of one man and one woman in the holy estate of matrimony," which was—he quoted from Francis Lieber—"the sure foundation of all that is stable and noble in our civilization." The court thus confirmed congressional power to legislate monogamous morality, and applied immigration law to reinstate the sexual double standard, when social behavior was defying both. Confident that Americans "almost universally held" its own view, the court ignored the expanding spectrum of sexual behavior.[5]

The third case involved wife abuse. Congress had enacted a married women's property and earnings statute for the District of Columbia. One of its provisions declared that wives had the capacity to sue "as fully and freely as if they were unmarried" for harms to themselves (torts, in legal language). On the basis of this law, an abused wife in the nation's capital sued her husband to recover damages for his tort of assault and battery on her. Had she been successful, her victory would have registered an enormous change in the institution of marriage. Suits *between* husband and wife (interspousal suits) were anathema to the doctrine of marital unity. Back in 1792, the jurist James Wilson had explained why: the "beautiful and striking" principle of marital unity presumed that "between husband and wife, there subsist or may subsist no difference of will or of interest." Wilson put "the matrimonial state" at a "far remove" from legal intervention except in "very pressing emergencies." This legal doctrine, which "like a candid and benevolent neighbour," Wilson wrote, would "presume . . . all to be well," implemented the husband's right to be the decision-maker in his household. The law trusted the husband's "hon-our" to exercise his marital governance justly.[6]

The common law had supported a husband's right to correct his wife with reasonable physical force, but in the post–Civil War period state courts no longer defended that prerogative. Judges called the husband's common-law right "a relic of barbarism that has no place in an enlight-ened civilization," "a rude privilege," a "brutality found in the ancient common law," a "revolting precedent." The discourse of Christian civi-lization directly confronted a husband's traditional prerogative to disci-pline his wife by blows. Christian civilization's claim to supremacy relied on its high valuation and protection of wives, and judges in the late nine-teenth century abjured physical compulsion, but they did not substan-tially change the law's support of the husband's marital governance. Instead, they rewrote his authority, and the resulting hierarchy between husband and wife, by keeping the law's interference away from the inti-macy of the household domain. Just as Wilson had a century earlier, they stressed the public interest in shielding interactions between husband and wife from public view. It was "better to draw the curtain, shut out the public gaze, and leave the parties to forget and forgive," a much-cited North Carolina decision said.[7]

In the 1911 case *Thompson v. Thompson,* a majority of the justices on the U.S. Supreme Court endorsed this approach. They refused to believe that Congress intended the District of Columbia married women's statute "to revolutionize the law governing the relation of husband and wife as between themselves." They rejected the "radical and far-reaching" reading that a wife could sue her husband "for injuries to per-son or property as though they were strangers." Allowing interspousal tort suits would encourage wives and husbands to bring marital spats into the public spotlight, unnecessarily and inappropriately. Without even glancing at the way such public restraint perpetuated male dominance in the married couple, the court alluded to divorce as the remedy available to a battered wife suffering "atrocious wrongs."[8]

The conservatism of this decision mirrored and intensified the previ-ous ones. For the third time in a few years the court acted to preserve both marital unity and the husband's dominance (and would again in 1915, in response to Ethel Mackenzie's attempt to keep her citizenship despite her marriage to a foreigner). The court's view of an ongoing marriage as an intimate zone insulated from legal interference offered the wife no resources, outside of her personal charms, to deal with a problematic relationship: she was either to endure or to seek a divorce. Yet this harsh view—veiled in a rhetoric of household intimacy and liberty—laid the groundwork for far different meanings about the privacy of the married couple that would be summoned into life a half-century later.

In its strictures, the high court was responding to many pressures on public understandings of marriage. Despite the court's intent to say otherwise, new behaviors in the early twentieth century had begun to blur the sharp lines of monogamous morality and had disrupted conventions of marital unity. In the always-contentious area of marriage across the color line, the 1910s and 1920s were explosive. In 1912, the marriage of the heavyweight boxer Jack Johnson, who was African American, to Lucille Cameron, a seventeen-year-old white prostitute, made sensational national news. The marriage came on the heels of Johnson's defeat of the "great white hope," Jack Jeffries, in a championship match interpreted across the nation as a contest for racial supremacy. Cameron's parents attempted to charge Johnson with abduction, portraying their daughter as an innocent girl who came to the city, was snared into a life of sin, and succumbed to Johnson only because she was drunk. The federal government tried to show that Johnson and his friends ran an interstate prostitution ring. Because the couple had traveled across state lines, Johnson was successfully prosecuted under the Mann Act and had to spend a year in prison.[9]

In the year after the couple married, fourteen state legislatures introduced bills to institute or strengthen bans on racial intermarriage, though none passed in northern states. Congress introduced a bill for the District of Columbia and returned to it several times in the teens and twenties, without achieving it (although the House passed it twice). Some southern congressmen hoped to pass a constitutional amendment against racial intermarriage. The Johnson-Cameron marriage became such a flashpoint, touching off this renewed effort, because more and more frequent mixed marriages loomed on the horizon as the "Great Migration" of African Americans from the south proceeded. Mixed couples became more visible, especially in New York City's celebrated Harlem. African Americans such as W. E. B. Du Bois, a founder of the National Association for the Advancement of Colored People in 1909 and the editor of its journal, did not favor intermarriage but opposed the bans because they provided a "magna charta of concubinage and bastardy" to white men, giving them license to exploit black women sexually without feeling any obligation.[10] Black voters' pressure had much to do with the failure of new bans to pass in the north. Nonetheless, thirty states still nullified and/or punished marriage between whites and blacks in 1930— many of them, mainly in the west, treating marriage between whites and Asians the same way. Marriage was the most criminalized form of racially related conduct.[11] Although these laws inhibited and stigmatized mixed couples, the behavior banned had leeway to advance elsewhere. Legislators knew they were making a prescriptive statement in passing or strengthening such laws; they could only contain, not eliminate the conduct they were stigmatizing.

If sexual norms, marital unity, and separation between black and white were all challenged by transformations taking place in the new century, the old relation between marriage and political citizenship was even more directly undercut. After three quarters of a century of suffragists' efforts, the U.S. Constitution was amended, in 1920, to prohibit sex discrimination in voting. Women now could enter the voting booth and the political parties as putative equals whether they were wives or not. The prior relation between marriage and citizenship became "as archaic as the doctrine of ordeal by fire" once women had the ballot, a Massachusetts congressman remarked.[12] Wives, voting as individuals, could no longer be presumed to be represented by their husbands. In a clear insistence on this position, women activists moved quickly to eliminate the federal laws that bound a wife's nationality to her husband's and took away the citizenship of American women who married foreigners.

The result was the Cable Act, or Married Women's Independent Nationality Act, of 1922. Reflecting the reluctance of Congress to give up its long-term priority for the male citizen as family head and also the racial nationalism of immigration restriction, the act did not free a wife's citizenship entirely. An American woman who married a foreigner and stayed put in the United States would now remain the citizen she was. But she would lose her citizenship if she lived in her husband's country as much as two years, and she could not retain it at all if she married a man "ineligible for citizenship"—an Asian, a polygamist, or an anarchist. An American man suffered no such consequences for similar choices. His earlier privilege to endow a foreign-born woman with American citizenship by marrying her was revoked in the act, however; instead, his wife would have to undergo naturalization as other immigrants did, but she need be in the country only one year, instead of the standard five, to do so.[13] Even while supportive congressmen insisted that "the right of the woman to be an independent American citizen in her own right" was indisputable, "because the nineteenth amendment to the Constitution has settled that for all time," still the Cable Act contained inequalities that kept the principle of a wife's political individuality from being fully realized. These were eventually corrected with a series of legislative revisions, hard fought for by women's pressure groups, in 1930, 1931, and 1934.[14]

Even stronger hesitations dogged women's accession to jury service. Jury service was a political right that had always been linked to voting capacity. Accordingly, a ripple of state statutes enabling women to be jurors followed ratification of the nineteenth amendment, as if this were obvious and right. But by 1923—in tandem with politicians' assessment that women were not going to vote as a bloc—this initial rush had stopped, and it became very, very difficult for advocates of equal jury service to make headway. Major states, including New York, Massachusetts, and Illinois, resisted women's jury service until the late 1930s. Wyoming and Colorado, which had granted women the ballot very early (in 1870 and 1893, respectively) did not permit women to serve on juries until the 1940s.

Decisions in the numerous court cases resulting from the protracted struggle showed two alternative readings of the relation between women's enfranchisement and their jury service. Some judges assumed that women's admission to the vote immediately entitled them to full political participation and the consequent obligations. But others strongly contended that the exclusion of women from juries could persist after the nineteenth amendment was ratified because the ballot was a discrete right, not inherently capable of transforming women's political character. This bisected view of the meaning of enfranchisement suggested that in public policy there was a deep ambivalence about women's citizenship. Opponents of women's jury service sometimes claimed that women were unsuitable because they were irrational and emotional. More often, they argued that jury service conflicted with women's more important responsibilities to be at home serving the needs of their husbands and children. Opponents thus took for granted that "women" were "wives," and gave more weight to marital and domestic obligations than to women's obligations as citizens. By 1938, twenty-six of the forty-eight states and the District of Columbia called women to jury service, but of those, only eleven required women to serve on equal terms with men. Men's service was mandatory (with very limited exceptions), while women could easily exempt themselves by claiming domestic responsibilities. Predictably, juries with very few women members resulted.[15]

The nineteenth amendment might have been expected to transform the legal and political status of wives more thoroughly, given the prior importance of the husband's political representation of his wife, but continuity in the economic relation of husbands to wives minimized the transformation. A bisected vision of women workers paralleled the two readings of women's admissibility to juries. The "working girl" was a figure of some style and independence by 1920, when about one quarter of all women over fourteen were in the labor force. Many commentators in the 1920s equated women's enfranchisement with total emancipation. Unprecedented feats by women athletes, explorers, movie stars, authors, and politicians made headlines. Individual women in politics, law, medicine, journalism, photography, the arts, and the media were celebrated, while the great majority of women wage-earners in low-paid and repetitive work were less remarked. In one view, women at work looked common enough in the 1920s, and some outstanding achievers visible enough, that the whole employment field seemed open to female aspiration and success. This view seldom noticed the sex segregation of the labor market, which confined all but exceptional women to a few kinds of jobs.[16]

Alongside glamorous incarnations of the "working girl," unpaid housekeeping was still commonly regarded as women's inevitable vocation. This bisected vision was not entirely distorted, for relatively few women were regularly employed *after* they married. The proportion was increasing, but only 12 percent of wives with husbands present were in the labor force as of 1930. Marriage and motherhood were assumed to be every woman's hope, and despite some brave advocates' attempts to prove the contrary in the 1920s, marriage and motherhood were viewed as inconsistent with full-time employment for all but the economically pressed. Heralded modern labor-saving equipment did not prevent housekeeping and childrearing from being a full-time job. Ninety percent of urban housewives spent thirty-five hours or more per week on their tasks, a 1920s study showed, and rural housewives even more. Many wives at home took part in what now is called the underground economy, keeping boarders or lodgers, exchanging services with others, and so on, but they were rarely considered to be "working" and were not counted by census-takers that way.[17]

Because of the increased employment of women workers, however, the vocation of wife-and-motherhood could now be seen as chosen rather than prescribed. Women had alternatives. If a woman married, the consequences could be viewed simply as her individual choice, just as the Supreme Court had said Ethel Mackenzie's choice, which led to deprivation of American citizenship, was hers to make. Directives from social scientists and popular romance magazines rehabilitated marriage as an exciting venture in which sexual satisfaction for both partners became a prime index of marital harmony. Two investigators of young women's views in 1930 concluded that "the modern union of man and woman is visioned as a perfect consummation of both personalities that will involve every phase of mutual living."[18]

Women's continuing vocation in marriage was now portrayed in terms of modernity and choice. Some voices countered this ideal view: in novels of social realism by intellectual women and those on the left, for example, in occasional complaining articles in women's magazines, and in the urban blues sung by African American women, more sardonic views of marriage could be seen and heard. "Marriage is too much of a compromise; it lops off a woman's life as an individual," wrote one politically active woman who remained unmarried. "Yet the renunciation too is a lopping off," she continued, genuflecting to expectations for "normality."[19]

The working-out of "modern marriage" was far from painless. Twentieth-century wives exercised far more legal and economic autonomy than their mothers and grandmothers had: by the mid-1930s virtually all the states had laws on their books enabling a wife to own her own property and to inherit an estate free of her husband's debts, to sue in court and make contracts (enabling her to conduct business on her own), to write a will, and if her husband deserted her, to act as a single woman economically. Judges ordinarily awarded mothers custody of children in cases of separation or divorce. Yet the modern wife's freedom from economic and other constraints was incomplete. The nineteenth amendment did not fully dismantle coverture. Laws to ensure that a wife's earnings belonged to her (rather than her husband) spread at a much slower pace, and more unevenly, than the lifting of other property constraints, because of the assumption that a husband owned his wife's labor. This foundation of the marriage bargain epitomized both the reciprocality and the economic inequality between husband and wife. Every state legally obliged the husband to support his wife, and his ownership of her labor corresponded to his support obligation. By the mid-1930s, twenty-eight states had explicitly granted the wife her wages when she worked for a third party, and only two states had explicitly denied the wife's right to her own earnings, while the rest hedged or complicated the question.[20] But the sticking point, where the hand of the past showed itself most, was not her work in an office or shop or factory—it was her household labor, traditionally seen as her husband's domestic right. Even in states that had passed married women's earnings statutes, courts strongly tended to interpret a wife's household work as belonging to her husband, whether she was undertaking tasks for family members or keeping boarders or lodgers or washing laundry as a way to generate income.

Legal writers who meant to stress the economic emancipation of the wife had to concede that "the courts have jealously guarded the right of the husband to the wife's service in the household," as part of the legal definition of marriage.[21] Judges saw the wife's service as a necessary corollary to the husband's ongoing legal obligation to support her. The laws requiring husbands' support—although by no means wholly effective inside marriage or out—had consequences in the labor market and in marital roles. Municipal officials and social workers saw new reason for enforcement of husbands' support obligations when millions of immigrants were being assimilated into American life in the early twentieth century. The frequency of men's desertion of their wives and families became a public issue, as charitable societies addressed themselves to the needs of poor mothers and children. These groups emphasized husbands' support obligations not only for the immediate purpose of reducing the need for public relief of female-headed households, but also for the longer-term purpose of making immigrant working-class men conform to American standards for marriage and the domestic environment.

Charities, social workers, and child defenders sought out "shiftless fathers" and "cowardly husbands" and upbraided them to mend their irresponsibility. In response to public concern, most states made their laws harsher, setting higher fines or longer imprisonment for the husband who failed to support his wife and children. Many made nonsupport a felony rather than a misdemeanor. States allowed deserted wives to testify against their husbands in court, something previously impossible because coverture maintained that such testimony was self-incrimination, the two spouses being one person legally. Reformers pressured states to designate "family courts" to hear domestic relations cases and especially to enforce men's duties of support. Advocates and legislators emphasized that the husband did not simply owe support to his chosen partner; it was his public obligation. In implementing the support laws, courts looked to a man's public obligation (set by the state) more than to the wife's quality of life. When family courts ordered separation and support for abused wives, the husband had to make his payment to the court, rather than to the wife. The wife's own obligation of service did not go unnoticed. Harsh as they were on husbands, charity workers often blamed the deserted wives just as much, accusing them of failing to create the kinds of comfortable American homes in which husbands would want to stay put.[22]

Laws making it a crime for the husband to shirk his obligations were strengthened further by many states during the Depression decade. Nonsupport cases, heard at family courts, served mainly to discipline wayward men among the working poor in an effort to keep public funds from being spent on their families.[23] Implementation was always a problem. Three basic routes existed to bring the husband in line. A retailer who had given goods to a wife on credit could sue to collect from the husband. A person who was helping the wife financially, such as a relative, could bring a civil suit against the husband to recover costs. Third, the wife could get a court decree mandating her husband to pay, and have criminal sanctions brought if necessary. Both the second and third modes, the ones usually used, had a catch: both presupposed that the wife and husband were living apart. Because courts were chary of intervening in an intact marriage, the husband's obligation to provide was rarely legally enforceable unless a marriage had effectively ended.[24] If an unsupported wife obtained a court decree, there was no guarantee that her husband would deliver. If he was jailed for nonsupport, that hardly helped her (though he could be put on probation, on the condition that he work to support the family). When a middle-class wife went to court over nonsupport, the case was usually a prelude to divorce—and in some states a ground for it. As in *Thompson v. Thompson* at the Supreme Court earlier, the remedy for "atrocious wrongs" was still divorce, though it was not a remedy that could guarantee a vanished man's support of his ex-wife.

The innovation of "mothers' aid" or "mothers' pensions" in this era of commotion over marital desertion manifested a similar logic, emphasizing the economic substructure of marriage rather than offering alternatives to it. These state programs were meant to help "deserving" single mothers raise children in their own homes, to prevent children from being shunted to institutions, and to minimize child labor. Advocates thought that poor children without fathers would fare better at home with their mothers than in asylums or foster homes. They wanted the state (not private charities) to take the lead in providing the funds.[25] Because of very widespread popular pressure, especially from middle-class women's clubs, mothers' aid programs spread like wildfire to almost every state in little more than a decade, beginning in 1911. The terminology of mothers' pensions expressed the most visionary advocates' wish to honor mothering as a labor on behalf of the public welfare. With the world's eyes focused on World War I, advocates argued that mothers performed as crucial a service to the state as soldiers did, so pensions were warranted.

Some radical women imagined state funding of motherhood as the way to eliminate women's economic reliance on men and inaugurate sexual freedom and childbearing unattached to marriage. That version was not the one put into practice. Mothers' pensions marked a significant breakthrough by taking up public responsibility for some level of economic welfare, but the programs left unfulfilled the promise to support single mothers and children with respect. The aid did not go to deserted wives, or unmarried mothers, but to widows. Advocates realized that political realities required compromise. Legislators would not accept programs that appeared to negate marriage or to lift the onus of support from a man's shoulders. The social work leader Mary Richmond cited marital unity in opposing aid to deserted mothers, arguing that it was "absurd to go into a home and do for it what the legal and recognized head . . . has deliberately shirked . . . and then to suppose . . . that you have not interfered between man and wife."[26] Aid to widows, on the other hand, brought in the state to supply the husband's place as provider after his death, sustaining his wife's appropriate economic dependency and childrearing role.

The "pensions" amounted more to a token than a sufficiency. The funds budgeted by states and counties were meager, never enough to cover all applicants. The grants were not enacted as a right of mother-citizens but rather as a response to need, and recipients were closely supervised to monitor continuing need and appropriate use. Local control in defining who was "deserving" made for highly variable coverage, enrolling high proportions of white immigrant mothers in the hope that the supervision accompanying the aid would serve as an Americanizing purpose, while discriminating against African American applicants in the south.[27]

When the economic crisis of the Great Depression hit, new federal programs reinvoked the economic pattern of marital relationship in place at the state level. From the government's perspective, the huge problem of unemployment in the Depression called for bolstering men as providers, and women as their wives and dependents. President Franklin D. Roosevelt's administration reinforced that emphasis in responding to the Depression. The New Deal's mode of connecting social and economic welfare to political citizenship, necessary and promising at it was, did not bode equality between husbands and wives.

Millions lost their jobs in the 1930s and either remained jobless or took positions far inferior to their previous ones. Although women composed a quarter of the labor force, the focus of public concern about unemployment was working *men,* understood as providers for their families. Wives with paid jobs became the target of economic discrimination, on the widely accepted though fallacious thinking that the unemployment crisis would be solved if married women left the labor force. This outcry failed to recognize that the jobs men lost or sought were not the ones held by wives or by women at all, except in the case of some high-ranked professionals. Over 90 percent of women wage-earners were clustered in "women's work" in a very few occupations. Nonetheless, many private and public employers (public school systems, for instance) fired or refused to hire married women. Single women or widows, seen as having to support themselves, escaped most of this hostility, but those in desirable professional positions did not always escape being replaced by men.

When governments at any level removed married women from public sector jobs, it was an important signal to the nation about priorities in employment. The U.S. Congress fostered the exclusionary trend with Section 213 of the Economy Act of 1932, which prohibited two people of the same family from holding federal employment at the same time. Although it was gender-neutral in its language, in practice Section 213 meant dismissing from federal jobs those wives whose husbands also worked for the government, because the wife's job was almost always the lower-paid one and the one to be sacrificed. Nearly all of the fifteen hundred persons fired the first year that Section 213 went into effect were women. Women's organizations sprang into action opposing it, but five years of persistent lobbying were required before Section 213 was eliminated. Meanwhile a crop of state legislatures imitated its intent. As late as 1939, legislatures in twenty-six states were considering bills to bar married women from state jobs. Meanwhile, Depression poverty and male unemployment actually drove more married women to seek jobs. The negative climate meant that they got what others viewed as undesirable and ill-paid jobs—cleaning office buildings at night, for example. Amidst the condemnation, the proportion of wives in the labor force rose faster than ever before, going up from 12 percent to 17 percent during the 1930s.[28]

Although putting the onus on married women workers may have diffused discontent, it had grave consequences for women workers. The diatribes against wives earning meant that the "working girl" was the only approved female wage-earner—someone passing through a phase of her life, for whom paid work was fleeting and not a continuing need and right, who could manage without equal work and did not merit the same say in government or in union policy as the "working man." This mindset assumed that women with husbands belonged at home; a wife who persisted in working must be motivated either by dire need or callous personal selfishness. Movies in the Depression decade played with this theme, starting with a glamorous, assertive "working girl" heroine who by the end of the film had usually opted for marriage and domesticity.

Working men's welfare was at the center of popular and social-scientific commentary and at the heart of New Deal domestic policies.

Studies addressing the social consequences of the economic crisis bore titles such as *The Unemployed Man and His Family*. When President Roosevelt asserted that government had an "inescapable obligation" to "protect the citizen in his right to work and his right to live" no less than "in his right to vote," he sketched a prospect of social citizenship that began with the "right to life" and the "right to make a comfortable living" owed to every *man*.[29] Attempts in federal agency after agency to shore up the nation's individuals and families during the economic crisis addressed the husband-father as the principal wage-earner and citizen.

Except for grants of military pensions, the New Deal was the first time since the Freedmen's Bureau that the federal government offered jobs or job substitutes to its citizens at all. These programs showed that marriage still underlay civic status. The vast majority of New Deal–instigated benefits went to men as individuals who were or would be husbands, fathers, and providers for families, and to women, if at all, as wives or widows. Women were seldom excluded outright (except from the army-like Civilian Conservation Corps), but as individuals and potential wage-earners they received only a tiny fraction of what men did. The Works Progress Administration job-creation program, for example, served a far smaller number of women than their proportion in the labor force dictated. This disparity stemmed less from sex discrimination as such than from the expectation that benefiting men's employment would benefit women's welfare, because women as wives were men's dependents.

New Deal policy innovations revivified the fading connection between citizenship and marital role through economic avenues. These choices diluted the formal political equality of women and deeply imprinted marriage on citizenship entitlements, while refiguring what those entitlements were. Arguably the most important and lasting was the Social Security Act of 1935. This omnibus act had two major categories: social insurance and public assistance. In the social insurance category, which included unemployment compensation and the retirement benefits we still call "Social Security," recipients were envisioned as able-bodied (white, male) workers insuring themselves against untoward circumstances. In the public assistance category, which included aid to the blind and financial help for the indigent elderly not covered by Social Security, the recipient was imagined to be needy and dependent. Aid to Dependent Children (ADC), later renamed Aid for Families with Dependent Children (AFDC), or what now call "welfare," was in the public assistance category.[30]

From their inception, the social insurance programs were superior in payments and in reputation. They were known as programs that were not need-based but were financed by beneficiaries' contributions. Unemployment compensation and retirement benefits were premised on wages and on objective criteria for qualification. They were entitlements based on participation in paid employment. Public assistance, by contrast, was attuned to nonworkers or unpaid workers, was based on need rather than right, and was comparatively inferior in benefits and reputation. ADC, the assistance program reaching the most people, took mothers' aid as its model—continuing local administration and discretion over recipients, scrutinizing and supervising their lives to guarantee continuing deservingness. In return for a scanty stipend, a recipient had to be certified "a proper person, physically, mentally, and morally fit to bring up her children." This brought motherhood under surveillance, as had been true when the Union first instituted pensions for Civil War widows.

Both tracks of the Social Security Act confirmed marital roles, without being explicit about it. Retirement and unemployment insurance made no reference to gender or race, and employed wives could pay in and utilize both, and did. But the old-age insurance coverage in the 1935 act was partial, covering only about half of all workers by excluding part-time, seasonal, agricultural, domestic, philanthropic, and government employees (including teachers), and the self-employed. These were exactly the areas where women wage-earners, and African American and Latino men as well, were concentrated. More than 60 percent of women wage-earners were left uncovered, as though they were unearning wives. A far more even-handed proposal lay before Congress at the time, but languished: An alternative bill sponsored by Farmer-Labor Party congressman Ernest Lundeen proposed a federal system of insurance for loss of wages through sickness, accident, old age, or maternity for all categories of workers, without discrimination by race, sex, age, origin, or politics.[31] The Social Security Act that passed, after the wheeling and dealing and bargain-trading of Congress, helped most those who needed help the least: white male employees with year-round work. These were the citizens whose "right to work" and "right to make a comfortable living" as well as "right to vote" the New Deal would try to guarantee. The priority given to the male citizen in the New Deal thus echoed the prominence of the (white) male immigrant in immigration policy of the early part of the century.

The shape and spirit of social policy in the United States were fatefully ordained by the Social Security Act's inherent differentiation between the male citizen-husband-provider and the female citizen-mother-dependent. Seventy years before in the Freedmen's Bureau, husbands' responsibilities had given reason to reward men as citizens, and also to police them. The Social Security program rewarded men for taking on family responsibilities, while state-level apparatus policed them if they faltered in delivering support. When amendments to Social Security were made later in the 1930s, the intent to reward the male citizen-worker became still clearer. Revising the system to pay out slightly more and improve the standard of living possible for some Americans, policymakers did not extend coverage to excluded groups but rather gave more privileges to the citizen-worker-husbands who were already covered. Amendments passed in 1939 created "survivors' benefits" for the wives and minor children of men who died before the age sixty-five (so long as the wife did not remarry). They also increased a man's retirement benefit by 50 percent if his wife lived with him, once she reached the age of sixty-five. A wife who had worked in covered employment could choose to collect the benefits accrued from her own contribution, or the benefits her husband would get on her behalf. Typically, an employed wife earned so little and her years of employment were so relatively few that 50 percent of her husband's benefit was more than her own whole benefit, and she chose the larger amount. (In 1996, men's and women's earning powers were still so disparate that nearly two thirds of women on Social Security collected as wives rather than earners.)[32]

Among wage-earners contributing through the payroll tax, all women and unmarried men were subsidizing old-age benefits for the wives of married retirees and for both the wives and children of retirees who died young. The added benefit did not belong to the wife, really; the check for 150 percent was sent to the husband, recognizing his continued performance as a provider, rather than the service of his wife. If the couple divorced—no matter how many years they had been married and no matter how close to the age of sixty-five the divorce occurred—the 50 percent supplement disappeared. Similarly, the survivors' benefits paid to wives and children of covered male employees were not their own but entitlements for the male worker posthumously, honoring him by keeping his family from penury. The wife of a covered male worker who died would get these Social Security benefits, while an unmarried mother—or the widow of a man whose work had not been covered—was eligible only for ADC, or "welfare."

Policy-makers' and congressmen's endorsement of these benefits for a male worker's family members was especially remarkable because the supplements contradicted the highly championed "equity" principle of the retirement benefit system. Being purposely tied to workers' contributions, retirement insurance was distinguished from a "dole," justified as harmonizing with the cherished American value of self-reliance. President Roosevelt said at the time it was "not charity"; the payroll taxes gave contributors "a legal, moral, and political right to collect their pensions and their unemployment benefits." Workers would receive benefits in proportion to what they paid in—this was "equity." But the supplements added in 1939 meant that at sixty-five a married man who had worked right beside a single man for the same number of years, and paid the same amount in, got 50 percent more out of the system.

The policy-makers who crafted the amendments recognized that single men and all women contributors were being overtaxed, so to speak. They saw this as a useful incentive to men to marry and have families, and to women to be stay-at-home wives and mothers rather than entering the labor force. An "adequacy" function (what we would today call "welfare" function) was intended in the supplement, for the extra 50 percent would allow older couples a higher standard of living than the man's benefits alone could. Congress continued to insist on the equity of the contributory system in passing the amendments. Federal officialdom saw no violation of principle because their "common sense" allowed greater reward to the husband-citizen-workers than to others. The nation's political and economic reliance on male-headed monogamous families for well-being made this *ipso facto* equitable.[33]

Between family courts and New Deal innovations such as the Social Security Act, public policy embraced differing and unequal roles for husband and wife. Neither state nor nation ever guaranteed that men could or would earn sufficient income to support their families—and often they did not. Yet New Deal remedies for economic depression assumed the male earner to be primary and granted entitlements of social or economic citizenship principally to men as providers and to women as their loyal dependents. The nation-state itself reiterated a gender order of citizens in which men were defined as individuals, workers and husband-providers, and women were defined as wives and mothers first.

Both men and women helped to draft New Deal public policy. The women involved, who formed a network around Eleanor Roosevelt, were themselves career-oriented and mostly self-supporting. Of an identifiable group of influential women policy-makers and reformers, two thirds had never been married, and even fewer had children. A quarter of them were involved with same-sex relationships. But they did not take themselves as the norm. Almost all these women thought that a full-time career could not be sustained successfully by a wife and mother. They assumed that most women wanted husbands and children, and would pursue only ill-paid or part-time employment at best. For the benefit of child nurture they preferred shoring up the husband-father's wages and security to increasing the mother's opportunities in the labor market. They did not push public policy to disrupt the pattern in which husbands remained principal earners and wives were homemakers and childrearers.[34]

The New Deal's broader conception of citizenship, extending from the political into the economic and social realms, made the line between federal public authority and the private economy harder than ever to draw. Federal social provision renewed the economic substructure of marriage, and revivified social and economic features of marital unity just when legal writers were calling it legally archaic, "foreign to modern statutes."[35] The early part of the new century had seen many opposing tides, the highest being the enfranchisement of women. Women's and men's arenas of possible accomplishment now overlapped far more. Marriage ideals had become less hierarchical amidst the language of true love and companionate partnership; more wives were in the labor force; in legal terms the wife's personal identity was freer of her husband's imprint; and a wider spectrum of sexual behavior had become acceptable. Yet the economic bedrock held fast below, and on it stood the public architecture of marriage.

8

PUBLIC SANCTITY FOR

A PRIVATE REALM

*N*ew perspectives on marriage occasionally glinted in the 1940s, hastened by World War II, a global event of unprecedented magnitude. The war was a forcing ground of new departures in many areas, including gender and racial inequalities, national values, and international relations. Postwar rethinking, reneging on some new trends and extending others, could never return to the earlier habits.

The year after Allied victory, Alfred Hitchcock's thriller *Notorious* presented a tale of wartime patriotism that pushed aside the canons of sexual respectability and trumped the sacredness of marriage. Ingrid Bergman plays the protagonist, the daughter of a convicted Nazi sympathizer who is herself loyal to the United States. Right after her father's conviction for treason and his suicide, the government recruits the daughter to take on a mission for her country. The task to be accomplished is specific to sex, and Bergman's sex appeal makes it possible. She is persuaded by federal agent Devlin (played by Cary Grant) to infiltrate her father's pro-Nazi circle by reacquainting herself with an older man who has always fancied her. Patriotically, she overcomes her own distaste and becomes intimate with this older man, even agreeing to accept his proposal of marriage so as to guarantee her access. (Conveniently, the marriage makes her sexual impropriety premarital, instead of promiscuous). Not one of the federal officials is taken aback at the idea of her vowing marriage in pursuit of her intelligence mission; none of them asks what will happen to the mismatched couple in the future. Devlin, assigned to monitor her actions, approves her "notorious" behavior because it is in the service of her country. He falls in love with her, of course. When he says to his superior that she is "no lady," he means it as a compliment, for she is sacrificing her personal life to aid the war effort while "ladies" play bridge. The happy ending of the film avoids even the contemplation of divorce, because her pro-Nazi husband is handily shot by his own associates, freeing her to love Cary Grant—and to marry him, the audience can imagine.

Although it was not a typical signal from the postwar silver screen, *Notorious* epitomized the often conflicting public messages about marriage at the time. The film's narrative justified a calculated, instrumental use of marriage vows in the service of duty to country. Its hard-boiled recognition that marriage was a constructed, manipulable, often expedient structure vied with more predictable contemporaneous portrayals of true love conquering all obstacles to unite destined mates. The decade of the 1940s looked both forward and backward. Adults in those years may have thought they had lived through a revolution in sexual morality: sexual attraction had become the stock in trade of sophisticated entertainment; illicit sexual affairs were conversational fare. Far from undermining monogamous marriage, however, the sexual liberality introduced had mainly injected talk about sex into ordinary discourse, and lessened the stigma on premarital sex. Common sense still dictated that heterosexual love meant marriage—not something else. A middle-class girl and her boyfriend would hardly think of "living together" before marriage, even if they were in love, and sexually intimate (in private). A sexual double standard still condemned women far more than men for extramarital sex, and it was effective even if not quite as harsh or morally freighted as in the past.

With marriage seen as more companionate, more flexibly defined, less hierarchically structured than in the past, sexual fulfillment was an acknowledged reason *to* marry, even apart from having children. In response to economic duress during the Depression, far more couples practiced methods of birth control, leading the American Medical Association to endorse contraception. The federal appellate judiciary likewise recognized the separation of marital sex from childbearing, in the late 1930s, by overruling the classification of birth control as "obscene." This decision decriminalized birth control at the federal level, though numerous states retained their own limitations or prohibitions.[1]

When the Census Bureau reported in 1940, it classified family data for the first time into three "types." The first, called the "normal" family, had a male head residing with his wife (with or without other persons); the second type was all other male-headed families, and the third was all female-headed families.[2] In seeing more than one type of family, the bureau was acknowledging social diversification, although in naming the first one normal (and by implication the others abnormal), it was revivifying traditional expectations in the form of social science. The economic framework of marriage, its essential public aspect, prescribed that husbands would be the primary earners in families and wives their economic dependents (and principal childrearers), whether or not they also earned. An entanglement of economy, society, and state kept this framework stable while advice columns, imaginative literature, and popular media dwelt on keeping "true love" alive in the intimate unity of the married pair. The availability of divorce could make marrying and staying married seem purely volitional—yet divorce represented a failure, "un-American" enough, so to speak, that a male politician might have to sacrifice high aspiration if he was divorced (and a female politician had better be single or widowed).

The presence of wives in the work force had barely dented the mass conviction that a woman was free to choose *either* marriage and family *or* vocational ambition—and she was predicted to choose the first, if she was "normal." Wives' entry into the labor market because of husbands' unemployment during the economic crisis of the Depression only exaggerated the widespread assumption that a working wife represented family difficulty. One study of children raised during the 1930s concluded that this generation, as adults in the 1950s, saw a wife and mother in the labor force as a signal of family trauma.[3] A small minority of women had the strength and conviction to consider themselves capable of self-support and to pursue artistic, intellectual, or professional work while also marrying and even becoming mothers, but the far greater majority put their capabilities and intellectual energies into part-time employment or volunteer and community work that they could fit around what was felt to be their first responsibility to husband, children, and home.

The predictability of marriage could not fail to be affected by the enormous consequences of World War II on the home front nonetheless. The infusion of federal dollars into war production brought the country out of economic despair. Fifteen million new jobs were created as the annual federal budget soared from about $9 billion in 1939 to $100 billion in 1945. This created flush times for the ordinary worker, whose average annual earnings rose from $754 to $1,289.[4] Fostering geographical mobility as well as a rising economy, military service and jobs in defense industries in distant towns drew people away from their homes, away from the eyes of watchful known neighbors. Social alarms sounded about young people's excessive freedoms, about servicemen's live-for-the-day attitude, about juvenile delinquency among "latchkey children" whose mothers were at work. But there was money to spend, and it was very important to keep up morale by stressing that whatever might seem ominous was temporary, and that on the whole the American people were pulling together toward victory.

Whether they migrated voluntarily or were uprooted, Americans mixed together in new locations with strangers of different regions, religions, and ethnic derivations, fostering a new cosmopolitanism; new group allegiances could form, as they did among lesbians and gay men in the military. Some permanent demographic changes resulted. The 1940s saw more African Americans move to the urban north and west than had relocated during the prior three decades of the "Great Migration." Jobs in war production doubled black men's employment in manufacturing, gave black women their first real alternatives to domestic and agricultural employment, and likewise drew Latinos, native Americans, and Asian Americans into the urban-industrial nation.[5]

The long tradition of a racial barrier to citizenship for Asians began to break down during the war, although political and popular discourse at the same time viciously stereotyped the Japanese war enemy as savage and subhuman. The quarantining of Japanese aliens and Japanese American citizens in internment camps raised anti-Asian injustice to a new official height. Quite a different policy trajectory began toward China, a war ally of the United States. The Chinese exclusion laws were repealed in 1943. A tiny, token quota of Chinese-born individuals (105 per year) were allowed into the United States to reside and pursue citizenship, and the same opening to India and the Philippines followed. Chinese American male citizens' insistence on their right to have their wives with them provoked a further liberalization, embodied in the War Brides Act of 1945. Chinese-born men who had become U.S. citizens by serving in the armed forces were allowed to bring their Chinese wives and children into the United States outside the usual quota. The next year, Congress extended this quota waiver to Chinese wives of all American citizens.[6]

Although these exceptions had been made, all other Asian immigrants were still prevented from entering the United States. Hundreds of American GIs wanted to marry Japanese women when the United States occupied Japan after victory, but would not have been able to bring them home. This situation forced the issue of Japanese exclusion. Congress in 1947 was persuaded to pass the Soldier Brides Act, which waived racial inadmissibility of wives or fiancées of American citizens married before or within thirty days of the legislation. The time limit on the bill created hardships. Men in the military had to have their superiors' permission to marry, and the American command in Japan remained slow and ungenerous in authorizing white soldiers to marry Japanese brides, on grounds of racial disapproval. Sometimes officers cited the existence of state laws criminalizing marriages between whites and Asians as reason to deny their permission.[7]

By 1948, however, a historic change had taken place. In *Perez v. Sharp*, a suit brought by a white woman and black man who were refused a marriage license, the California Supreme Court struck down that state's ban on marriage of a white person "with a Negro, mulatto, Mongolian, or member of the Malay race." It was the first time since Reconstruction that a state court had declared such a law unconstitutional. Because the

California court said that the marriage ban violated the fourteenth amendment's guarantee of equal protection of the laws, the decision was a signal precedent, leading about half of the other states with bans on racial intermarriage to revoke them.[8]

A rhetoric of racial and religious tolerance and cultural pluralism had come to the fore during the world war, championing the diversity of America's population in contradistinction to Nazi "racial" volkishness. The democratic public rhetoric of the war decade, the economic prosperity, and the fact that African American soldiers had risked their lives for their country, spurred rising expectations and inspired protests against tenacious discriminations. Presidents Roosevelt and Truman both made gestures to address African Americans' demands for racial justice. The United States had strong global and domestic motivations to appear more racially even-handed during the wartime alliance with China, and afterward, once Cold War competition for the allegiance of third world began. There were visible results in immigration policy: in 1952, Congress removed "race" as a reason to bar admission, naturalization, or citizenship for immigrants, and established tiny quotas for all Asian countries.[9]

The impact of the war on gender relations was more noticed at the time. Twelve million men went into war service, and women's employment—especially the employment of wives and mothers—reached dramatically new highs. For the first time, industries welcomed women into what were seen as men's manufacturing jobs at nearly men's pay. Women workers made up 35 percent of the civilian labor force by 1944. In the absence of men, women found doors suddenly open to them in higher education and in the professions; the army and navy admitted women for the first time into their own services rather than into auxiliaries; and women's organizations gained some modest victories. During the war the judiciary committees of both houses of Congress even voted favorably on the equal rights amendment (first introduced twenty years earlier), but it failed on the Senate floor to achieve the requisite two-thirds margin.

At the same time that it catapulted millions of women into unprecedented opportunities, the war also cemented and enhanced the disparity between the sexes in the most basic ways. Men bore the most dangerous and heroic burdens of the war. Only a small number of women served in the military. Their participation, while a very significant (and controversial) benchmark, could be seen as exceptional and did not force reevaluation of differences between the sexes. More generally, the public discourse that encouraged women to take on new challenges during the war contained implicit conditions. Goaded to contribute to war production and applauded when they did, women were nonetheless supposed to be replacing men only "for the duration." Employers and public officials and journalists stressed that women workers must be eager to return to their homes and to see their jobs filled by returning men. No matter how extraordinary women's war jobs were, recruiters portrayed women's motivations in taking them as traditional feminine desires to help their men, to safeguard their children, to answer local needs, and to support national well-being. This way, even taking up pathbreaking occupations need not challenge long-held convictions about women's essential identity as sweethearts, daughters, wives, and mothers.[10]

As women stepped partway into men's shoes and earned man-sized pay, they were constantly reminded to retain their femininity, meaning their appeal to men. The theme song "Rosie the Riveter," celebrating a woman war worker, prominently included the line "Rosie's got a boyfriend, Charlie—he's a Marine." During the 1930s when men's employment had been so insecure, cultural reinforcements of masculinity had appeared, especially stressing heterosexual desire. The new men's magazine *Esquire*, for example, affirmed men's prowess as desiring subjects with the prerogative to gaze at women as sexual objects and to take the sexual initiative.[11] During the war years the U.S. government used visions of women's attractiveness to bolster men's morale, cooperating with Hollywood to make "pin-ups" of movie stars a visual component of the wartime landscape. Millions of photographs of female stars were distributed, coming to adorn the walls of barracks, the bulkheads of ships, and the fuselages of planes. Soldiers' favorites among the pin-ups suggested that it was not sexiness alone but visions of marriage, family, and the comforts of home that appealed in these feminine icons. At one point there were twenty thousand requests per week for Betty Grable standing coyly in a swimsuit; her image with graph lines superimposed was used to teach map-reading skills. Her photograph, in the hands of five million servicemen by war's end, was not exotic or torrid. It was an idealized image of the girl next door, blond and healthy, "straight-arrow, chintz-tablecloth" as her studio said. After Grable married bandleader Harry James and had a baby, her image became even more popular and soldiers' demands for it far exceeded requests for pin-ups of the sultry Rita Hayworth. Wives and sweethearts back home eagerly participated by sending pin-up poses of themselves to the men at the front. A wartime bargain between American men and women was being forged: women would retain their allure, and men would fight to defend their freedom to marry themselves to that femininity, and to the home comforts and rewards of fatherhood it promised. One veteran told Betty Grable, "There we were out in those dirty damn trenches. Machine guns firing. Bombs dropping all around us. We would be exhausted, frightened, confused and sometimes hopeless about our situation. When suddenly someone would pull your picture out of his wallet and then we'd *know* what we were fighting for."[12]

Though men were being sent to distant locations, wartime courtships made marriage thrive. More than a million more marriages than were expected took place between 1940 and 1943. The war years halted the Depression's demographic slide, lowering the average age at marriage and beginning to inflate the birth rate. The public rhetoric of war, while dwelling on the defense of democratic freedom against Nazi aggression and Japanese imperialism, emphasized the intimate, private, and familial aspects of the American way of life, centering on heterosexual love and marriage. On a radio program called "To the Young," for example, sponsored by the federal government and broadcast on all stations in 1942, a young male voice could be heard saying, "That's one of the things this war's about." To which a young female voice responded, "About us?" And the reply from the young man was: "About *all* young people like us. About love and gettin' hitched, and havin' a home and some kids, and breathin' fresh air out in the suburbs . . . about livin' and workin' *decent*, like free people."[13] Government recruitment efforts, Hollywood, and the

War Advertising Council harmonized as one on this theme. The Union Central Life Insurance Company pictured the war as a "fight to keep our country a safe place for the wives we love, a place where our children can grow up free and unafraid." The Eureka vacuum cleaner company assured women war workers that they were fighting "for freedom and all that means to women everywhere. You're fighting for a little house of your own, and a husband to meet every night at the door . . . for the right to bring up your children without the shadow of fear."[14]

In public sentiments and popular culture the American way of life was signified and virtually constituted by marriage and family ties. The Academy Award for Best Picture of 1944 went to the film *Since You Went Away*, described on screen as the story of that "unconquerable American fortress, the American Home." Claudette Colbert played the wife on the home front, mothering her two daughters alone while her husband served his country. Well known to audiences as the irrepressibly kooky and rebellious single woman starring opposite Clark Gable in *It Happened One Night* of 1934, Colbert in this wartime film showed no transgressive desires for sexual freedom or independence. She took a job in a munitions factory to express support for her absent husband and her courageous children, without diminishing her primary sense of herself as mother and wife. And she was rewarded: the final scene shows her receiving a Christmas letter saying that her husband is coming home.

Civic dialogue during the war years, in which Hollywood participated, thus reemphasized the private and public double-sidedness of the institution of marriage. Marriages and the families they created were private experiences so precious that they amounted to a public necessity worth fighting for. This mainstream vision beamed from a blockbuster film of 1946, *The Best Years of Our Lives*. The story of three veterans returning to the same town at war's end, the film won seven Academy Awards and grossed more money than any previous film except *Gone with the Wind*. It addressed the postwar reintegration and reemployment of veterans, which was seen as the major domestic problem of the time. The returning men were welcomed, of course, as heroes. Yet they composed a potentially volatile population. In putting their lives on the line for their country they had been exposed to horrific violence, had lived apart from "normal" society for years, had lost buddies and perhaps limbs, and had been trained to kill. Memories of the Depression put the question of peacetime employment on almost everyone's mind, with danger envisioned if veterans felt out of place, idle, unrewarded.[15]

The Best Years of Our Lives dramatized this situation in the intertwined narratives of Al, a middle-aged upper-middle-class banker who was an army sergeant; Fred, a younger working-class soda jerk who had gained glamor and authority as a bombardier and captain; and a still younger Homer, a lower-middle-class naif whose tour of duty in the navy had left him with hooks where his hands used to be. Veterans' ability to gain suitable employment and thereby sustain a peacetime version of manhood and a viable economy formed a central underlying theme in the film, while the men's relationships with their wives or wives-to-be carried the emotional freight. Homer (played not by a professional actor but by a veteran really disabled) endowed the movie with a compelling poignancy, but all the men showed anxiety, confusion, and some bitterness as well as hopefulness in their attempts to communicate and to readjust. The three appeared more comfortable with one another (although they had only met on the transport home) than with their erstwhile loved ones.

The film's linking of men's work to marriage was clear from an early scene. During an anxious shared taxi ride home, Fred remarked that he did not want to be "rehabilitated" but only wanted a good job, and his wife. The equation of the veteran's readjustment with a job and a wife expressed not only Hollywood's penchant for the romantic angle but the dominant societal prescription as well. Veterans were to be reintegrated into civilian life by marshaling those same private obligations that the war had been fought to defend. In 1945 and 1946 a literature on demobilization streamed from government pamphlets, newspapers, professional journals, popular magazines, fiction, and books with titles like *Readjustment or Revolution* and *Soldier to Citizen*. These assumed that men would be reacclimated within the private sphere of family, kinship, friendship, and community, and stressed that veterans hoped and deserved to recapture the traditional marital constellation, with the father/husband the provider and protector, and the wife/mother the sympathizer and nurturer.

These texts commonly inundated women with advice, saying that they had "the biggest morale job in history"; that "the personal side of reconstruction is women's work"; that the wife of the ex-GI was the "indispensable person" in his adaptation to civilian life. Many writers insisted that veterans both needed and desired feminine women who would be sensitive and adjust their interests and desires to those of their men. Wives and girlfriends were counseled to make the veteran feel secure, tolerate his outbursts, refrain from questioning his decisions and from nagging. They were asked to be self-abnegating for the time being and warned to balance their recently discovered competence and independence against the needs of their returning men.[16] In *The Best Years of Our Lives,* all three female partners of the veterans enacted this role. They managed to be sexual and maternal at the same time, strong yet accommodating, wise and humorous, patient and understanding—and they appeared to do so naturally and willingly, out of freely offered love and the belief that it was best for them as well as for their men and for the nation. The film harmonized with the "adjustment" literature, addressing the need to shore up men's sense of themselves through intimate relationships, and wrapping this psychological approach around the core intention to sustain men's economic primacy.

The postwar reconstruction of marital roles took place through very material benefits as well as through public discourse. In the 1944 GI Bill of Rights, the nation as a whole, embodied in the federal government, took more responsibility for veterans' economic well-being than for any previous subgroup of citizens. All veterans were included, but since the 350,000 women who served made up just about 2 percent of all military personnel, the bill's largesse went overwhelmingly to men. The GI Bill gave veterans a year of unemployment compensation (twice the normal length of benefits); paid for their higher education and job training; subsidized their medical care; awarded them pensions; gave them preference above any other contenders for civil service jobs; and loaned them mortgage funds to buy houses.[17] These entitlements supported and enhanced men's roles as husband-heads of households, as property-owners, as job-holders and providers, as persons of superior education and training who could excel in the vastly expanding white-collar economy.

Through the 16 million men who had served, the GI Bill dispensed privileges to as much as a quarter of the population—the veterans, their wives, and their children—and at the same time confirmed the rightness of a family model in which the male head was the most secure and best-skilled provider in the household. A significant revision to the federal income tax fortified this public policy. Direct taxation of individuals by the federal government had been allowed only since a constitutional amendment in the World War I era, and the threshold for paying tax was initially set so high that only 5 percent of Americans were affected by it. During World War II, however, federal expenditures forced the threshold down, so that the number of Americans required to pay jumped from 7 million in 1940 to 45 million in 1945. The income tax became a much broader-scale concern.[18]

In the original mandate for the federal income tax, marriage played no role: everyone was taxed as an individual. But after considerable wrangling during the war decade, Congress in 1948 allowed a combined return for married couples that gave them a great tax advantage. Two different trajectories fed into this change. The Treasury Department for decades had wanted to require every married couple to be taxed as a unit. Its aim (devised when only the wealthy paid tax) was to maximize tax revenue. Treasury officials knew that wealthy men handed off income-producing assets such as stocks and bonds to their wives, who were then taxed as individuals themselves, in effect dividing the husband's income between two taxpayers. Attributing income to the wife resulted in a lower overall tax for the couple, because tax rates were graduated, or "progressive"—income at higher levels was taxed at a progressively higher rates. If the marital household were the standard tax unit, this maneuver would not be possible.

Another impetus for the joint return came from community-property states. In the eight states (mainly in western areas formerly colonized by

Spain) with legal codes influenced by civil law as well as common law, the assets and earnings of husband and wife were considered "community" property in the marriage, meaning jointly owned. An income-earning husband in such a state could attribute half his income to his non-employed wife, and the federal tax on both became far lower than what his would be if the income were attributed to him alone. Community-property rules made this a standard procedure, which became enormously appealing during the war, when the tax rate on the highest income topped 90 percent. Some couples moved their residences to community-property states to take advantage of it, and many state legislatures discussed changing their property regimes in order to retain and attract residents.

For one-earner couples, the appeal of something like the community property rule was undeniable. Differences between states on this issue was causing unrest. The halls of Congress rang with discussions about instigating federal tax consideration for married couples. Women's groups, meanwhile, protested loudly that the Treasury Department's proposal to make the marital household the tax unit would reinvigorate coverture, by erasing the economic persona of the employed wife. The upshot was a compromise called income-splitting. It was not instituted until the huge budget drains of the war subsided, for it supported marital unity in the economic arena at the expense of lost tax revenue. Under the income-splitting plan, which mimicked the practice in community-property states, the sum of a couple's incomes was divided in two, one half attributed to each spouse, with each taxed at the individual rate. In response to women's groups' objections, "married filing jointly" was made optional rather than mandatory. But it was so advantageous it was hard to decline. In 1948, a couple filing jointly faced the same graduated rates as an individual, a tremendous advantage to the married pair, especially where only one spouse earned. The tax on a single income split between husband and wife turned out to be far lower than the individual's tax would have been. Any married couple filing jointly got a lower combined tax than if they had filed as individuals, whether one or both were employed. This model of the joint return, which lasted from 1948 to

1969, had no "marriage penalty," but did have a "singles' penalty." A bachelor might have to pay twice as much federal tax as a married man who made the identical income but supported an unemployed wife.

Like the Social Security system, the new federal income tax arrangement rewarded the married over the unmarried and most generously rewarded "normal" families with husband/fathers who were primary earners, building in (again) a national commitment to this family model. Where husband and wife were both employed but he earned far more (the usual situation), the overall tax burden for the couple was lower than it would have been for them as two single individuals, but it was the husband's tax that had been reduced. Income-splitting brought down the tax rate on the bigger salary while actually increasing the tax burden on the lower-earning spouse, because her income, added "on top" of the primary income, was being taxed at a higher rate in the graduated rate structure than it would have been if she had filed as an individual.

The "married–filing-jointly" provision was ostensibly gender-neutral, but in the existing structure of the economy, its results were gender-skewed. Employed women earned far less than men, on average, because of the limited arenas where they were hired. The joint return supported the labor market's definition of husbands as primary earners and wives as secondary earners by taxing wives' already lower income at a higher marginal rate, making wives' employment less appealing financially. Thus even the marital tax privilege included a disincentive for wives to think of themselves as earners.

As the American economy rose to unprecedented heights of prosperity in the postwar decade, encouraging consumers to buy and families to send more than one member to work, wives and mothers took jobs in proportions higher than ever, but the potential for their employment to gain parity with their husbands' was repeatedly compromised. Even institutions favoring women's participation in the work force and the public arena, such as the National Manpower Council, insisted that this "must not detract from the importance of their roles as wives and mothers."[19] Cultural prescriptions for women to see themselves first as nurturant wives and mothers positioned them as secondary earners if they sought employment. The structure of the joint return reiterated the same priority and helped to perpetuate it.

Although in these major respects the nation's public policies seemed to line up uniformly, there were some hints of change in the official attitude on marriage. One glimmered in a U.S. Supreme Court decision in 1946, where the court had to decide whether it was constitutional to use the Mann Act to convict Mormon men who had moved their plural wives from one state to another. Originally directed against commercialized sex, the elastic language of the Mann (or White Slave Traffic) Act had since been stretched by zealous U.S. district attorneys to justify prosecuting those engaged in other sorts of "immoral" libertinism, even consensual sexual liaisons between adults who happened to cross state lines (as Jack Johnson and Lucille Cameron had done).[20] The 1946 case did not consider all expanded uses of the Mann Act, but centered on determining whether Mormon polygamy was a practice of debauchery, lewdness, and immorality within reach of the federal law. Justice William O. Douglas's opinion for the majority was literally a throwback, quoting phrases from nineteenth-century anti-Mormon decisions such as *Reynolds v. U.S.* But Justice Frank Murphy's dissent took quite a new tack. He refused to condemn polygamy as "odious" and called it "one of the basic forms of marriage," the practice of which, historically, had "far exceeded that of any other form." Referring to anthropological findings that monogamy, polygyny, polyandry, and group marriage were four forms of marriage sanctioned by human cultures, he maintained that even if Mormon polygyny was distasteful, it was "a form of marriage built upon a set of social and moral principles" and ought to be recognized as such. It was not "in the same genus" as prostitution or debauchery.[21] Without disfavoring monogamy, Murphy's dissent showed broad-ranging and even-handed respect for various forms of marriage, introducing an unprecedented comparative and relativistic perspective to the nation's highest court.

The dissent was one small indication that the decade of World War II formed an important turning point. Even while public policy fortified the "normal" family, challenges to the long-prevailing model of marriage could not be prevented. The understanding of marital union as lifelong and synonymous with morality continued to be battered by divorce, which had flagged briefly during the Depression only to rise thereafter. Perception of a boom in divorces right after the war sparked renewed concerns. During the war and the postwar period, the U.S. Supreme Court resolved the long-troublesome issue of the variances among different states' divorce rules. If, for instance, an unhappy spouse went from home in New York (where adultery was the only ground for divorce) to Las Vegas, and took advantage of Nevada's liberal grounds and mere six-week residency requirement to get a divorce, did New York have to honor the termination? In transformative decisions between 1942 and 1957, the court moved toward national acceptance of "migratory" divorce.

The series of U.S. Supreme Court cases also outlined a national policy on treatment of post-divorce situations, most important, establishing that the state where divorced partners lived could take jurisdiction over payment of alimony and child support whether or not the divorce had been granted there. Divorce had become a fact of life, so recognized a feature of the American marital landscape that the various states concerted their efforts to deal with its economic consequences. Most of them adopted a model law (nicknamed the "Skipping Pappy" Act) to enable a divorced parent to pursue a nonpaying former partner over state lines.[22] Thus divorce policies altogether focused state concern on the "broken" family's economic support. Like federal programs for Social Security and income tax, the states' efforts to prevent divorced spouses and their children from falling into poverty stemmed from a view of marriage as an economic bargain in which the public had a stake. The prominence of child support as an issue in divorces helped to place public emphasis on the institutional character of the family.[23] By making divorce more feasible, states had not backed out from their role as a third party in marriage but had backed in to the family as a whole.

Divorce remained an adversarial process in which one partner had to prove that the other had failed to meet the terms set by the state. It was well known by the 1950s, however, that couples colluded to present divorce suits as the fault of one, rather than the wish of both, in order to terminate their marriages. Leading lawyers were concerned that these subterfuges corrupted the legal process. If the state's definitions were causing widespread deceit in obtaining divorces, respect for the law was thereby undermined, and a more realistic approach was called for. As early as 1948 the American Bar Association's section on divorce recommended moving to a no-fault principle, pointing out that 85 to 90 percent of divorces were uncontested and therefore denoted marital breakdown on both sides.[24]

With similar motivation, the American Law Institute (ALI, a body of elite lawyers who monitored the profession, reviewed legislation, and proposed model codes) recommended drastic changes in criminal laws on extramarital sexual behavior. Monogamy had been the dividing line between sexual morality and immorality in the law for hundreds of years. Laws criminalizing fornication, adultery, sodomy, and "unnatural practices" such as oral sex commonly stood on states' books. Yet as Alfred Kinsey's pathbreaking and well-publicized studies *Sexual Behavior in the Human Male* (1948) and *Sexual Behavior in the Human Female* (1953) revealed, extramarital and "deviant" practices (including homosexual experience) were far more common among Americans than had ever been admitted. The very irregular and selective enforcement of state laws against extramarital sex made the same point indirectly.

The ALI argued that laws on sexual conduct should be brought into conformity with accepted behavior. In its proposed model criminal code, no consensual sexual conduct carried criminal sanctions. The presence or absence of consent (and not the presence or absence of legal monogamy) was the decisive issue.[25] The ALI recommendation attempted to take traditional monogamous morality out of the law, by calling a sex act a crime only if it was nonconsensual and thus invaded personal liberty. The ALI's revolution stopped at the door of the marital household, however, preserving the marital exemption in the definition of rape. In the letter of the law, a man could not rape his own wife. The ALI did not propose change in the traditional assumption that a woman's consent to marry was consent to all future sexual acts with her husband.[26] Nonetheless, like Justice Murphy's dissent in the 1946 case on Mormons, the ALI proposals in the 1950s were straws in the wind blowing in a future direction.

These blurrings of the legal equation between morality and lifelong monogamy made nonmarital sex more thinkable without reducing public esteem for marriage itself. The public meaning that World War II had placed on private domestic lives continued into Cold War politics. In confrontations with the Soviet Union and its socialist allies, American propaganda and Americans themselves often translated their political economy into private aspirations, linking capitalism and representative democracy to personal choices in marrying, having children, buying a home, and gaining access to a cornucopia of consumer goods. Vice President Richard Nixon's famous "kitchen debate" with Soviet Premier Nikita Khrushchev, which took place in Moscow at the opening of the American National Exhibition in 1959, conveyed in a nutshell the American point of view on the contrast between the two systems. The exhibit showcased American recreational and consumer goods, including a furnished and equipped six-room ranch-style house. In the two leaders' much-reported verbal contest, sparked by Nixon's championing of American washing machines, the vice president made clear that what distinguished the United States—what it had to offer the world—was the freedom to pursue the good life at home.[27]

Where mid-nineteenth-century judges and other public spokesmen had hardly been able to speak of marriage without mentioning Christian morality, mid-twentieth-century discourse saw the hallmarks of the institution in liberty and privacy, consent and freedom. Marriage and family and all the emotional and material comforts of home were personally chosen private freedoms and at the same time public emblems of the nation, essential to its existence and defense, just as they had been during war. The U.S Supreme Court set these linkages into constitutional interpretation at mid-century. Justice Douglas led in referring to "the intimacies of the marriage relationship" as emblematic of "the privacy that is implicit in a free society." In a 1961 dissent in a birth control case, he said this privacy was intrinsic to "the constitutional scheme under which we live," as contrasted to a "totalitarian regime."[28] (The term "totalitarian," used in the 1940s to refer to both fascism and communism, had become a virtual synonym for Soviet communism at the time Douglas wrote, in 1961.)

Justice Douglas here fused the protection of marital intimacy with the political principles of American democracy, to provide a crucial underpinning of modern constitutional doctrine on privacy rights.[29] His words, written in dissent in 1961, foreshadowed the 1965 decision that freed birth control for married couples from state interference. Striking down Connecticut's ban on birth control because it invaded the "innermost sanctum" of the marital bedroom, the court in *Griswold v. Connecticut* found that "fundamental" rights of privacy, marital choice, and family creation were implied in the Constitution's guarantees of liberty.[30]

Griswold's constitutional rearticulation of marriage as a fundamental right formed an important background to another historic case two years later, *Loving v. Virginia*. This decision closed the long history of race-based legislation on marriage by striking down Virginia's law that made marriage between a white and a nonwhite person a felony. The Supreme Court had held back from ruling on this flashpoint issue when given opportunities in 1955 and 1964, but in the aptly named *Loving* case in 1967, the court rejected the century-old argument that bans on marriage across the color line imposed equally on both races, and called such laws an effort to maintain white supremacy, insupportable in view of the fourteenth amendment. Marital intimacy was not the deciding point, but the opinion reiterated clearly that marriage was a "fundamental freedom."[31]

Chief Justice Earl Warren, who wrote the unanimous decision in *Loving*, had been governor of California in 1948, when *Perez v. Sharp* had struck down the state's denial of racial intermarriage. His leadership on the court produced an era of great judicial creativity on questions of sexuality and marriage no less than on race. Just six years after *Griswold*, the court struck down a Massachusetts law that prohibited the prescription or sale of contraceptives to unmarried people. This case, *Eisenstadt v. Baird*, pronounced a historic reversal, since it denied the state's right to distinguish between citizens of differing marital status. Invoking the principle of equal protection of the laws, the court said that Massachusetts, allowing birth control to married persons, could not fairly bar the unmarried. Rather than tying privacy in reproductive decision-making to marital intimacy the *Eisenstadt* decision made it a more portable, individual right: "the right of the *individual,* married or single, to be free from unwarranted governmental intrusion into matters so fundamentally affecting a person as the decision whether to bear or beget a child."

Refusing to deny to single persons the privacy that married couples were granted, the Supreme Court in *Eisenstadt* moved toward displacing marriage from the seat of official morality. The court's view of equal protection for married and single individuals rejected traditional marital unity with the comment, "The marital couple is not an independent entity with a mind and heart of its own, but an association of two individuals each with a separate intellectual and emotional makeup."[32] In 1971 when Justice William J. Brennan wrote these words, the social landscape of the United States had been vastly changed by social protest movements for civil rights, black power, and women's equality, by countercultural unrest, and by confrontations over the nation's war in Vietnam and young men's resistance to the military draft. The Civil Rights Act of 1964 had been in force for several years, attacking race discriminations in public life and employment more vigorously than at any time since Reconstruction and making the analogous concept of sex discrimination legally efficacious for the first time.[33] The high court's decisions on sex and marriage were just keeping pace with the upheavals in society. Social as well as legal changes were about to uncouple morality from marriage, to knock marriage from its position of preeminence as "pillar of the state."

9

MARRIAGE REVISED
AND REVIVED

$\mathcal{A}$ phenomenon such as President William Jefferson Clinton—a leader who remained popular and in office despite public knowledge of his sexual strayings outside marriage—had never been seen in American politics before the 1990s. Public faithfulness to lifelong monogamy had previously been the rule. As recently as the 1960s, the fact of having been divorced kept Nelson Rockefeller from the Republican presidential nomination. Certainly, earlier presidents had been rumored to have had affairs and even to have fathered children out of wedlock, but the details remained covert and the accusations remained unproved. President Clinton's plural affronts to his wife were revealed in public as flamboyant instances of disrespect for the institution of marriage. His behavior was always controversial, and maligned by many long before he was impeached. Yet Clinton was not repudiated by the majority of the sovereign people for his infidelities.

Clinton was able to hang on to political credibility because of the judgment that his sexual transgressions were between him and his wife—a burden on his conscience but not one that affected his capacity to carry on as president. Even the most stalwart prosecutors of Clinton, such as Republican Congressman Henry Hyde of Illinois, maintained that sexual misconduct was not at issue, because "infidelity is a private act"—whereas the president's putting his hand on the Bible and swearing to tell the whole truth but failing to do so was a *public* act that threatened to undermine the rule of law. An implicit question shadowed the proceedings nonetheless: could a president untrue to his marriage vows keep his other vows to the public? The impeachment imbroglio could not have begun had not Clinton's unfaithfulness signaled an alarm to the nation. If monogamous fidelity is nowhere prescribed as a presidential duty, everyone knew, despite Hyde's demurral, that Clinton's sexual misconduct was inextricable from the prosecution's case. His insults to the institution of marriage flew in the face of long-held national values. His lying testified to his own presumption that such behavior in a president was inadmissible.

As compared to President Thomas Jefferson's, or Franklin Roosevelt's, or John Kennedy's rumored infidelities, however, Clinton's did become a matter of public record without toppling him because of the way the majority of the people understood marriage at the end of the twentieth century. Clinton attracted frequent condemnation for his moral failings and embarrassing lack of self-restraint. He escaped rejection, however, because the majority generously (or cynically) tolerated a wide range of behavior in couples, seeing husbands and wives as accountable principally to each other for their marital performance. The debacle of the impeachment forced explicit public cognizance of marital conduct as private and of marital infidelity as too common a failing to prompt civic excommunication.

The public forgiveness of Clinton's sexual misadventures can only be understood against the background of a generation's seismic shift in marriage practices. Drastic eruptions and reorientations began in the 1960s, with a sexual revolution that deserved that name. As much as 1950s tremors had given some hints, emancipatory claims based on sex burst out from the nourishment given by 1960s political movements. The New Left, the antiwar movement, black power, women's liberation, and gay liberation—along with the hippies and flower children who constituted themselves the counterculture—all fused dissident politics with purposeful cultural disobedience and devil-may-care hijinks centering on defiance of sexual norms.

Making sexual nonconformity a political statement, this younger generation enacted the bold propositions of their predecessors of the

1910s and 1920s, welcoming sexual initiatives from women as well as from men, demolishing sanctions on premarital relationships and attempting to do the same for extramarital and cross-racial sex. The mass marketing of the birth control pill enabled sex to be more decisively separated from pregnancy than ever before, severing a link in the chain between sex and marriage. Once dissidents opened the way, advertisers, merchandisers, and entertainers extended the sensational commercial possibilities for sex to the mass public. Sexual allusions, acts, and fantasies became ever more clearly exploitable commodities. Sexual behavior was transported into the civil sphere. Youth culture in the 1960s linked sexual disclosure with authenticity and brought into full light the equation between personal freedom and sexual freedom that had rumbled and murmured among "free lovers" and bohemians for at least a century. Same-sex love came "out" with this new exposure. Within a decade, sex between the unmarried no longer caused expressions of shock or dismay. Love became sufficient justification, and, increasingly, the search for personal fulfillment or pleasure sufficed to explain sexual indulgence.

The sexual revolution was not unique to the United States. Extraordinary shifts in sexual and marital practices and in the shape of households were taking place all over the industrialized world. A French demographer named Louis Roussel, looking at trends across North America, Europe, Japan, Australia, and the Soviet Union in the late 1980s, identified 1965 as a rare axis of change. In the subsequent fifteen years, a whole set of demographic indicators was reshuffled. Among the billion people encompassed in these nations, rates of formal marriages and of births tumbled; divorces and the proportion of births outside formal wedlock both shot up. The increases and decreases were substantial and even spectacular, often 50 percent or more. In Roussel's view, this quick and shared change in behavior marked a profound cultural transformation, which he called the "banalization" of previously condemned behavior.[1] His awkward neologism captured something. A person had formerly been cast outside the pale of ordinary respectability by living coupled but unmarried or by having children outside of marriage. Even divorce had cast a blight on personal character. But now these behaviors were so common as to arouse no negative comment—or any comment at all.

In the United States, the number of unmarried-couple households recorded by the Census Bureau multiplied almost ten times from 1960 to 1998. It grew more than five times as fast as the number of households overall. The General Social Survey, conducted every year since 1972 by sociologists of the National Opinion Research Center at the University of Chicago, reported in 1999 that cohabitation had become the "norm" for men and women as their first form of heterosexual living (as well as for post-divorce unions). Almost two thirds of those born between 1963 and 1974 first cohabited, without marrying.[2]

At the twentieth century's close, marriage could no longer be considered the predictable venture it once had been. People living alone composed a quarter of all households in 1998. This reflected growth in the elderly population who were widows and widowers, but it also showed marriage itself losing ground. The proportion of adults who declined to marry at all rose substantially between 1972 and 1998, from 15 percent to 23 percent. The divorce rate rose more furiously, to equal more than half the marriage rate, portending that at least one in two marriages would end in divorce. In the Pacific states, which have tended to lead the nation, the ratio between divorces and marriages in the mid-1990s was closer to 7 to 10. Only 56 percent of all adults were currently married in the late 1990s, down from three quarters in the early 1970s. This general percentage, skewed by the majority white population, masked the markedly lower rate of current marriage among African American adults (about 40 percent). Yet men and women broke taboos in the way they married as well by not marrying—crossing the color line to choose each other. In the three decades after the *Loving v. Virginia* decision, mixed couples tripled from 2 percent to 6 percent of all marriages. Most of these had one black and one white partner, but the fastest growing type of mixed marriage was between an African American and another nonwhite partner.[3]

Along with the decline in marriage overall, the birth rate dropped, from more than 3.5 births per woman in 1960 to about 2 births per woman in the mid-1990s. The household without children, rather than with children, was the norm (62 percent) in the United States. What had been typical adult status in the long past—married, with minor children—described barely more than one quarter of adults in 1999, the General Social Survey found. Children's parents were unmarried far more often than in the past; unmarried mothers accounted for almost one third of births in 1998, compared to about 5 percent in 1960. White women's rate of unmarried childbearing more than doubled after 1980. Black women's rate moved up only 2 percent during the same years, so that where their rate had been 4 or 5 times that of whites in 1960, in the late 1990s it was only about twice as high. As a result of both nonmarriage and divorce among women with children, one fifth of family-based households of whites were female-headed in the 1990s, as were almost three fifths of black families and almost one third of Hispanic families.

Women workers were edging toward being half of all workers at the end of the twentieth century. Not depending on men to provide their economic support, three quarters of all women were in the labor force, including more than 60 percent of married mothers of children under the age of six. The instability of marriages and marriage rates only partly explained this development. Vivid activists for women's rights burst onto the scene in the 1960s, and their efforts cascaded through the decades, deeply inflecting the trends in work and family life. Theorists of women's liberation in the 1960s and 1970s resurrected overt public critique of marriage while demanding equal rights and equal access in the public sphere. Feminists deepened public awareness of sex discrimination by inventing the concept of "sexism." Kate Millett's phrase "sexual politics" expressed the new sensitivity to power asymmetries between men and women, husbands and wives.[4]

Claiming that "the personal is political," feminist consciousness-raising groups transformed women's daily-life perceptions of the reason for their subordination from individual failings to systematic sexual inequality. The statement also intended to disrupt the assumption that "private" and "public" were really separate realms, because the association of women with private life reflected and helped to maintain inequality by making women marginal to the public arena, where recognized achievement took place. Some feminists reappraised the public interest and public welfare involved in women's work of household care and childrearing, intending to make these visible and valued. Others revived the previous century's metaphor of the wife as implicit slave. They made a public issue of the social devaluation of unpaid household work, while also protesting against demeaning women by confining their talents to housekeeping, childminding, and personal services to men.[5]

Remaining legal constraints on wives in the business world unraveled. Because the 1964 Civil Rights Act included "sex" as an unwarranted basis for discrimination, and because judges were subsequently persuaded to reinterpret the fourteenth amendment's guarantees of "due process of law" and "equal protection of the laws" to apply to gender, feminist-instigated suits in the 1970s were able to dismantle the battery of sex distinctions in employment and education and—finally—jury service.[6] Social Security and military benefits became gender-neutral, so that they still gave special privilege to married couples, but made either spouse equally able to gain benefits for his or her partner. Sex difference was not wholly unseated as a valid legal category, however. Supreme Court decisions did not make the constitutional standard for scrutinizing sex classifications as strict as the standard for examining race, which was considered a "suspect" classification not to be employed without compelling reasons. Women's reproductive and childrearing roles counted heavily in keeping sex differentiation alive in the law—as well as in feminists' losing the battle to add an equal rights amendment to the Constitution.

State legislatures, too, contributed to the moral and legal reframing of marriage, by reforming divorce law. In less than two decades, beginning in the mid-1960s, the adversary principle in divorce was virtually eliminated. California first adopted "no-fault" divorce in 1969 and within four years at least thirty-six states had made it an option. By 1985 every state had fallen into step, not always under the rubric of "no-fault" but offering essentially the same thing, that a couple who had proven incompatible could end their marriage. By and large, these reforms were seen as procedural—along the lines of the American Bar Association observations and recommendations much earlier to make law congruent with practice. They were not pushed by any particular social movement. Yet the innovation of no-fault divorce, or divorce on the ground of "irretrievable breakdown" of the marriage as defined by the spouses, indicated a major shift.[7] Earlier, the petitioner for divorce had to show that the other spouse failed to uphold state-defined obligations by committing adultery or desertion or another legislatively set deviation from marriage. No-fault divorce implied instead that the state should refrain from passing judgment on performance in an ongoing marriage and allow the partners to decide whether their behavior matched their own expectations; if it did not, the marriage could be legally dissolved.

Feminist activists did not speak for the no-fault principle but did press for subsequent reforms treating post-divorce arrangements such as child custody, child support, alimony. and the division of marital assets.[8] Custom if not legal doctrine for the preceding century had typically awarded custody of children of "tender years" to the mother, and expected child support from the father. Divorce reforms intended to see the roles of both husband and wife more gender-neutrally, with both able to be earners and caring parents. Most states revised their law and practice to make joint custody and child support from both parents the standard, to be tailored to each situation. Alimony was made gender-neutral as a result of a U.S. Supreme Court decision of 1979. In corollary, virtually every state took up the principle that the material assets belonging to either spouse should be seen as belonging to both when a marriage ended. Dividing marital property "equitably" between husband and wife upon divorce was meant to credit the unpaid work that the typical non-employed homemaker put into the partnership, and it also benefited ex-husbands who had been supported by their wives' earnings or assets.

These divorce reforms not only intended to treat men and women equally but also addressed the state's interest in securing adequate support after divorce for all family members. While state authorities were giving the initiative back to couples to say that their marriage was over, they did not opt out of the post-divorce provision arrangements. A judge had to approve the terms of economic support and care for children before a divorce could be made final. The reform of custody and support arrangements reiterated that the government's stake in marriage and divorce in the late twentieth century was economic far more than it was moral. Knowing the extent of women's wage-earning and hearing feminist demands for sex equity, legislatures and courts made post-divorce support obligations for children, which had earlier rested on the man of the family, reciprocal and formally gender-neutral. Amidst finger-pointing at the federal dollars expended on "welfare" (public assistance through the Aid to Families with Dependent Children program of the Social Security Act), Congress by 1971 designed new methods to get support from delinquent fathers when children were in their mothers' custody and receiving public assistance, and instituted incentives for welfare mothers themselves to earn wages. By 1988, welfare reforms placed responsibility for children's support on both parents.[9]

The state's interest in post-divorce support obligations converged with the phenomenon of unmarried cohabitation to produce a signal case in California in 1976, from which the term "palimony" was born. When the actor Lee Marvin and the former singer with whom he had been living for seven years broke up, she sued for support, averring that the couple had an oral agreement that entitled her to rely on his continued support. The trial court rejected her suit because their cohabitation included sex, and there was an older California precedent calling a contract for sexual services invalid—against public policy because it amounted to prostitution. On appeal, however, the California high court cited "the prevalence of nonmarital relationships in modern society and the social acceptance of them" as reason to move beyond the assumption that a cohabiting relationship including sex had to be "meretricious," meaning as unworthy as prostitution. Recognizing an implied economic contract between the pair (Marvin had agreed to support her, she to give up her career to keep house) and considering it actionable in court, the court therefore remanded the case for rehearing.

This case was rightly seen as a landmark, because it overcame the moral disapproval of extramarital sex enshrined in the earlier precedent and allowed the economic aspect of a cohabiting relationship to be recognized legally. But the court carefully minimized its innovation. The opinion anticipated and deflected criticism, by denying that its approach would discourage marriage and by refusing to qualify the Marvins' arrangement as a common-law marriage (abolished in California in 1895). It explicitly did not grant to cohabitors any of the privileges of legal spouses under California's Family Law Act, and instead likened the implied contract between the Marvins to an agreement between business partners or joint venturers—whose economic arrangements had resort to the courts.

Michele Marvin (she used his name as if they were married) won a right but not much recompense, as it turned out. Upon rehearing, she won only $104,000 from the millionaire actor and when he appealed, her award was overturned. None of the divorce reforms of the 1970s and 1980s closed the gap that could yawn between equitable principle and the outcome of a given case, where the partner advantaged by money and power had every likelihood of getting the better deal. The Marvin case also predicted that in the courts, unmarried partners would be held accountable for the economic obligations without reaping the larger legal privileges of husband and wife.[10]

The idea that couples could redefine marriage on their own terms resounded appealingly through the 1970s nonetheless. To reinvent marriage, why not make it a malleable arrangement—extend its founding principle of consent between the couple to all the terms of the relationship, allowing the contractual side of the hybrid institution to bloom. This orientation could be seen in new toleration of extramarital sex in the 1970s. As unmarried cohabitation became more acceptable and lesbians and gay men defied "compulsory heterosexuality" (in Adrienne Rich's phrase), adultery also came out of the shadows. Earnest inquirers and hedonists assailed the hypocrisy of minimizing the commonness of adultery. Amidst handwringing over the meaning of sexual fidelity in mutual commitment, a rash of books burst out, bearing titles such as *Beyond Monogamy; Couplings and Groupings; The Extramarital Sex Contract; The Fragile Bond: Marriage Now; Marriage and Its Alternatives; Beyond Open Marriage; Loving Free;* and *The Love Contract: Handbook for a Lib-*

erated Marriage. If conventional respectability said that monogamous fidelity was required by church and state as well as by love of one's spouse, many in the 1970s came to think that only the spouse really mattered. Neither "open marriage" nor "swinging" made much headway, but the view that partners themselves were the judge of sexual fidelity in their marriage became much more widespread.

A contractual emphasis in marriage appealed to feminists as the main hope for restructuring the institution to shed its history of inequality. Some feminists recommended that couples devise their own private contracts to substitute for the state's prescription of marital obligations. Unlike earlier centuries' prenuptial contracts, which were intended to stabilize the descent of rich couples' assets, feminist contracts in the 1970s set out the obligations and rewards of the ongoing marriage—what husband and wife would owe each other in financial support, housework, childcare, sex, and so on. The content of "model" contracts testified to concern that the heavy weight of marital convention would drag any marriage down the old path, regardless of the couple's initial good intentions. This contractual approach reaccentuated the element of consent in monogamy, which had always been central to its prominence as a public institution. Like the Supreme Court's finding (in *Griswold v. Connecticut*) that constitutional protection of "liberty" freed birth control from state interference, this reinvention of marriage employed a longstanding principle to new effect.

The courts responded by taking couples' prenuptial contracts seriously, and also those composed once the couple was married. The principle that courts would assess spousal contracts dealing with post-divorce arrangements for fairness, and would enforce them, was well established by the 1990s—but there were limits. A court would not allow a wife to contract away her marital obligation to serve her husband's needs, nor a husband his obligation to support the wife. In 1993 a California appeals court refused to support a wife's claim to collect assets from her husband's estate as compensation for taking care of him at home as he had begged, after he suffered a stroke, rather than placing him in a nursing home (as she preferred to do). He had agreed to increase his bequest to her if she cared for him at home, but his will did not follow through. The court, finding "sickbed bargaining" offensive and "antithetical to the institution of marriage as the Legislature has defined it," would not award the wife the compensation she sought. Citing precedents from 1937 and 1941, the majority opinion emphasized that the wife's care for her husband was simply part of her "marital duty of support"—even in the face of a dissenting colleague's objection that this "smack[ed] of the common law doctrine of coverture." Thus the traditional marriage bargain survived in skeleton form to the end of the twentieth century.[11]

The contractual emphasis moved understandings of marriage toward the private side, and there was another strong reason for feminists to see intimate relationships as private. The legal argument for women to exercise freedom of choice over childbearing, or "reproductive rights," rested on privacy. The decisions in *Griswold* and *Eisenstadt* had used reasoning about privacy to remove state constraints on birth control, but abortion remained criminal. Feminist efforts to change that led to *Roe v. Wade*, the U.S. Supreme Court decision of 1973 that freed abortion (for the first trimester of pregnancy) from state restrictions. The opinion rested on a woman's right to consider privately, with her doctor, whether she would bear a child.[12]

Feminist legal strategies had to work both sides of the private/public divide that marriage inhabited, however. To defend reproductive choice, as in *Roe*, or to try to secure equalitarian marriages, it was necessary to see intimate decisions taking place in a sheltered private realm. But in order to protect wives and daughters from being overpowered physically by the men in their households, feminists wanted to bring public authority into the private domestic sanctum. The doctrine of domestic privacy, allowing the home to be curtained off from public scrutiny, could work just like the old assumption of marital unity to maintain superior power in the hands of an abusive husband. If domestic violence was going to be prosecuted and if a husband's exemption from rape charges for coercing his wife into sex was going to be eliminated, then the zone of domestic privacy had to be opened up and the notion that "a man's home is his castle" unseated.[13]

Both of those intentions have been substantially accomplished in the law since the 1970s. Almost everywhere, legislation and police directives allow public authorities to breach the "sacred precincts" in order to arrest violent men. The effectiveness of these provisions is far less certain. Habitual legacies of inequalities between wives and husbands hang on after laws are changed, and these legacies are enacted not only in the "bonds of love" between couples but also in police responses and jury attitudes. Yet the stance of public authorities affects these habits. For example, a Los Angeles Police Department officer who dealt with domestic violence said of wife-batterers: "when two big guys come to their houses, handcuff 'em and take them down to the station for the night, they start to wonder whether or not it's really OK to hit their wives."[14]

The downfall of the marital rape exemption has to be seen as a very significant emblem of change. Of all the legal features of coverture, this right of the husband to his wife's body was the longest lasting. Through the 1970s sweep of legal sex discriminations from the law, it was not moved. Not until 1984, after at least a decade of feminist arguments, did a New York appellate court overturn that state's marital rape exemption—then other states followed. As in the *Eisenstadt* case allowing birth control to single persons, the force of an equal protection argument turned the tide: if the man in an *un*married cohabiting couple could be prosecuted for rape but a husband could not, the two couples were not experiencing equal protection of the laws.[15]

Dissolving the husband's privilege, this decision eliminated a historically central feature of marriage in the law, and subsequent developments showed that states were putting their public force behind the denial of marital unity. The law of marriage no longer gave bodily possession of the wife to her husband. This change announced a new norm of the wife's self-possession, with the potential to reframe the roles of both marriage partners. Marital rape was not altogether blended in to the category of rape, however. While all states criminalized it, at least a third of them distinguished marital rape from other forms. The police, lawyers, judges, and juries involved in prosecuting marital rape tend to make assumptions that exonerate the husband. Still, no state of the

United States any longer puts a husband's right to coerce his wife into sex in the definition of marriage.[16]

It could be contended, then, that by the 1980s the states and the nation had let go their grip on the institution of marriage along with their previous understanding of it. States' willingness to prosecute marital rape and wife abuse formed the most recent items in a trail of evidence, including the unchaining of morality from formal monogamy, the demise of the fiction of marital unity, and the institution of no-fault divorce. State legislatures and courts had moderated their former definitional role and resuscitated their much earlier willingness to treat couples "living together" as if they were married, at least in economic terms. The families of unmarried couples are treated as families in court. Parents' rights over children do not diminish—nor do their enforceable responsibilities for support—just because of birth out of wedlock. This public willingness to see marriage-like relationships *as* marriage is driven by the aim of guaranteeing economic support by family members, thereby minimizing demands on public assistance, but it also diversifies social views of family relationships.

This alteration in the relation between marriage and the state might be called "disestablishment," if the term can be borrowed from the history of religion. A national church supported by church taxes or tithes in the past was called the "established" religion or religious "establishment," and the ending of that special status for one religion was called disestablishment. Disestablishment did not mean that piety or religious institutions disappeared. On the contrary, the consequence more often was that religious sects proliferated, while no single model was, any longer, supported and enforced by the state. By analogy one could argue that the particular model of marriage which was for so long the officially supported one has been disestablished.[17] Continuing the analogy to religious disestablishment, one could say that with the weight of the one supported faith lifted, plural acceptable sexual behaviors and marriage types have bloomed. The situation today bears some similarity to eighteenth- and early nineteenth-century America, before a strong national standard descended, when laws regulating marriage were on the books everywhere but the more effective validation of marriage came from local communities.

Community then was geographical, whereas now it may be more cultural or ideological, ethnic or occupational. Couples who are not following the conventional model look for endorsement from like-minded communities, and expect to be left alone by others whom they are not harming, since marriage is understood as a private choice. This stance has allowed hundreds and perhaps thousands of fundamentalist Mormons in Utah and Arizona to revive polygamy.[18] The open practice of polygamy—unprosecuted although it is illegal as well as officially disapproved by the Church of the Latter-Day Saints—signals not only disestablishment but also the evaporation of the political role of marriage as ballast for the form of governance. Courts, the legal arm of the state, are interested in economic support functions. The formality and conformity of marriage-like arrangements matter far less in the law now than in the past, because support can be traced through cohabitation and biological parenthood. And no state needs to work through household heads to locate or govern family members: the interweaving or intrusion of government presence in the lives of individuals through their employment, schooling, immigration, taxation, social welfare, travel, and so on, has advanced so far that all are already in the state's grasp.

These remarkable and probably irrevocable transformations in the marital landscape have not been uncontested. Political and ideological backlash has been in the mix since the mid-1970s. The emergence in American politics of a New Right, strongly allied with Protestant fundamentalism and centered simultaneously on "family values" and embrace of the free market, responded in part to the apparent disestablishment of traditional marriage. This reactionary movement was successful in blocking ratification of the equal rights amendment and in cutting back on reproductive rights and denying government funding to abortion for Medicaid clients. One major way the New Right mobilized its numbers was by heightening alarms that conventional gender differences were facing destruction and possible homosexual takeover. This vocal minority, effective beyond its numbers in electoral politics in the 1980s and

1990s, still made a vivid connection between the stability of conventional Christian-model monogamy and the health of the nation-state. Alarms about the degradation of family life in the United States have sounded from many political angles, but only partisans of the New Right (and not all of them) openly voice the desire to reinstate a patriarchal model of marriage with the husband/father as the provider *and* the primary authority figure.

The conservative family politics of this backlash conflicts with its economics, ironically. The economic values championed by the right— the free market, individual accumulation of property, and a higher and higher standard of consumption—have been instrumental in undermining the marriage model in which the husband/father earns the family income and his wife and children are his dependents. The late-twentieth-century free market ethic inspired higher consumption than the old-style one-earner family could typically achieve. Ever-expanding desire to be able to buy urged wives and mothers into the labor force and multiplied two-earner families. Even with unemployment very low in the late 1990s, the rising standard of living (or of longing) cultivated by advertisements and the absence of publicly provided services such as health care vaporized the illusion of a single "family wage" except for the families of the uppermost male earners. The national government was no longer willing to mimic the family wage in assisting the poor, as the original Social Security Act once did. The Aid to Families with Dependent Children program once offered father-like assistance to poor children whose mothers were not gainfully employed, but the reorientation from "welfare" to "workfare" definitively discontinued that practice. Offered incentives in 1967 and 1971 to pursue employment or job training, welfare mothers since 1994 have been required to do so, in order to continue receiving aid for their children. As much as this shift reflected a punitive social outcry against welfare recipients' drain on the public purse, it also indicated that the family wage concept had lost credibility.[19]

Despite the extensive gains made by the New Right both culturally and politically, it seems dubious that conventional legal marriage can recover the primacy it once had. Economic reasons for two-earner families and feminist transformations of self-understanding make that unlikely. Houses hold unrelated groups, cohabiting couples, multigenerational rather than couple-based households, single-person households, and single adults raising children. Government entities have been able to look past the formalization of marriage because support obligations can be enforced without it. Besides, since transgressive forms of sexuality have been allowed into the open, they will not be tucked back behind the curtains—not without a nationwide religious revival. Free expression and commercial exploitation of adolescent sexuality, nonmarital cohabitation, and extramarital affairs have become, if anything, more and more banal, as the majority reaction to President Clinton's dalliance with Monica Lewinsky ineffably demonstrated. The boundaries of acceptable heterosexual behavior generally follow lines of consent rather than marriage— with adultery a partial exception. Though acknowledged to occur, and even shrugged at, marital infidelity was pronounced to be always wrong by about 80 percent of adults at the end of the century, a figure rising back from a low of about 70 percent in the combative 1970s.[20]

Bring same-sex marriage into view, however, and the suitability of the disestablishment parallel fails. If disestablishment of formal and legal Christian-model monogamy were real, public authorities would grant the same imprimatur to every kind of couple's marriage. That has not happened. Opponents of same-sex marriage have drawn a line in the moving sand of disestablishment. Marriages between two women or two men can be validated *only* by like-minded communities, not by formal public authorities. (Clergy members, including Unitarian-Universalists, reform Jews, and various Protestants, have stepped increasingly into the breach to perform religious ceremonies of marriage—without legal standing— for same-sex couples.)[21] The morality that the law has dropped or soft-pedaled with respect to consensual heterosexual acts still lives in the law's prosecution of homosexual behavior. As late as 1986, the U.S. Supreme Court upheld a Georgia law under which two consenting male homosexuals were arrested for what they did in private and at home. In 1996, Supreme Court Justice Antonin Scalia grouped murder, polygamy, and homosexuality together as kinds of inherently reprehensible conduct against which he assumed laws could constitutionally "exhibit 'animus.'"[22] Both prosecution of homosexual behavior and resistance to same-sex marriage show that the profound transformation of disestablishment has *not* taken place.

Lesbians and gay men seek legal marriage for some of the same reasons ex-slaves did so after the Civil War, to show that they have access to basic civil rights. The exclusion of same-sex partners from free choice in marriage stigmatizes their relationship, and reinforces a caste supremacy of heterosexuality over homosexuality just as laws banning marriages across the color line exhibited and reinforced white supremacy. Tailoring their legal arguments to current constitutional doctrine, same-sex couples have underlined the association of marriage with consent and with privacy rights. A 1998 superior court ruling in Alaska accentuated that interpretation, setting off sirens in some camps and cheers in others. The Alaska state constitution explicitly guarantees the right to privacy as well as equal protection of the laws. Two gay men who were denied a marriage license sued the state, asserting that its disallowance of same-sex marriage violated their constitutionally assured rights.

The judge in the Alaska case called the "right to choose one's life partner" constitutionally "fundamental," a privacy right that ought to receive protection whatever its outcome (even a partner of the same sex). "Government intrusion into the choice of a life partner encroaches on the intimate personal decisions of the individual," Judge Peter Michalski wrote. "The relevant question is not whether same-sex marriage is so rooted in our traditions that it is a fundamental right"—the focus of earlier judicial inquiry—"but whether the *freedom to choose* one's own life partner is so rooted in our traditions." The judge's reasoning here followed directly from the long tradition of mutual consent as basic to marriage and, more immediately, from the logic of the *Griswold* and the *Eisenstadt* cases on birth control. Although opponents of same-sex marriage had claimed that its exclusion was not a sex discrimination because members of both sexes were equally prevented (an argument paralleling earlier justifications of bans on black-white marriage as symmetrical for both races), Judge Michalski thought it obvious that prohibition of same-sex marriage *was* a "sex-based classification," subject to close scrutiny for discriminatory intent or impact. "If twins, one male and one female, both wished to marry a woman and otherwise met all of the Code's requirements," he said, "only gender prevents the twin sister from marrying." He did not make a definitive ruling but ordered further hearings in order to see whether the state had a "compelling" interest in preventing same-sex marriage.[23]

This Alaska case came in the wake of a Hawaii Supreme Court ruling in 1993 that showed even more starkly the distance traveled since Joel Bishop's mid-nineteenth-century certainty that marriage involved "one man and one woman united in law for life" in a civil status whose source was "the law of nature."[24] The Hawaii opinion characterized marriage as a "state-conferred legal partnership status, the existence of which gives rise to a multiplicity of rights and benefits reserved exclusively to that particular relation." This description—also emphasizing "the state's role as the exclusive progenitor of the marital partnership"—cut the institution loose from Christianity and nature and instead put its birth in the legislature.[25]

The Hawaii approach reduced conventional heterosexual marriage to just one of many possible state-conferred forms. Although this opinion, like the one in Alaska, dwelt much on the privacy rights of individuals in marriage choice, its emphasis on the "state-conferred" character of the institution of marriage had the more radical potential. Hawaii's action sparked opponents of same-sex marriage to organize politically. In 1996 and 1997, twenty-four states passed legislation banning recognition in their territory of same-sex marriages (even if validated elsewhere). To prevent the transformation looming in Alaska and Hawaii, advocacy groups worked to amend those states' constitutions to declare marriage legal only between a man and a woman, and through referenda in 1998, mobilized voters in both states to trump the courts' opening to same-sex marriage.

By the spring of 2000, a total of thirty-five of the fifty states had legislated their unwillingness to recognize same-sex marriage. Despite the Golden State's reputation for sexual liberalism, more than three fifths of voters there endorsed the resolution that "only marriage between a man and a woman is valid and recognized in California." Yet simultaneously Vermont created a legal status called "civil union" for same-sex couples. The state high court, using reasoning about equal protection of the laws, declared in December 1999 that same-sex couples deserved access to the benefits that heterosexual couples gain from marrying. Even though Catholic, Mormon, and conservative groups mobilized in opposition, in April 2000 Vermont enacted a historic law, reserving "marriage" to one man and one woman but allowing a same-sex couple in the state the identical rights and protections in "civil union."[26]

Conservative advocacy groups, intending to preempt validation of same-sex marriage by state referenda and constitutional amendments, were fashioning symbolic statements as much as pragmatic instruments. So were the large majorities in both houses of Congress who had ushered through a "defense of marriage act" with very unusual speed in 1996. The Defense of Marriage Act was not a complex piece of legislation. It was a "modest proposal" based on "common sense," according to one Senate sponsor. The act did two things. First, it explicitly defined the words "marriage" and "spouse" in federal law as involving one man and one woman. Second—and far more questionable constitutionally—it provided that no state would be required to give effect to a same-sex marriage contracted in another state, despite the constitutional rule that each state should give "full faith and credit" to the public acts of others. Advocates of the bill saw the threat looming from Hawaii the way that opponents of divorce had seen the threat of Indiana's liberality in the 1850s: if any same-sex couple could go to Hawaii to be married, and return to their home state to live, then Hawaii was strong-arming the other states, setting marriage policy for the nation. The Defense of Marriage Act struck preemptively against that possibility. Advocates contended that Congress had the power to do so, because it could prescribe how "full faith and credit" should be effected.[27]

Congressional rhetoric on behalf of the Defense of Marriage Act, relying more on pronouncement than on reasoning, undercut the idea that disestablishment of the traditional institution of marriage was well under way. The bill's supporters announced that traditional heterosexual marriage was "the fundamental building block of our society"; that nature and the Judeo-Christian moral tradition commanded or comported with it; that it was the basis of "civilization." One or two said homosexuality was immoral, a perversion, based on lust; more often the fear was expressed that licensing same-sex marriage would start the descent down a slippery slope to licensing polygamy, incest, even marriage to animals. The most fervent urged that the disparity between homosexual and heterosexual relationships could not become a matter of moral indifference. To treat the two as moral equivalents was to "completely erase whatever boundaries that currently exist on the definition of marriage and say it is a free-for-all, anything goes."[28]

These expressions of anxiety may have resulted from pondering the unsentimental (yet undeniable) words of the Hawaii ruling. Congressman James M. Talent of Missouri summed up a predominant viewpoint among the bill's supporters when he declared, "it is an act of hubris to believe that marriage can be infinitely malleable, that it can be pushed and pulled around like silly-putty without destroying its essential stability and what it means to our society, and if marriage goes, then the family goes, and if the family goes, we have none of the decency or ordered liberty which Americans have been brought up to enjoy and to appreciate."[29] He voiced a tension that had been present ever since legislators began altering the terms of marriage in the 1840s with married women's property acts and new grounds for divorce. Legislators had jealously guarded their power, yet hardly wanted to admit that marriage was "state-conferred"—that they themselves, rather than nature or God, defined its outlines. They tried to have it both ways with marriage in political discourse—picturing it as a rock of needed stability amidst eddies of change, while also acting to define and redefine marital obligations.

In the 1996 debate as in the past, observance of Christian-model monogamy was made to stand for customary boundaries in society, morality, and civilization; the nation's public backing of conventional marriage became a synecdoche for everything valued in the American way of life. One of the co-sponsors of the bill preferred the language of the 1885 Supreme Court to the Hawaii approach, saying it was "vital" to protect "our Nation's traditional understanding of marriage" as the "union for life of one man and one woman in the holy estate of matrimony."[30] Those who opposed the Defense of Marriage Act also had American values to marshal on their side, however. They reasoned that marriage was a basic right that should not discriminate on the basis of gender, that the American values of liberty and the pursuit of happiness should apply to couples of the same sex. They invoked the social value of love between partners who chose each other and contended that Congress should not step into the making of private relationships. Citing the extensive changes in sexual and familial practice that had transpired (harmlessly, they thought) during the past century, opponents of the bill saw no threat to other families in allowing two adults of the same sex to make a legal commitment to each other. They championed the diversity of households flowering in the United States and condemned the Defense of Marriage Act as a measure of Republican partisanship, an appeal to fear and bigotry and intolerance. Congressman Patrick Kennedy of Rhode Island said, for instance, that the bill was "not about defending marriage. It is about finding an enemy. It is not about marital union. It is about disunion, about dividing one group of Americans against another." Opponents drew analogies between the civil rights deprivations suffered in the past by African Americans and those currently imposed on homosexuals, and specifically between earlier bans on cross-race marriage and the continuing illegality of same-sex unions.[31]

Bypassing opponents' reasoning, partisans of the bill argued unstintingly that because marriage had been heterosexual since "time immemorial" the Congress had to assure its remaining so. Where public authorities a century earlier had been primed to defend Christian-model monogamy from free love, interracial coupling, polygamy, self-divorce, and commercial sex, now the Congress found heterosexuality the crucial boundary to maintain. The bill passed the House by a vote of 342 to 67 (with 22 not voting and 2 "present") and the Senate by 85 to 14.[32] As had often been the case in previous legislative contentions over marriage forms, the debate on the Defense of Marriage Act revealed a cultural contest being waged between the majority and a nonconforming minority. Senator Jesse Helms's speech epitomized the strongly ideological stance of the bill's supporters, condemning "homosexual extremists" for eviscerating the nation's "moral stamina." Calling marriage "sacred," Helms proclaimed that "the moral and spiritual survival of this Nation" was at stake in the measure and that the vote would decide "whither goeth America."[33]

Putting the nation's imprimatur on one man and one woman in sacred union, Congress signified its concern for more than heterosexuality alone. Further assumptions wrapped in the word "marriage" reverberated loudly in the contemporaneous welfare reform law. The federal act that fulfilled President Clinton's promise to "end welfare as we know it" was called the Personal Responsibility and Work Opportunity Reconciliation Act of 1996 (formally a set of revisions in public assistance under the Social Security Act). It answered years of polemics against welfare clients for purportedly taking unfair advantage of an overgenerous system. The act replaced "welfare" with "workfare," by putting federal public assistance to needy mothers and fathers in the form of block grants to states, contingent on the states' providing the recipients (in the words of the act) "with job preparation, work, and support services to enable them to leave the program and become self-sufficient."[34]

This reform responded to the rise in caseloads under the Aid to Families with Dependent Children. An average of 3.3 million children received AFDC benefits monthly in 1965, and 9.3 million in 1992. Not a simple issue of public expenditures, however, the case against "welfare as we know it" made economic concerns inseparable from racial, gender, household, and marital questions. Almost two decades of white conservatives' fingerpointing at black single mothers—especially teenagers—fueled the principal arguments for workfare, despite the fact that most mothers receiving assistance were white.

The Personal Responsibility and Work Opportunity Act (PRWO) zeroed in on marriage as a solution to the ballooning welfare caseload. While the main lineaments of the bill mandated work requirements and the means to chase down deadbeat dads, the bill opened with the normative claims "(1) Marriage is the foundation of a successful society. (2) Marriage is an essential institution of a successful society which promotes the interests of children." According to the social science analysis incorporated in the act, the availability of public assistance for poor and unemployed single mothers had allowed the men who fathered children to forget about marrying the women they made pregnant, and to shirk financial responsibility for their children. In this view, "welfare" encouraged shiftless women to get pregnant in order to be supported by the public purse in female-headed households. Their children, lacking responsible employed fathers as worthwhile role models, were doomed to making this cycle of nonmarriage and illegitimacy and consequent poverty and dependence on public assistance repeat itself.

Proponents of welfare reform brought together social facts—the increases in welfare caseloads, births out of wedlock, and female-headed households in poverty—and, by linking these to male irresponsibility, female profligacy, and marital failure, considered them all consequences of the welfare system. Female-headed households with children are far poorer, on average, than married-couple households, but proponents of the Personal Responsibility act spoke as though the marriage ceremony itself magically solved the problem of poverty. Proponents assumed rather than probed what were the reasons behind the correlation between marriage and greater economic stability. They did not give equal attention to highly relevant and complex issues of sex segregation and racial stratification in the labor market; they did not question how far the rise in illegitimacy and female-headed households, and the decline in marriage, were larger phenomena not caused by welfare. They said "get a job!" and "get married!" The Personal Responsibility and Work Opportunity Act offered substantial incentives to states to reduce out-of-wedlock pregnancies (especially among teenagers) while lowering abortion rates—as if wedded parents would always be adequate parents, and would not split up or fall into poverty.

The tenor of the Personal Responsibility and Work Opportunity Act (and even its title) faintly echoed the tenets of the Freedmen's Bureau, in linking legal marriage to the requisite ethic of hard work and reinforcing normatively the husband's and father's responsibility to support his dependents. Just as the model of marriage in which the husband is the provider and the wife his dependent lingered in federal veterans' and Social Security benefits and income tax provisions, it hovered behind the PRWO's emphasis on the desirability of marriage, despite the requirement for mothers to seek employment. The mother no less than the father was addressed as someone who must take "personal responsibility" for supporting herself and her children. This approach made paid work a requirement and an emblem of full citizenship for both women and men. Nonetheless, the attention given to marriage upheld the vision that a woman *could* be a full-time mother at home, by marrying a man able and willing to make her and the children his dependents. In pursuit of its aim to reduce welfare caseloads through private support, the Personal Responsibility and Work Opportunity Act echoed centuries of enforcement of the husband's obligation to provide. Like the Defense of Marriage Act, it sought to impose majority norms of marriage on a minority, for the ostensible benefit of the nation. Yet there was a catch. The methods of implementing the Personal Responsibility and Work Opportunity Act— like those used to enforce federal welfare provisions since Civil War pensions were instituted—brought public oversight into the personal lives of the poor. The national value placed on marital and familial privacy did not extend to families in need of help. Welfare mothers and fathers could not enjoy a "private realm of family life where the state cannot enter."[35]

These two major acts of Congress in the late 1990s, along with the myriad marital obligations and benefits in the federal legal apparatus, illustrated the national government's continuing investment in traditional marriage. If the federal battery of veterans' benefits, immigration preferences, Social Security, taxation policies, and so on gave principally financial boons, perhaps that was more meaningful than anything else in a dollar-driven culture. One tax privilege for married couples became problematic, however, as two-earner couples increased and wives' incomes grew closer to husbands'. The married-filing-jointly option for federal income tax, revised in the 1960s to eliminate its original "singles' penalty," continued to benefit married couples with one earner and those couples whose two incomes were quite disparate—because it was designed with provider/dependent couples like that in mind. As couples' earnings approached equivalency, though, joint filing disadvantaged them—they owed more tax than they would if they were unmarried and filed two individual tax returns. This "marriage penalty" ignited a great deal of criticism for being unfair and for contradicting public policy by discouraging marriage. Less noticed has been its especially negative impact on African Americans. In a higher proportion of African American married couples than of white couples both husband and wife earned incomes, and a higher proportion of black couples than white couples were near-equal earners.[36] While federal "workfare" proponents were castigating black teenage mothers for not marrying, federal tax policy was attaching a particular disincentive to marriage in the African American community.

Contested and contradictory as they were, the marriage bonus and penalty persisting in tax law illustrated the economic framework for marriage that public authority had long been fostering. Equal-earning spouses griped about the marriage penalty, giving rise to stories of couples who divorced on December 31 to qualify for single-earner status for the year and remarried on January 1—but the penalty was outweighed by the many other legal advantages of marriage. Legal marriage remains a privileged public status, buttressed by government policies that allow and inspire people to have confidence in it. It *does* bring with it— for better or worse—all the presumptions that a cohabiting arrangement has to prove, in court or out.

Despite sweeping reformulations in intimate relationships in the past quarter century, one can doubt whether most Americans' "common sense" about marriage has vastly changed. So flayed and scorned in the 1960s and 1970s, conventional and legal marriage like the phoenix has arisen from its ashes, even alongside innovations and deviations. It is the main theme around which the variations take place. Even with no-fault divorce common, marriage commands greater respect from popular opinion and implies a greater commitment than "living together." The position of legal marriage above comparable relationships resists toppling. Contestation over same-sex marriage has, ironically, clothed the formal institution with renewed honor. Not all lesbian and gay rights activists aim for same-sex marriages, since many—lesbians, especially—see the institution as too mired in inequality to be desirable, but those who do advocate marriage have brought its civil rights and rewards back into public discourse and have portrayed its promise of stable mutual commitment as a benefit to society as well as to the couple. Their opponents, who cannot imagine extending the license to marry to same-sex couples, nonetheless employ the same rhetorical strategies in lauding the institution itself.[37]

The resiliency of belief in legal marriage as the destination of a love match and as a safe haven begs for explanation, even when hyperbole about love seems to demand none. Love is exalted in our society—it is the food and drink of our imaginations. Sexual love has even more of a halo, because we assume that an individual's full subjectivity blossoms in the circle of its intimacy. But where does marriage stand, when there is widespread awareness that half of all marriages end in divorce? Alarmists declare certainly that marriage is withering, but its firm grip is more of an enigma. Even with failed marriages staring them in the face, individuals still hope to beat the odds. The belief persists that a couple have achieved the ultimate reward, the happy ending, by adding the imprimatur of public authority and making their relationship formal and legal. Dating services certainly advertise it this way, promising to introduce "Mr. Right" and "Ms. Right" to each other. Splendid, elaborately detailed weddings have swelled in popularity, as though the money spent on a wedding is ballast destined to keep the marriage afloat.[38]

The preeminent stature of marriage in public opinion is not unwarranted because it still *is* a public institution, building in material rewards along with obligations. History and tradition cement the hold of marriage on individual desires and social ideals. Marriage also continues to appeal subjectively, despite the alternatives visible, because of the relief it seems to offer from the ineffable coercions and insistent publicity of the postmodern world. At the opening of the twenty-first century, individuals face overwhelming techniques of surveillance, record-keeping, and publicity wielded by government, medical authorities, marketing firms, and telecommunications media. Government agencies, directives, incentives, and regulations intersect with private enterprise and ubiquitous advertising; daily headlines and talk show hosts blare out the secret sexual and medical grotesqueries of public figures; formerly hidden bodily orifices become the subject of performance art; and outerwear looks like underwear. In an era of aggrandizement by both nation-states and global corporations and of instant access via the World Wide Web, personal well-being seems to require marking off a boundary of privacy from the welter of public compulsions.

Marriage can be imagined as setting this boundary and providing private liberty inside it. When freedom is understood to reign mainly in private choices, marriage becomes reconfigured, enhanced. Traditionally a "yoke," marriage more recently and paradoxically signifies freedom in a chosen space—a zone marked off from the rest of the world. While it promises to defend against the sense of estrangement haunting our cosmopolitan world, marriage can now also symbolize freedom. Constitutional doctrine since the 1940s has predicted this outcome, allying privacy with personal liberty and putting public authority behind that alliance. Consent in marriage—less critical than it once was as a analogy for government in the United States—has greater resonance in the private domain.

If marriage harmonizes the seeming opposites of choice and dependability—the promise of an arena of freedom along with security of a very loving and personal kind—then that is a key to its hold on the imagination. Yet—hasn't the record shown that public authorities thoroughly shape the institution, infusing it with aims not personal at all? Is the liberty associated with marriage an illusion? That will depend not only on luck and love but also on the character of public directives. Marriage remains inextricably public *and* private, both faces of the institution as paired as the couple is. The patchworked emotions and practices with which individuals endow their unions color the evolving institution, and the values and requirements incorporated into it by official policy furnish citizens' imaginations as well as setting them to their marital tasks. If public authorities arrayed various marriage definitions—and if private intimacy would also nurture generous attention to the public interest— then the institution might be replenished. The ideal of a reciprocal commitment between two people that unites public honor with private meanings of freedom might be revivified.

NOTES / ACKNOWLEDGMENTS / INDEX

ABBREVIATIONS USED IN THE NOTES

AAG	Assistant Adjutant General
AAAG	Acting Assistant Adjutant General
AHR	*American Historical Review*
AQ	*American Quarterly*
BRFAL	Bureau of Refugees, Freedmen, and Abandoned Lands
CG	*Congressional Globe*
CR	*Congressional Record*
Exec. Docs.	*Executive Documents*
FS	*Feminist Studies*
H.R.	House of Representatives
JAH	*Journal of American History*
LJ	*Law Journal*
LR	*Law Review*
P	Press
Sen.	Senate, Senator
U	University
USCT	U.S. Colored Troops
WMQ	*William and Mary Quarterly*, 3d ser.

In citations of congressional materials the number of the Congress and the session is in the form 38/2, meaning 38th Cong., 2d sess.

Introduction

1. *Prince v. Massachusetts,* 321 U.S. 158, at 166 (1944).

2. See Maura Strassberg, "Distinctions of Form or Substance: Monogamy, Polygamy, and Same-Sex Marriage," *North Carolina LR,* 75 (1997), esp. 1571–75, on Hegel's view of the ethical bond between the marrying couple and the public.

3. Report to the Honorable Henry J. Hyde, chairman, Committee on the Judiciary, House of Representatives, "The Defense of Marriage Act," dated Jan. 31, 1997, Federal Document Clearing House, General Accounting Office, GAO/OCG 97–16, 1997 WL 67783. Most of the myriad references stem from sections on Social Security, federal income tax and estate and gift taxes, and veterans's benefits.

4. Karl M. Llewellyn, "Behind the Law of Divorce," part 2, *Columbia LR,* 33 (1933), 277.

5. *Loving v. Virginia,* 388 U.S. 1 (1967), 6, n. 5.

6. Martha Minow, "We, the Family: Constitutional Rights and American Families," *JAH,* 74:3 (Dec. 1987), 959–83; see also Lee Teitlebaum, "Family History and Family Law," 1985 *Wisconsin LR,* 1135–48; Nayan Shah, "Paradoxes of Inclusion and Exclusion in American Modernity: Formations of the Modern Self, Domicile, and Domesticity," paper prepared for the OAH-NYU conference Internationalizing the Study of American History, sponsored by the Organization of American Historians and New York University, July 4–7, 1999, Florence, Italy.

7. On state-level marital policies during the nineteenth century, Michael Grossberg's *Governing the Hearth: Law and the Family in Nineteenth-Century America* (Chapel Hill, U of North Carolina P, 1985) is indispensable; Jill Elaine Hasday, "Federalism and the Family Reconstructed," *UCLA LR,* 45:5 (June 1998), 1297–1400, confirms the federal role from a contemporary standpoint.

8. See Roderick Phillips, *Putting Asunder: A History of Divorce in Western Society* (Cambridge and New York, Cambridge UP, 1988), 25–27, 34–35, 194–206; John R. Gillis, *For Better, For Worse: British Marriages, 1600 to the Present* (New York and London, Oxford UP, 1985), 139–41; Mary Ann Glendon, *The Transformation of Family Law: State, Law, and Family in the United States and Western Europe* (Chicago, U of Chicago P, 1989), 15–27.

9. George Elliot Howard, *A History of Matrimonial Institutions*, 3 vols. (New York, Humanities P, 1964: orig. 1904), summarizes the founding marital regulations of all the colonies and states. See, on Virginia, Kathleen M. Brown, *Good Wives, Nasty Wenches, and Anxious Patriarchs* (Chapel Hill, U of North Carolina P, 1996), 91–93; on Texas, Hans W. Baade, "The Form of Marriage in Spanish North America," *Cornell LR*, 61 (Nov. 1975), 9–12; on the French and the Bolshevik revolutions, Phillips, *Putting Asunder*, 208–09, 535–36.

10. Joel Prentiss Bishop, *Commentaries on the Law of Marriage and Divorce*, vol. 1, 4th ed. (Boston, Little Brown, 1864), 2. See Carol Weisbrod, "Family, Church, and State: An Essay on Constitutionalism and Religious Authority," *Journal of Family Law*, 26:4 (1987–88), 741–70; Phillips, *Putting Asunder*, 134–35, 159; Howard, *Matrimonial Institutions*, 2:129; Grossberg, *Governing the Hearth*, 66.

11. See Susan Moller Okin, *Women in Western Political Thought* (Princeton, Princeton UP, 1979); Carole Pateman, *Sexual Contract* (Stanford, Stanford UP, 1988); Brown, *Good Wives*, 126–27; Toby L. Ditz, "Ownership and Obligation: Inheritance and Patriarchal Households in Connecticut, 1750–1820," *WMQ*, 47:2 (April 1990), 235–65.

12. Quotation from "Marriage and Divorce," *Southern Quarterly Review*, 26 (1854), 351. On continuities see Norma Basch, "Invisible Women: The Legal Fiction of Marital Unity in Nineteenth-Century America," *FS*, 5:2 (Summer 1979), 346–66; Reva B. Siegel, "The Modernization of Marital Status Law: Adjudicating Wives' Rights to Earnings, 1860–1930," *Georgetown LJ*, 82:7 (Sept. 1994), 2127–2211; Christopher Tomlins, "Subordination, Authority, Law: Subjects in Labor History," *International Labor and Working-Class History*, 47 (Spring 1995), 56–90; Defense of Marriage Act debate in *CR* 104/2, vol. 142, no. 102, July 11, 1996.

13. See Robert A. Ferguson, *Law and Letters in American Culture* (Cambridge, Harvard UP, 1984); Michael Grossberg, "Institutionalizing Masculinity: The Law as a Masculine Profession," in *Meanings for Manhood*, ed. Mark C. Carnes and Clyde Griffen (Chicago, U of Chicago P, 1990), 133–51.

14. I am indebted to Philip Corrigan and Derek Sayer, *The Great Arch: English State Formation as Cultural Revolution* (London, Basil Blackwell, 1985), e.g.,

4–5, 198–200, for their analysis of public authorities' shaping of a moral order; see also William J. Novak, *The People's Welfare: Law and Regulation in Nineteenth-Century America* (Chapel Hill, U of North Carolina P, 1996), esp. 152–56, 216. On the relation between law and society, see Robert Gordon, "Critical Legal Histories," *Stanford LR,* 57 (1984); Hendrik Hartog, "Pigs and Positivism," *Wisconsin LR,* 4 (July 1985), esp. 932–34; Tomlins, "Subordination."

1. An Archaeology of American Monogamy

1. Clifford Geertz, "Common Sense as a Cultural System," in his *Local Knowledge: Further Essays in Interpretive Anthropology* (New York, Basic Books, 1983), 84.

2. Dorothy Ross, *The Origins of American Social Science* (New York, Cambridge UP, 1991), 36–37.

3. Baron de Montesquieu [Charles-Louis de Secondat], *The Spirit of the Laws,* trans. and ed. Anne M. Cohler et al. (Cambridge, Cambridge UP, 1989), 270, 316; and see Anne Cohler's introduction, xxvi-vii, on Montesquieu's influence on the founders, which all scholars credit, e.g., Henry F. May, *The Enlightenment in America* (New York, Oxford UP, 1976), 282; Robert A. Ferguson, *Law and Letters in American Culture* (Cambridge, Harvard UP, 1984), 42–43. *Spirit of the Laws* was held by more American libraries during the years between 1750 and 1813 than any other work of political theory; David Lundberg and Henry F. May, "The Enlightened Reader in America," *AQ,* 28 (Summer 1976), 262–93.

4. Robert G. McCloskey, ed., *The Works of James Wilson* (Cambridge, Harvard UP, 1976), 600–01; Hendrik Hartog, "Marital Exits and Marital Expectations in Nineteenth Century America," *Georgetown LJ,* 80:1 (Oct. 1991), 95–129; Carole Pateman, "The Shape of the Marriage Contract," in *Women's Views of the Political World of Men,* ed. Judith Stiehm (Dobbs Ferry, N.Y., Transnational Publications, 1984), 77.

5. G. B. Harrison, ed., *Shakespeare: The Complete Works* (N.Y., Harcourt, Brace and World, 1948), 363; I have changed "froward" to "forward."

6. John Winthrop, "On Civil Liberty," quoted in Linda K. Kerber, *Toward an Intellectual History of Women* (Chapel Hill, U of North Carolina P, 1997), 200, 203; and in Mary Beth Norton, *Founding Mothers and Fathers* (N.Y., Knopf, 1996), 317–19.

7. See Lawrence Stone, "The Rise of the Nuclear Family," in *The Family in History,* ed. Charles Rosenberg (Philadelphia, U of Pennsylvania P, 1975), 13–59;, Sarah Hanley, "Engendering the State: Family Formation and State Building in Early Modern France," *French Historical Studies,* 16:1 (1989), 4–27;

Mary Lyndon Shanley, "Marriage Contract and Social Contract in Seventeenth Century English Political Thought," in *The Family in Political Thought,* ed. Jean Bethke Elshtain (Amherst, U of Massachusetts P, 1982).

8. Norton, *Founding Mothers,* 17–19, 38, 58–59, 401; David Flaherty, "Law and the Enforcement of Morals in Early America," *Perspectives in American History,* 5 (1971), 56–59; Jane Kamensky, *Governing the Tongue* (New York, Oxford UP, 1997), 99–126.

9. Edwin G. Burrows and Michael Wallace, "The American Revolution: The Ideology and Psychology of National Liberation," *Perspectives in American History,* 6 (1972), 168–79; Melissa A. Butler, "Early Liberal Roots of Feminism: John Locke and the Attack on Patriarchy," *American Political Science Review,* 72:1 (March 1978), 135–50; Shanley, "Marriage Contract and Social Contract"; Susan Moller Okin, "Women and the Making of the Sentimental Family," *Philosophy and Public Affairs,* 11:1 (1981), 65–88; Linda J. Nicholson, *Gender and History: The Limits of Social Theory in the Age of the Family* (New York, Columbia UP, 1986); Carole Pateman, *The Sexual Contract* (Stanford, Stanford UP, 1988).

10. I rely on Burrows and Wallace, "The American Revolution," 165–306, and Jay Fliegelman, *Prodigals and Pilgrims: The American Revolution against Patriarchal Authority, 1750–1800* (New York, Cambridge UP, 1980), especially 120–30, for discussion of familial analogies in Revolutionary argument.

11. See Susan Moller Okin, *Justice, Gender, and the Family* (New York, Basic Books, 1989).

12. On the Scottish moralists, see May, *Enlightenment,* 342–47; Rosemarie Zagarri, "Morals, Manners, and the Republican Mother," *AQ,* 44 (June 1992), 192–215, and "The Rights of Man and Woman in Post-Revolutionary America," *WMQ,* 55:2 (April 1998).

13. Quotations from Burrows and Wallace, "The American Revolution," 194, 211–2, 213, 215. See also Joan Gunderson, "Independence, Citizenship, and the American Revolution," *Signs,* 13:1 (Aug. 1987), 59–77, on the impact of this rhetoric on women's citizenship.

14. I am indebted to Fliegelman, *Prodigals and Pilgrims,* 123–29, (quotation from Mayhew on 126) and to Jan Lewis, "The Republican Wife: Virtue and Seduction in the Early Republic," *WMQ,* 44 (Oct. 1987), 689–721, for my discussion of Revolutionary-era marriage references.

15. "Letters on Marriage" (1775) reprinted in *The Work of the Rev. John Witherspoon* (Philadelphia, 1802), 4:169; other quoted fragments and article titles are to be found in Lewis, "Republican Wife." See also Norma Basch, "From the Bonds of Empire to the Bonds of Matrimony," in *Devising Liberty:*

Preserving and Creating Freedom in the New American Republic, ed. David Thomas Konig (Stanford, Stanford UP, 1995), 229–34; Fliegelman, *Prodigals,* 123–24. On the other side of the Atlantic, in British publications, practical advice on finding the right mate did not differ markedly, but where British spokesmen were most concerned with marriages as anchors of society, Revolutionary Americans saw them also as models for the ship of state.

16. Webster quoted in Carroll Smith-Rosenberg, "Dis-Covering the Subject of the 'Great Constitutional Discussion,' 1786–1789," *JAH,* 79:3 (Dec. 1992), 841–73; *The Weekly Museum* (New York), March 16, 1793.

17. See Anne M. Cohler, *Montesquieu's Comparative Politics and the Spirit of American Constitutionalism* (Lawrence, UP of Kansas, 1988), esp. 12–17; Diana J. Schaub, *Erotic Liberalism: Women and Revolution in Montesquieu's Persian Letters* (London, Rowman & Littlefield, 1995); Mary Lyndon Shanley and Peter G. Stillman, "Political and Marital Despotism: Montesquieu's *Persian Letters,*" in *The Family in Political Thought,* ed. Jean Bethke Elshtain (Amherst, U of Massachusetts P, 1982), 66–79.

18. See Gordon Wood, *The Creation of the American Republic* (New York, Norton, 1969).

19. Schaub, *Erotic Liberalism,* 25–31; Fliegelman, *Prodigals,* 24.

20. *Massachusetts Magazine* quoted in Jan Lewis, "Motherhood and the Construction of the Male Citizen in the United States, 1750–1850," in *Constructions of the Self,* ed. George Levine (New Brunswick, Rutgers UP, 1992), 162; "On Love," *New-York Magazine,* June 1791; Witherspoon, *Letters,* 166, 162; *The Royal American* of 1774 quoted in Fliegelman, *Prodigals,* 127.

21. See, e.g., Thomas Gisborne, *An Enquiry into the Duties of the Female Sex* (London, Cadell, 1797), 23.

22. Kames quoted in Zagarri, "Morals, Manners," 201. I am indebted to Zagarri's essay for the analysis of manners.

23. James Tilton, quoted in Zagarri, "Morals, Manners," 205.

24. Entry of June 2, 1778, in *Diary and Autobiography of John Adams,* ed. Lyman H. Butterfield (Cambridge, The Belknap P of Harvard UP, 1962), 4:123.

25. *Spirit,* 316, 270.

26. My discussion of the novel is indebted to Shanley and Stillman, "Political and Marital Despotism," Cohler, introduction to *Spirit,* and Schaum, *Erotic Liberalism.*

27. "On Love," *New-York Magazine,* June 1791.

28. William Paley, D.D., *The Principles of Moral and Political Philosophy* (Boston, Benj. Mussey, 1852), quotations from 185, 194–95. See Wendell Glick, "Bishop Paley in America," *New England Quarterly,* 27 (1954), 347–54; Donald

H. Meyer, *The Instructed Conscience: The Shaping of the American National Ethic* (Philadelphia, U of Pennsylvania P, 1972), 7–8; D. L. LeMahieu, *The Mind of William Paley: A Philosopher and His Age* (Lincoln, U of Nebraska P, 1976); M. L. Clarke, *Paley: Evidences for the Man* (Toronto, U of Toronto P, 1974), esp. 153–62; and Maxwell Bloomfield, *American Lawyers in a Changing Society, 1779–1876* (Cambridge, Harvard UP 1976), 86, 105–06.

2. Perfecting Community Rules with State Laws

1. Stephen Skowronek, *Building a New American State: The Expansion of National Administrative Capacities, 1877–1920* (Cambridge, Cambridge UP, 1982); Richard L. McCormick, "The Party Period and Public Policy: An Exploratory Hypothesis," *JAH*, 66 (1979), 279–98; Richard John, *Spreading the News: The American Postal System from Franklin to Morse* (Cambridge, Harvard UP, 1995), 1–20, quotation from the historian John Murrin on 18.

2. Stephanie Coontz, *The Social Origins of Private Life* (New York, Verso, 1988), 41–72, offers a good summary of native American families; see also Carole Shammas, "Anglo-American Household Government in Comparative Perspective," *WMQ*, 52:1 (Jan. 1995), 104–44.

3. Quotations from southwestern state court cases in James Hugo Johnston, "Documentary Evidence of the Relations of Negroes and Indians," *Journal of Negro History*, 14:1 (Jan. 1929), 41.

4. See Francis Paul Prucha, *The Great Father: The United States Government and the American Indians* (Lincoln, U of Nebraska P, 1984), 1:135–48, 151.

5. See Joan Jacobs Brumberg, "Zenanas and Girlless Villages: The Ethnology of American Evangelical Women, 1870–1910," *JAH*, 69:2 (1982), 347–71; Patricia Grimshaw, *Paths of Duty: American Missionary Wives in Nineteenth-Century Hawaii* (Honolulu, U of Hawaii P, 1989).

6. Jedidiah Morse, *Report to the Secretary of War . . . on Indian Affairs* (New-Haven, 1822), esp. 12, 72–75. (quotation on 75); William G. McLoughlin, *Cherokee Renascence in the New Republic* (Princeton, Princeton UP, 1986), 68–71; Prucha, *Great Father.*

7. The U.S. made 378 treaties for land cession by native groups between 1778 and 1868. Francis Paul Prucha, *Americanizing the American Indians* (Cambridge, Harvard UP, 1973), 55; Arnold J. Lien, *The Acquisition of Citizenship by the Native American Indians,* Washington U Studies, vol. 13, Humanistic Series, no. 1 (1925), 141–42, 146, 169–71; James H. Kettner, *The Development of American Citizenship, 1608–1870* (Chapel Hill, U of North Carolina P, 1978), 292–94; McLoughlin, *Cherokee Renascence,* esp. 330–333.

8. Two states instituted bans on Indian-white marriage during the colonial period (but Virginia eliminated it before the Revolution); five more had added them by 1855; five others added them in the Civil War and postwar era: and Louisiana adopted a ban in 1920. See David H. Fowler, *Northern Attitudes towards Interracial Marriage* (New York, Garland, 1987), appendix.

9. On courts representing state authority, see Michael Grossberg, "Crossing Boundaries: Nineteenth-Century Domestic Relations Law and the Merger of Family and Legal History," *American Bar Foundation Research Journal*, 1985:4, esp. 818, 830–32; Christopher L. Tomlins, *Law, Labor, and Ideology in the Early American Republic* (Cambridge and New York, Cambridge UP, 1993), 16, 21–23; Skowronek, *Building a New American State;* on states' authorizing marital ceremonies, see Michael Grossberg, *Governing the Hearth* (Chapel Hill, U of North Carolina P, 1985), 65–82.

10. See Joel A. Rogers, *Sex and Race: A History of White, Negro, and Indian Miscegenation in the Two Americas,* (New York, Helga Rogers, 1942), 2:153–198; and Daniel R. Mandell, "Shifting Boundaries of Race and Ethnicity: Indian-Black Intermarriage in Southern New England, 1760–1880," *JAH,* 85 (Sept. 1998), 466–501.

11. Mary Frances Berry discusses this case in "Judging Morality: Sexual Behavior and Legal Consequences in the Late Nineteenth-Century South," *JAH,* 78:3 (Dec. 1991), 841–42, and *The Pig Farmer's Daughter and Other Tales of American Justice* (New York, Knopf, 1999), 39–40.

12. Grossberg, *Governing the Hearth,* emphasizes the dominance of judge-made law in domestic relations.

13. See Kermit Hall, *The Magic Mirror: Law in American History* (New York, Oxford UP, 1991), 153–55; Grossberg, *Governing,* 69–102; Otto E. Koegel, *Common Law Marriage and Its Development in the United States* (Washington, D.C., John Byrne, 1922); John E. Semonche, "Common Law Marriage in North Carolina: A Study in Legal History," *American Journal of Legal History,* 9 (1965), 324–41; Maxwell Bloomfield, *American Lawyers in a Changing Society, 1779–1876* (Cambridge, Harvard UP, 1976), 106–10; Norma Basch, "Relief in the Premises: Divorce as a Woman's Remedy in New York and Indiana, 1815–1870," *Law and History Review,* 8:1 (Spring 1990), 1–24; Hendrik Hartog, "Marital Exits and Marital Expectations in Nineteenth Century America," *Georgetown LJ,* 80:1 (Oct. 1991), 95–129; Lorena S. Walsh, " 'Till Death Us Do Part': Marriage and Family in Seventeenth-Century Maryland," in *The Chesapeake in the Seventeenth Century: Essays on Anglo-American Society,* ed. Thad W. Tate and David L. Ammerman (Chapel Hill, U of North Carolina P, 1979), 129–30; Guion Griffis Johnson, "Courtship and Marriage Customs in

Ante-Bellum North Carolina," *North Carolina Historical Review,* 8 (1931), 384–402; Chilton L. Powell, "Marriage in Early New England," *New England Quarterly,* 1 (1928), 330–33; Hans W. Baade, "The Form of Marriage in Spanish North America," *Cornell LR,* 61 (Nov. 1975), esp. 78–79; Darlis A. Miller, "Cross-Cultural Marriage in the Southwest: The New Mexico Experience, 1846–1900," *New Mexico Historical Review,* 57:4 (1982), 344–45; all giving evidence of informal marriages.

14.Walsh, "Till Death," 129–30; Allan Kulikoff, " 'Throwing the Stocking:' A Gentry Marriage in Provincial Maryland," *Maryland Historical Magazine,* 71:4 (Winter 1976), 516–17; Daniel Blake Smith, *Inside the Great House: Planter Family Life in Eighteenth-Century Chesapeake Society* (Ithaca, Cornell UP, 1980), 151–53.

15. Quoted in Semonche, "Common Law Marriage in North Carolina," 332.

16. Rev. Henry Addison quoted in Grossberg, *Governing,* 68, and Walsh, "Till Death," 129–30, and see 139–40; Sally D. Mason, "Mama, Rachel, and Molly: Three Generations of Carroll Women," in *Women in the Age of the American Revolution,* ed. Ronald Hoffman and Peter J. Albert (Charlottesville, UP of Virginia, 1989), 244–92.

17. Richard J. Hooker, ed., *The Carolina Backcountry on the Eve of the Revolution: The Journal and other Writings of Charles Woodmason, Anglican Itinerant* (Chapel Hill, U of North Carolina P, 1953), 7, 15, 48 (1766). In 1753 Parliament in England attempted to end informal and clandestine marriage by passing the Hardwicke Act, rendering a marriage null and void unless the ceremony was performed by an Anglican minister in church in front of two witnesses, and preceded by the posting of banns for three successive weeks or the purchase of a license. But the act was never implemented in the colonies; see Shammas, "Anglo-American Household Government," 127; Stephen Parker, *Informal Marriage, Cohabitation, and the Law, 1750–1989* (New York, St. Martin's, 1990), 29.

18. *Weaver v. Cryer,* 12 N.C. 337 (1827), and *Archer v. Haithcock,* 51 N.C. 421 (1859), quoted in Johnson, "Courtship and Marriage Customs"; see also Semonche, "Common Law Marriage ," esp. 320–42; and Laura F. Edwards, " 'The Marriage Covenant Is at the Foundation of All Our Rights': The Politics of Slave Marriages in North Carolina after Emancipation," *Law and History Review,* 14:1 (Spring 1996), 111–16.

19. Grossberg, *Governing,* 200–15.

20. See Margaret Burnham, "An Impossible Marriage: Slave Law and Family Law," *Law and Inequality,* 5 (1987); and Grossberg, *Governing,* esp. 130–32.

21. See Brenda Stevenson, *Life in Black and White: Family and Community in the Slave South* (New York, Oxford UP, 1996), 140–42; Edwards, "'Marriage Covenant,'" 111–16; cf. Norma Basch, *Framing American Divorce* (Berkeley, U of California P, 1999), 48–49.

22. On marriage implying freedom, see Lea Vandervelde, "Mrs. Dred Scott," esp. 1041 and 1104–05, and Justice Curtis's dissenting opinion in *Dred Scott v. Sandford*, 60 U.S. (19 How.) 393, 397–98, 600–01 (1857).

23. Grossberg, *Governing*, 129–32; Jones quoted from *The Religious Instruction of the Negroes in the United States* (1842) in Herbert Gutman, *The Black Family in Slavery and Freedom, 1750–1925* (New York, Random House, 1976), 295–6; on N.Y., see Edgar J. McManus, *A History of Negro Slavery in New York* (Syracuse, Syracuse UP, 1966), 65–67, 178, and George Elliot Howard, *A History of Matrimonial Institutions* (New York, Humanities P, 1964; orig. 1904), 2:453.

24. Orlando Patterson, *Slavery and Social Death: A Comparative Study* (Cambridge, Harvard UP, 1982), 5–7; *The State v. Samuel*, 19 N.C. 177 (1836); *Alvany v. Powell*, 54 Jones (1 Jones Eq.) 35 (1854). The latter case affirmed the inheritance rights of the children of a slave freed by her master, because Justice Richmond Pearson (who became Chief Justice five years later) would not apply to a slave the common-law rule that children born outside wedlock could not inherit.

25. See Eugene Genovese, *Roll, Jordan, Roll: The World the Slaves Made* (New York, Vintage, 1972); Gutman, *The Black Family;* Stevenson, *Life in Black and White;* Ann Patton Malone, *Sweet Chariot: Slave Family and Household Structure in Nineteenth-Century Louisiana* (Chapel Hill, U of North Carolina P, 1992).

26. See Genovese, *Roll*, 458–81; Malone, *Sweet Chariot*, 224–25. Stevenson, *Life in Black and White*, 228–33; Donna L. Franklin, *Ensuring Inequality: The Structural Transformation of the African-American Family* (New York, Oxford UP, 1997), 3–25.

27. From the 1842 narrative of Lunsford Lane, quoted in Albert J. Raboteau, *Slave Religion: The "Invisible Institution" in the Antebellum South* (New York, Oxford UP, 1978), 228, and see 125, 183–87; cf. William Wells Brown's novel *Clotel or, the President's Daughter,* ed. William Edward Farrison (New York, Carol Publishing, 1969: orig. 1853), 59–61, quoting answers from the Shiloh Baptist Association and the Savannah River Association.

28. John Gillis, *For Better or Worse: British Marriage, 1600 to the Present* (New York and London, Oxford UP, 1985), 185–209, 233–35; Bridget Hill, *Women, Work, and Sexual Politics in Eighteenth-Century England* (Oxford, Basil

Blackwell, 1989), 174–220; Anna Clark, *The Struggle for the Breeches* (Berkeley, U of California P, 1995), 42–51; Parker, *Informal Marriage*, 54–58; Rachel G. Fuchs and Leslie Page Moch, "Pregnant, Single, and Far from Home: Migrant Women in Nineteenth-Century Paris," *AHR*, 95 (Oct. 1990), 1007–32; Katherine A. Lynch, *Family, Class, and Ideology in Early Industrial France: Social Policy and the Working-Class Family, 1825–1848* (Madison, U of Wisconsin P, 1988), 90–91.

29. See *Nichols v. Stewart*, 15 Tex. 226 (1855), for a case of self-divorce and wife purchase; Baade, "Form of Marriage," esp. 5–8, 49–50, 78–79, 84–89; William R. Swagerty, "Marriage and Settlement Patterns of Rocky Mountain Trappers and Traders," *The Western History Quarterly*, 11:2 (April 1980), 159–80; John Mack Faragher, "'The Custom of the Country': Cross-Cultural Marriage in the Far Western Fur Trade," in *Western Women: Their Lands, Their Lives*, ed. Lillian Schlissel et al. (Albuquerque, U of New Mexico P, 1988); Susan Johnson, "Sharing Bed and Board: Cohabitation and Cultural Difference in Central Arizona Mining Towns, 1863–1873," in *The Women's West*, ed. Susan Armitage and Elizabeth Jameson (Norman, U of Oklahoma P, 1987), esp. 80–81; Miller, "Cross-Cultural Marriage"; Richard Griswold del Castillo, "La Familia Chicana: Social Changes in the Chicano Family of Los Angeles," *Journal of Ethnic Studies*, 3 (Spring 1975), 47.

30. See Harriet Chappell Owlsley, "The Marriages of Rachel Donelson," *Tennessee History Quarterly*, 36 (1977), 479–92; Norma Basch, "Marriage, Morals, and Politics in the Election of 1828," *JAH*, 80:3 (Dec. 1993), 890–919.

31. Caroline Johnson Harris, born a slave in 1843, recounted: "Didn't have to ask Marsa or nothin'. Just go to Ant Sue an' tell her you want to git mated. She tell us to think 'bout it hard fo' two days, 'cause marryin' was sacred in de eyes of Jesus. Arter two days Mose an' I went back an' say we done thought 'bout it an' still want to git married. Den she called all de slaves arter tasks to pray fo' de union." Aunt Sue also solemnized the marriage (in a broomstick ceremony) in this case. *The Negro in Virginia*, by the Writers' Program of the Works Progress Administration in Virginia (New York, Hastings House, 1940; reprint by Arno, 1969), 81.

32. See Merril D, Smith, *Breaking the Bonds: Marital Discord in Pennsylvania, 1730–1830* (New York, New York UP, 1991), 117–38; Clare A. Lyons, "Sex among the 'Rabble': Gender Transitions in the Age of Revolution, Philadelphia, 1750–1830," Ph.D. diss., Yale U., 1996; Brenda Stevenson, *Life in Black and White*, 140–42. Hartog, "Marital Exits," 95–98, 128–29, emphasizes that marrying meant "the public assumption of a relationship of rights and duties."

33. Quoted in David Montgomery, *Citizen Worker* (Cambridge and New York, Cambridge UP, 1993), 34.

34. Grossberg, *Governing,* 120–21; Susan E. Klepp and Billy G. Smith, "The Records of Gloria Dei Church: Marriages and 'Remarkable Occurrences,' 1794–1806," *Pennsylvania History,* 53:2 (April 1986), esp. 125–28; Timothy J. Gilfoyle, "The Hearts of Nineteenth-Century Men: Bigamy and Working-Class Marriage in New York City, 1800–1890," *Prospects,* 19 (1994), 135–60, esp. 148–49; Hartog, "Marital Exits," esp. 122–24; Norma Basch, "From the Bonds of Empire to the Bonds of Matrimony," in *Devising Liberty: Preserving and Creating Freedom in the New American Republic,* ed. David Thomas Konig (Stanford, Stanford UP, 1995), and "Relief in the Premises"; Lawrence Friedman, "Crimes of Mobility," in his *Crime and Punishment in American History* (New York, Basic Books, 1993), 197–201.

35. Gilfoyle, "Hearts of Men."

36. Ariela Dubler, "Governing through Contract: Common Law Marriage in the Nineteenth Century," *Yale LJ,* 107 (April 1998), 1887, stresses states' interest in private provision; Hartog, "Marital Exits"; *Rodebaugh v. Sanks,* 2 Watts 9, 10–11 (Pa. 1833), quoted in Grossberg, *Governing,* 74; *Sapp v. Newsom,* 27 Tex. 537 (1864), 540, quoted in Baade, "Form of Marriage," 78.

37. See Grossberg, *Governing,* esp. 65–83; *Archer v. Haithcock,* 51 N.C. 421 (1859), cited in Semonche, "Common-Law Marriage," 323–24; Larry A. Pacific, "Common Law Marriage in Mississippi," *Mississippi LJ,* 16 (1943), 40–65; Hendrik Hartog, *Man and Wife in America: A History* (Cambridge, Harvard UP, 2000), chap. 9.

38. Grossberg, *Governing,* 75–78; *Meister v. Moore,* 96 U.S. 76, 83, 81 (Oct. 1877); *Maryland v. Baldwin,* 112 U.S. 490, 494–95 (1884).

39. Colonial Delaware and South Carolina criminalized bastardy resulting from a black-white relationship, and colonial New York criminalized "adulterous intercourse," but not marriage. The 1724 "Black Code" promulgated by Louisiana's French royal governor forbade white subjects to marry blacks, and also forbade whites or free blacks to cohabit with slaves, under threat of heavy fines; a free black, however, could free a slave by marrying the person. Charles Gayarre, *History of Louisiana: The French Domination* (New York, Widdleton, 1867), 362–63, 531–32. Fowler, *Northern Attitudes,* 217–20, and appendix; see also George M. Fredrickson, *White Supremacy: A Comparative Study in American and South African History* (New York, Oxford UP, 1981), 100–08, 125–27, 145; Emily Field Van Tassel, " 'Only the Law Would Rule between Us': Antimiscegenation, the Moral Economy of Dependency, and the Debate over Rights after the Civil War," *Chicago-Kent LR,* 70 (1995), 873–926.

40. On Rome, see Gladys Harrison, "The Nationality of Married Women," *New York University Law Quarterly Review*, 9 (1932), 446; on England and Ireland, see J. Muldoon, "The Indian as Irishman," *Essex Institute Historical Collections*, 3 (Oct. 1978), 284; on Spanish America, see Gutierrez, *When Jesus Came, the Corn Mothers Went Away* (Stanford, Stanford UP, 1991), esp. 202, 315–17. Nazi Germany prohibited and criminalized marriage (and sex) between a German national of German blood and a Jew in a 1935 "racial law"; Kingsley Davis, "Intermarriage in Caste Societies," *American Anthropologist*, 43 (1941), 392–93. South Africa did not prohibit marriage and sex between black and white until the Nationalist regime instituted apartheid in 1948, according to Fredrickson, *White Supremacy*, 98.

41. Martha Hodes, *White Women, Black Men* (New Haven, Yale UP, 1998), 9, refuses to accept the term "interracial" marriage because it fixes "races"; she uses the phrase "marriage across the color line," which I borrow. On the courts' myriad difficulties in proving who was "white" and who "Negro or mulatto," see Eva Saks, "Representing Miscegenation Law," *Raritan* 8:2 (Fall 1988), 39–69.

42. Virginia Ingraham Burr, ed., *The Secret Eye: The Journal of Ella Gertrude Clanton Thomas, 1848–1889* (Chapel Hill, U of North Carolina P, 1990), 158 (Jan. 2, 1859). Davis, "Intermarriage," 381–86, argues that in caste societies, "hypergamy," or marriage between castes in which a lower-order woman assumes her spouse's caste upon marriage, can be allowed, to give upper-caste men more options; but this is precluded in a *racial* caste system because the lower-caste wife bears the marks of origin and the progeny cannot be passed off as of the higher caste.

43. Auguste Carlier, *Marriage in the United States*, trans. B. Joy Jeffries (New York, Leypoldt and Holt, 1867; reprint by Arno, 1972), 87.

44. *Armstrong v. Hodges*, 2 Ben. Monroe (Ky., 1841) 69, 70.

45. Fowler, *Northern Attitudes*, 167, 176–82. For the master artisan's worth, my thanks go to David Montgomery, and see his "Shuttle and the Cross," *Journal of Social History*, 5 (Summer 1972).

46. Fowler, *Northern Attitudes*, 154–55; Fredrickson, *White Supremacy*, 153; Lincoln-Douglas debate quoted in David Roediger, *The Wages of Whiteness: Race and the Making of the American Working Class* (London and New York, Verso, 1991), 142–43.

47. Fowler, *Northern Attitudes*, 156–65; Rowland Berthoff, "Conventional Mentality: Free Blacks, Women, and Business Corporations as Unequal Persons, 1820–1870," *JAH*, 76:2 (Dec. 1989), 773; Victoria Bynum, *Unruly Women: The Politics of Social and Sexual Control in the Old South* (Chapel Hill, U of North Carolina P, 1992), 97–98.

48. Civil cases (indicating consensual unions) outnumbered criminal cases in recorded appellate decisions, but there is no way to know whether the same was true at the trial level; Peggy Pascoe, "Miscegenation Law, Court Cases, and Ideologies of "Race" in Twentieth-Century America," *JAH*, 83:1 (June 1996), 50, n. 15; Berry, "Judging Morality," 839, 843. For examples of prosecutions, see Bynum, *Unruly*, 97–98; J. William Harris, *Plain Folk and Gentry in a Slave Society: White Liberty and Black Slavery in Augusta's Hinterlands* (Middletown, Wesleyan UP, 1985), 56–57. On long-term relationships between black and white individuals, see also John W. Blassingame, *Black New Orleans* (Chicago, U of Chicago P, 1973), 17–20, 202–210; Joel Williamson, *New People: Miscegenation and Mulattoes in the United States* (New York, Free P, 1980); Rogers, *Sex and Race;* Stevenson, *Black and White;* Hodes, *White Women, Black Men.*

49. Hodes, *White Women, Black Men.*

50. Thomas Brown, "The Miscegenation of Richard Mentor Johnson as an Issue in the National Election Campaign of 1835–36," *Civil War History*, 39:1 (1993), 5–30. The electoral vote for vice president was a tie, so the election went to the Senate, where the Democratic majority chose Johnson.

51. Joel Prentiss Bishop, *Commentaries on the Law of Marriage and Divorce* (Boston, Little Brown, vol. 1, 1864), 2.

52. Thomas Jefferson and Abigail Strong are quoted in Basch, "From the Bonds," to which I owe my view of Revolutionary-era divorce legislation.

53. Georgia statute quoted in George Elliot Howard, *A History of Matrimonial Institutions,* (New York, Humanities P, 1964; orig. 1904), 3:43–44.

54. Jefferson quoted in Basch, "Relief," 1; Lawrence M. Friedman, "Rights of Passage: Divorce Law in Historical Perspective," *Oregon LR,* 63 (1984), 654–55, emphasizes the economic point.

55. Carlier (who is not entirely reliable) believed the prohibitions on remarriage were easily evaded; *Marriage in the U.S.,* 116. Hartog, "Marital Exits," clarifies the adversarial nature of nineteenth-century divorce.

56. Jane Turner Censer, "Smiling through Her Tears": Ante-Bellum Southern Women and Divorce," *American Journal of Legal History,* 25 (1981), esp. 40–43.

57. Howard summarizes divorce legislation in *History of Matrimonial Institutions,* 3:3–160.

58. Howard, *Matrimonial Institutions,* 3:44–46; Roderick Phillips, *Putting Asunder: A History of Divorce in Western Society* (Cambridge and New York, Cambridge UP, 1988), 157, 400–02; Bloomfield, *American Lawyers,* 122; Lawrence B. Goodheart et al., " 'An Act for the Relief of Females . . . ': Divorce and the Changing Legal Status of Women in Tennessee, 1796–1860," *Tennessee*

Historical Quarterly, 44 (1985), esp. 340–41; Glenda Riley, *Divorce: An American Tradition* (New York, Oxford UP, 1991), 35; Censer, "Smiling," esp. 26–28; Norma Basch, *Framing American Divorce* (Berkeley, U of California P, 1999), 43–67; on the D.C. statute, see Martin Schultz, "Divorce in the South Atlantic States: Origins, Historical Patterns, and Recent Trends," *International Journal of Sociology of the Family,* 16 (1986), 234, 236. Historians no longer agree entirely that judicial divorce was more democratic than legislative petitions in the early period. "Pull" was required to succeed with a legislative petition, while moving divorce to the courts made it more widely accessible; but the expenses of a lawsuit may have been higher, and the system of applying to the legislature may have allowed an individual petitioner to succeed who would not have a case on statutory grounds. Richard H. Chused, *Private Acts in Public Places: A Social History of Divorce in the Formative Era of American Family Law* (Philadelphia, U of Pennsylvania P, 1994), 9–11, 109, disputes that the move to the courts constituted a liberalization.

59. See Howard, *Matrimonial Institutions,* vol. 3; quotation from Connecticut statute, 13; Karl N. Llewellyn, "Behind the Law of Divorce," *Columbia LR,* 33 (1933), 256–57, n. 12, n. 16; Martin Schultz, "Divorce in Early America: Origins and Patterns in Three North Central States," *Sociological Quarterly,* 25 (1984), 518–19.

60. For increases in divorce before 1860, see Schultz, "Divorce in Early America" and "Divorce in the South Atlantic"; Censer, "Smiling"; Chused, *Private Acts;* Riley, *Divorce,* 35–38, 60–65; Goodheart, "An Act"; on the 1850s, see James Harwood Barnett, *Divorce and the American Divorce Novel, 1858–1937* (New York, Russell and Russell, 1968), 24–29, including the newspaper citations and novel titles; *San Francisco Chronicle* of Feb. 2, 1854, quoted in Roger W. Lotchin, *San Francisco, 1846–1856* (New York, Oxford UP, 1974), 308, 293; on "divorce stories," see Basch, *Framing,* 147–86.

61. On Indiana, see Riley, *Divorce,* 62–66 (quotation from newspaper on 65). Between 1859 and 1873 Indiana increased its residency requirement and eliminated the omnibus clause.

62. Basch, *Framing American Divorce,* 53–56.

63. See Hartog, "Marital Exits," and *Man and Wife in America;* Basch, "Relief," 16; Basch, *Framing,* 43–67.

64. Richard H. Chused, "Married Women's Property Law: 1800–1850," *Georgetown LJ,* 71:5 (1983), 1359–1425, is the most complete treatment; also very helpful are Norma Basch, *In the Eyes of the Law: Women, Marriage, and Property in Nineteenth-Century New York* (Ithaca, Cornell UP, 1982), and "Invisible Women: The Legal Fiction of Marital Unity in Nineteenth-Century

America," *FS,* 5 (1979), 356–59; 1–32; Suzanne D. Lebsock, "Radical Reconstruction and the Property Rights of Southern Women," *Journal of Southern History,* 43 (May 1977), 195–216; Michael B. Dougan, "The Arkansas Married Woman's Property Law," *Arkansas Historical Quarterly,* 46 (Spring 1987), 3–26; Peter W. Bardaglio, *Reconstructing the Household: Families, Sex, and the Law in the Nineteenth-Century South* (Chapel Hill, U of North Carolina P, 1995), 31–34.

65. Chused, "Married Women's Property Law"; Basch, *In the Eyes* and "Invisible Woman"; Amy Dru Stanley, "Conjugal Bonds and Wage Labor: Rights of Contract in the Age of Emancipation," *JAH,* 75:2 (Sept. 1988), 471–500.

66. Helen Z. M. Rodgers, "Married Women's Earnings," *The Albany LJ,* 64 (1902), 384–86; Joseph Warren, "Husband's Right to Wife's Services," *Harvard LR,* 38 (Feb. 1925); Blanche Crozier, "Marital Support," *Boston University LR,* 15 (1935); Basch, "Invisible Woman"; Stanley, "Conjugal Bonds and Wage Labor," 495–98; Reva B. Siegel, "The Modernization of Marital Status Law: Adjudicating Wives' Rights to Earnings, 1860–1930," *Georgetown LJ,* 82 (Sept. 1994), 2127–2211; Bloomfield, *American Lawyers,* 114–15; Dougan, "Arkansas," 16–19.

67. Carole Shammas, "Re-assessing the Married Women's Property Acts," *Journal of Women's History,* 6:1 (Spring 1994), 9–30; Joan Hoff, *Law, Gender and Injustice: A Legal History of U.S. Women* (New York, New York UP, 1991), 127–31; Marylynn Salmon, "Republican Sentiment, Economic Change, and the Property Rights of Women in American Law," in *Women in the Age of the American Revolution,* ed. Ronald Hoffman and Peter J. Albert (Charlottesville, UP of Virginia, 1989), 474–75.

3. Domestic Relations on the National Agenda

1. *Noel v. Ewing,* 9 Ind. 37 (1857).

2. Peggy Cooper Davis, *Neglected Stories: The Constitution and Family Values* (New York, Hill and Wang, 1998), 30–40, 171–80, quotations of antislavery sentiment (including Stowe's) from 110 and 37; Ronald G. Walters, "The Erotic South: Civilization and Sexuality in American Abolitionism," *AQ,* 25 (May 1973), quotation from 192; see also Chris Dixon, *Perfecting the Family* (Amherst, U of Massachusetts P, 1997), esp. 21–45.

3. Bourne (1837), quoted in Amy Dru Stanley, "Home Life and the Morality of the Market," in *The Market Revolution in America,* ed. Melvyn Stokes and Stephen Conway (Charlottesville, UP of Virginia, 1996), 87–88; Ward quoted (sentences reversed) in Davis, *Neglected Stories,* 55. See Elizabeth B. Clark, "'The Sacred Rights of the Weak': Pain, Sympathy, and the Culture of Individual

Rights in Antebellum America," *JAH*, 82:3 (Sept. 1995), 463–93, and Karen Halttunen, "Humanitarianism and the Pornography of Pain in Anglo-American Culture," *AHR*, 100:2 (April 1995), 303–34.

4. T. Cobb, *An Inquiry into the Law of Negro Slavery in the United States of America* (1858), quoted in Karen Getman, "Sexual Control in the Slaveholding South: The Implementation and Maintenance of a Racial Caste System," *Harvard Women's Law Journal*, 7 (1984), 146. Orlando Patterson, *Slavery and Social Death: A Comparative Study* (Cambridge, Harvard UP, 1982), finds masters' sexual access to slave women characteristic of slave regimes.

5. See Michael P. Johnson, "Planters and Patriarchy: Charleston, 1800–1860," *Journal of Southern History*, 46 (Feb. 1980), 54.

6. Chesnut diary extract reprinted in *Root of Bitterness*, ed. Nancy F. Cott (New York, E. P. Dutton, 1972), 209.

7. Stephanie McCurry, *Masters of Small Worlds: Yeoman Households, Gender Relations, and the Political Culture of the Antebellum South Carolina Low Country* (New York, Oxford UP, 1995), 210; see also Elizabeth Fox-Genovese and Eugene Genovese, "The Divine Sanction of Social Order: Religious Foundations of the Southern Slaveholders' World View," *Journal of the American Academy of Religion*, 55:2 (Summer 1987), 211–33.

8. Ministers quoted by McCurry, *Masters*, 210–11, 217, and by Stanley, "Home Life," 86–87; see also Mitchell Snay, *The Gospel of Disunion: Religion and Separatism in the Antebellum South* (Cambridge and New York, Cambridge UP, 1993).

9. Quotation from Rev. Thornton Stringfellow, in Drew Faust, ed., *The Ideology of Slavery* (Baton Rouge, Louisiana State UP, 1981), 136.

10. Quotation from Anna Davison's diary, May 19, 1840 (Schlesinger Library, Radcliffe College); my thanks to Mary Maples Dunn for pointing this out. The Reverend Charles Colcock Jones attributed slaves' "degraded moral character" to a racial propensity for vice, to the fact that "they are *negroes*" (1842); quoted in Herbert Gutman, *The Black Family in Slavery and Freedom, 1750–1925* (New York, Random House, 1976), 295–96.

11. Benjamin M. Palmer [pastor, First Presbyterian Church, New Orleans], *The Family, in Its Civil and Churchly Aspects* (Richmond and New York, 1876)— a collection of prewar sermons, though published after the war. Thanks to Stephanie McCurry for suggesting this source. Historians of southern religion also neglect the denial of marriage to slaves; see Snay, *Gospel*. Not until the Confederacy's secession in 1861 was any substantial action taken to address the denial of marriage as contrary to God's law. At that point some congregations and denominations resolved to restore marriage to slaves; some governors and legis-

latures endorsed this position, to support the claim that slaveholding society was *more* moral than northern society based on free labor—but little of substance resulted. As a defender of the status quo in 1863 argued, "a legal recognition of marriage . . . would amount to a revolution in the status of the slave" because freedom to marry amounted to "a declaration of civil freedom"; "A Slave Marriage Law," *Southern Presbyterian Review,* 16 (Oct. 1863), 147–8. Drew Gilpin Faust, *The Creation of Confederate Nationalism* (Baton Rouge, Louisiana State UP, 1988), esp. 58–81; Willie Lee Rose, *Slavery and Freedom,* ed. William W. Freehling (New York, Oxford UP, 1982), 28; Eugene Genovese, *Roll Jordan Roll: The World the Slaves Made* (New York, Vintage, 1972), 52–53.

12. E.g., B. M. Palmer, *Family,* 11; George Fitzhugh, *Sociology for the South, or the Failure of Free Society* (New York, Burt Franklin, 1965; orig. 1855), 25. See Drew Gilpin Faust, ed. *The Ideology of Slavery: Proslavery Thought in the Antebellum South, 1830–1860* (Baton Rouge, Louisiana State UP, 1981), on southern treatises; Snay, *Gospel,* 82–87. Willie Lee Rose was the first to point out the "domestication of slavery," her phrase; see Genovese, *Roll, Jordan, Roll,* on "my family white and black."

13. McCurry, *Masters,* and "The Two Faces of Republicanism: Gender and Proslavery Politics in Antebellum South Carolina," *JAH,* 78:4 (1992), 1251–4.

14. McCurry, *Masters,* esp. 215; and "Two Faces"; Stanley, "Home Life."

15. See Nancy Leys Stepan, "Race, Gender, Science, and Citizenship," *Gender & History,* 10:1 (1998), 26–52; and Jacob Cogan, "The Look Within: Property, Capacity, and Suffrage in Nineteenth-Century America," *Yale LJ,* 107 (Nov. 1997), 473–98, on ideologies of "natural" differences.

16. Christopher Tomlins, "Subordination, Authority, Law: Subjects in Labor History," *International Labor and Working-Class History,* 47 (Spring 1995), 56–90.

17. McCurry, *Masters,* and "Two Faces," 1251; see also Elizabeth Fox-Genovese, *Within the Plantation Household* (Chapel Hill, U of North Carolina P, 1988); and Tomlins, "Subordination."

18. Fitzhugh, *Sociology,* 205–6. I was alerted to this remark by Stanley, "Home Life" 87.

19. See C. B. Macpherson, *The Political Theory of Possessive Individualism* (New York, Oxford UP, 1962); and Amy Dru Stanley, *From Bondage to Contract: Wage Labor, Marriage, and the Market in the Age of Slave Emancipation* (New York, Cambridge UP, 1998), 7.

20. See the views of Elizabeth Cady Stanton quoted in Blanche Glassman Hersh, *The Slavery of Sex* (Urbana, U of Illinois P, 1978), 199–200.

21. Stone, 1854, quoted in Hersh, *Slavery of Sex,* 198, 197; Rose, 1851, quoted in Françoise Basch, "Women's Rights and the Wrongs of Marriage in Mid-Nineteenth Century America," *History Workshop,* 22 (Fall 1986), 22.

22. Astell, *Some Reflections Upon Marriage,* quoted in Ruth Perry, "Mary Astell and the Feminist Critique of Possessive Individualism," *Eighteenth-Century Studies,* 23 (Summer 1990), 447, n. 10. *Roxana* reflected Astell's influence; see Ruth Perry, *The Celebrated Mary Astell* (Chicago, U of Chicago P, 1986), 330; see also Barbara Taylor, *Eve and the New Jerusalem* (New York, Pantheon, 1983), esp. 17–24.

23. See Eric Foner, *The Story of American Freedom* (New York, Norton, 1998); Edwin G. Burrows and Michael Wallace, "The American Revolution: The Ideology and Psychology of National Liberation," *Perspectives in American History,* 6 (1972), 165–306; Jay Fliegelman, *Prodigals and Pilgrims: The American Revolution against Patriarchal Authority, 1750–1800* (New York, Cambridge UP, 1980).

24. *Weekly Museum* (New York), Sept. 6, 1800; my thanks to Rosemarie Zagarri for pointing out the poem.

25. See Lydia Maria Child, *History of the Condition of Women, in Various Ages and Nations* (New York, 1835); Sarah Grimke, *Letters on the Equality of the Sexes and the Condition of Women* (Boston, 1838).

26. Reva B. Siegel "Home as Work: The First Women's Rights Claims concerning Wives' Household Labor, 1850–1880," *Yale LJ,* 103 (March 1994), 1073–1217; Basch, "Women's Rights"; Hersh, *Slavery of Sex;* Ellen C. DuBois, *Feminism and Suffrage* (Ithaca, Cornell UP, 1978); John Spurlock, *Free Love: Marriage and Middle-Class Radicalism in America, 1825–1860* (New York, New York UP, 1988), 141–42.

27. Frances Peters to Robert Peters, Feb. 22, 1851, quoted in Bertram Wyatt-Brown, *Southern Honor: Ethics and Behavior in the Old South* (New York, Oxford UP, 1982), 224; cf. Catherine Clinton, *The Plantation Mistress* (New York, Pantheon, 1982).

28. Halttunnen, "Humanitarianism."

29. Quotations from Stone in Ellen Carol DuBois, "Outgrowing the Compact of the Fathers: Equal Rights, Woman Suffrage, and the United States Constitution, 1820–1878," *JAH,* 74:3 (Dec. 1987), 842–43; Leslie Wheeler, ed., *Loving Warriors: Selected Letters of Lucy Stone and Henry B. Blackwell, 1853 to 1893* (New York, Dial, 1981), 186; and Basch, "Women's Rights," 25–26. Thomas Wentworth Higginson, who conducted the Stone-Blackwell wedding, published the words (and a defense) of the antilegal ceremony in two newspapers (one, Garrison's *Liberator*). The French traveler Auguste Carlier noted in

amazement this open flouting of the law; *Marriage in the United States*, trans. B. Joy Jeffries (New York, Arno, 1972; orig. 1867), 59–63.

30. Stanton quoted in Joan Hoff, *Law, Gender, and Injustice: A Legal History of U.S. Women* (New York, New York UP, 1991), 276.

31. John Spurlock, *Free Love: Marriage and Middle-Class Radicalism in America, 1825–1860* (New York, New York UP, 1988); Ann Braude, *Radical Spirits* (Boston, Beacon, 1989), esp. 117–41.

32. Spurlock, *Free Love; New York Daily Times*, Sept.8, 1855; T. L. Nichols and Mary S. Gove Nichols, *Marriage: Its History, Character, and Results* (New York, T. L. Nichols, 1854).

33. Speech of Julia Branch, "The Free Convention" [pamphlet], Rutland, Vt., 55. Spurlock, *Free Love*, esp. chap. 5.

34. Edward F. Underhill to the editor, *New York Daily Times*, June 25, 1858, 2; see Karen Lystra, *Searching the Heart: Women, Men, and Romantic Love in Nineteenth-Century America* (New York, Oxford UP, 1989).

35. "A Bad Book Gibbeted," *New York Daily Times*, Aug. 17, 1855, 2.

36. Blackwell to Lucy Stone, Sept. 17, 1855, in Wheeler, *Loving Warriors*, 147.

37. See Taylor, *Eve*.

38. Catharine Beecher, *A Treatise on Domestic Economy* (1841), excerpted in *Root of Bitterness*, ed. Cott, 175.

39. Taylor, *Eve*, xiv–xv; Louis J. Kern, *An Ordered Love* (Chapel Hill, U of North Carolina P, 1981), 4.

40. See Charles E. Nordhoff, *Communistic Societies of the United States* [1875] (New York, Dover, 1966), and John Humphrey Noyes, *History of American Socialisms* [1870] (New York, Dover, 1966).

41. *New York Daily Times*, Sept. 8, 1855.

42. The community began in Putney, Vermont, in the 1840s, and moved to Oneida in 1847 after Noyes was prosecuted for adultery. Complex marriage became known by 1850; Spurlock, *Free Love*, 82, 240, n. 12; Glenda Riley, *Divorce: An American Tradition* (New York, Oxford UP, 1991), 217, n. 24.

43. Sarah Barringer Gordon, "'Our National Hearthstone': Anti-Polygamy Fiction and the Sentimental Campaign against Moral Diversity in Antebellum America," *Yale Journal of Law and the Humanities*, 8 (Summer 1996), 295–350.

44. Sen. William Seward, April 9, 1856, quoted in Richard D. Poll, "The Mormon Question Enters National Politics, 1850–1856," *Utah History Quarterly*, 14 (April 1957), 124, and see 120–27; also see Orma Linford, "The Mormons and the Law: The Polygamy Cases," *Utah LR*, part 1, 9:1 (Summer 1964), 312–13.

45. Poll, "Mormon Question," 127; Eric Foner, *Free Soil, Free Labor, Free Men* (New York, Oxford UP, 1970), 130; Davis, *Neglected Stories*, 54–57.

46. Linford, "Mormons and the Law," 309–14; Richard S. Van Wagoner, *Mormon Polygamy: A History* (Salt Lake City, Signature, 1986), 83–87.

47. Several congressmen who linked polygamy with slavery were Roger A. Pryor of Va., John S. Millson of Va., April 2, 1860; Clement Vallandigham of Ohio, April 3, 1860; Lawrence Branch of N.C., April 4, 1860, *CG* 36/1 (36th Cong., 1st sess.), 1494, 1496, 1519, 1542; Sumner, June 4, 1860, *CG* 36/1, 2590–2603, quotations from 2592, 2596. Republicans continued to link slavery with polygamy and barbarism through the Civil War: see, e.g., *CG* 38/1, 2948. Conversely, antipolygamists condemned polygamy by calling it a form of slavery; Gordon, "Hearthstone," 325–26.

48. *CG* 36/1, April 3, 1860, 1519 (William H. Hooper of Utah excepted).

49. See the remarks by Pryor, April 2, 1860, *CG* 36/1, 1496. The southern polemicist George Fitzhugh had earlier portrayed Mormonism as a logical outcome of the pernicious northern values of "liberty, equality, and fraternity." "Shakers, and Oneida Perfectionists and Mormons," he wrote sardonically, "are the legitimate fruits of modern progress." Fitzhugh, *Sociology*, 195.

50. Etheridge, April 2, 1860, *CG* 36/1, 1496.

51. Pryor, April 2, 1860, *CG* 36/1, 1494.

52. See *CG* 36/1, April 5, 1860, 1559; *CG* 37/2, April 28, 1862, 1847–48; June 3, 1862, 2506–07.

53. See *CG* 38/1, March 28, 1864, 1439; June 14, 1864, 2948.

4. Toward a Single Standard

1. Sarah Barringer Gordon, "'The Liberty of Self-Degradation': Polygamy, Woman Suffrage, and Consent in Nineteenth-Century America," *JAH*, 83:3 (Dec. 1996), 838–39 (quoting Lincoln's famous remark of 1858); Lincoln's second annual message to Congress, 1862, quoted in Wai Chee Dimock, *Empire for Liberty* (Princeton, Princeton UP, 1988), 27; see also Nina Silber, "Intemperate Men, Spiteful Women, and Jefferson Davis: Northern Views of the Defeated South," *AQ*, 41 (Dec. 1989), 614–35; Norma Basch, *Framing American Divorce* (Berkeley, U of California P, 1999), 128–31.

2. See Anne Firor Scott, *The Southern Lady* (Chicago, U of Chicago P, 1970); Drew Gilpin Faust, *Mothers of Invention* (Chapel Hill, U of North Carolina P, 1996); Mary E. Massey, *Bonnet Brigades* (New York, Knopf, 1966); Catherine Clinton and Nina Silber, ed., *Divided Houses: Gender and the Civil War* (New York, Oxford UP, 1992).

3. Maris Vinovskis, "Have Social Historians Lost the Civil War? Some Preliminary Demographic Speculations," *JAH,* 76:1 (June 1989), 35–39.

4. *CG* 39/1, Feb. 2, 1866, 602.

5. Eric Foner, *Reconstruction: America's Unfinished Revolution, 1863–77* (New York, Harper & Row, 1988), 251–52; Ellen Carol DuBois, "Outgrowing the Compact of the Fathers: Equal Rights, Woman Suffrage, and the United States Constitution, 1820–1878," *JAH,* 74:3 (Dec. 1987), 844–60.

6. C. A. White, *CG* 38/2, Jan. 10, 1865, 215.

7. *CG* 38/1, April 7, 1864, 1465; April 8, 9, 1864, 1482–83, 1488–89; see Patricia Lucie, "On Being a Free Person and a Citizen by Constitutional Amendment," *Journal of American Studies,* 12 (1978), 343–58; Amy Dru Stanley, "Conjugal Bonds and Wage Labor: Rights of Contract in the Age of Emancipation," *JAH,* 75:2 (Sept. 1988), 471–81.

8. *CG* 36/1, April 2, 1860, 1498, 1500; *CG* 38/1, March 28, 1864, 1324; see also 1369, 1479.

9. On this parallel during Reconstruction, see Amy Dru Stanley "Home Life and the Morality of the Market," in *The Market Revolution in America,* ed. Melvyn Stokes and Stephen Conway (Charlottesville, UP of Virginia, 1996), and *From Bondage to Contract: Wage Labor, Marriage, and the Market in the Age of Slave Emancipation* (New York, Cambridge UP, 1998).

10. Helen E. Brown, *John Freeman and His Family* (Boston, American Tract Society, 1864, 1866; reprint New York, AMS Press, 1980), quotations on 67, 75–77; see also Clinton B. Fisk [assistant commissioner of the Freedmen's Bureau], *Plain Counsels for Freedmen: In Sixteen Brief Lectures* (Boston, American Tract Society, 1866; reprint New York, AMS Press, 1980), esp. 27, 40–41, 47.

11. *CG* 38/1, Feb. 23, 1864, 774.

12. Cf. Elsa Barkley Brown, "Negotiating and Transforming the Public Sphere: African American Political Life in the Transition from Slavery to Freedom," *Public Culture,* 7 (1994), 107–46.

13. See, e.g., Circular, HQ Asst. Comm. for the state of North Carolina, July 1, 1865, H.R., *Exec. Docs.*, 39/1 (39th Cong., 1st sess.), 1866, vol. 8, 2–3.

14. Ira Berlin and Leslie S. Rowland, ed., *Families and Freedom: A Documentary History* (New York, New P, 1997), 156; report by Col. John Eaton, Jr., chaplain of the 27th O.V. and Gen. Supt. of Freedmen, to Lt. Col. Jno. A. Rawlins, AAG, April 29, 1863 [K-89], also published in *Freedom: A Documentary History of Emancipation, 1861–1867,* ed. Ira Berlin et al., ser. 1, vol. 3, *The Wartime Genesis of Free Labor: The Lower South* (New York, Cambridge UP, 1990), 686–98. Instead of full archival citations for documents from the Bureau of Refugees, Freedmen, and Abandoned Lands such as this one, I have

given in brackets the numbers assigned to the documents by the Freedmen and Southern Society Project of the University of Maryland at College Park (a selection of 50,000 or more documents from the National Archives Record Group 105)—e.g., K-89 for the report just cited.

15. Herbert Gutman, *The Black Family in Slavery and Freedom, 1750–1925* (New York, Random House, 1976), 18; Laura F. Edwards, "'The Marriage Covenant Is at the Foundation of All Our Rights': The Politics of Slave Marriages in North Carolina after Emancipation," *Law and History Review*, 14:1 (Spring 1996), 90; chaplain, 54th Regt USCT, Little Rock, to Brig. Gen. L. Thomas, Feb. 28, 1865, in Berlin, ed. *Families*, 163–64; C. W. Buckley, Chaplain, 47th Regt. USCT, Vicksburg, to Lt. A. R. Mills, Aug. 1, 1864 [K-541], and Feb. 1, 1865 [K-508]; James Peet, Chaplain, 50th Regt. USCT, Vicksburg, to A. R. Mills, Sept. 30, 1864 [K-549]; see also [C 1014].

16. Quoted in Peggy Cooper Davis, *Neglected Stories: The Constitution and Family Values* (New York, Hill and Wang, 1998), 12.

17. Job S. Bass, Chaplain, 90th Regt. N.Y. Volunteers, to Maj. Gen. Ganks, commanding Dept. of the Gulf, New Orleans, June 17, 1864 [C 558]; Victor B. Howard, *Black Liberation in Kentucky: Emancipation and Freedom, 1862–1884* (Lexington, UP of Kentucky, 1983), 120–21; see the affidavit of Clarissa Burdett, March 27, 1865, in *Freedom: A Documentary History of Emancipation, 1861–67*, ed. Ira Berlin et al., ser. 1, vol. 1, *The Destruction of Slavery* (New York, Cambridge UP, 1985), 615–16.

18. Freedmen's Aid Society leaders in Boston, New York, Philadelphia, and Cincinnati to President Lincoln, Dec. 1, 1863, read into the *CG,* 38/2, Feb. 9, 1865, 690.

19. See *CG* 38/2, Feb. 22, 1865, 983–8. The bill creating the bureau passed as a war measure on March 3, 1865, after contentious discussion of the unprecedented extent of federal power involved; text in H.R., *Exec. Docs.*, 39/1, 1866, vol. 8, 81–82. See George Bentley, *A History of the Freedmen's Bureau* (Phila., U of Pennsylvania P, 1955); Donald G. Nieman, *To Set the Law in Motion: The Freedmen's Bureau and the Legal Rights of Blacks, 1865–1868* (Millwood, N.Y., KTO P, 1979).

20. H.R., *Exec. Docs*, 39/1, 1866, vol. 8, 16–18, 21–22, publishes Howard's initial circular announcing the policy and the rescinding of it; Foner, *Reconstruction*, 159; William S. McFeely, *Yankee Stepfather: General O. O. Howard and the Freedmen* (New Haven, Yale UP, 1968) esp. 102–09, 311, 320.

21. See H.R., *Exec. Doc.*, 39/1, 1866, vol. 8, 34–35, 64–65; for models of contracts, see 44–46, 60–61, 89–90. Freedmen were first "exhorted" to "select" their employers and contract with them; by December 1865 a bureau circular

said this was "imperative," and if they neglected to do so, bureau agents would "have the right, and it shall be their duty, to make contracts for them."

22. Unsigned editorial, "The Marriage Institution among the Southern Negroes," *New York Times*, Aug. 26, 1866, 4. Prior to Stanley, *From Bondage to Contract,* whose work highlights the bureau's concern with marriage, historians generally failed to recognize how important this issue was, but see McFeely, *Yankee Stepfather,* 131; Bentley, *History,* 86–87.

23. Laura Towne, a teacher at Port Royal, S.C., testimony to AFIC, file 3A, Dept. of the South [K-73]; see Willie Lee Rose, *Rehearsal for Reconstruction* (Indianapolis, Bobbs Merrill, 1964), 236; the AFIC final report is in *The War of the Rebellion: A Compilation of the Official Records,* ser. 3, vol. 4 (Washington, D.C., 1900), 328; see also ser. 2, vol. 3, 436.

24. Quoted in Berlin, ed., *Freedom,* ser. 1, vol. 3, 858–59. See also "The Future of the Sea Island People—the Immoralities Which They Practice—How They May Be Corrected," a letter from Beaufort, S.C., April 11, 1867, published in the *New York Times,* April 20, 1867.

25. O. O. Howard, Circular No. 5, May 30, 1865, H.R., *Exec. Docs.,* 39/1, 1866, vol. 8, 101–03, intended to assure "the unity of families and all the rights of the family relation"; see Oliver Otis Howard, *Autobiography of Oliver Otis Howard,* vol. 2 (Freeport, N.Y., Books for Libraries P, 1971; orig. 1907), 225, 223.

26. General Orders No. 8, "Marriage Rules," HQ Asst. Comm., BRFAL, S.C., Ga., and Fla., Aug. 11, 1865 [A-11033]; handwritten circular from the HQ of the 1st Colored Brigade, A.C., Chattanooga, Tenn., May 29, 1865 [C-2061]. Circular No. 1 issued by Brevet Maj. Gen. John B. Sanborn, head of the commission for regulating relations between freedmen in the Indian Territory and their former masters, Jan. 1, 1866, promised to uphold freedmen's marriages solemnized in Indian fashion, but warned that "the system of polygamy or plurality of wives" adopted by some freedmen must be abandoned, since it violated federal law [S-22].

27. Circular No. 7, Office of Asst. Comm., Miss., Vicksburg, July 29, 1865, H.R., *Exec. Docs.,* 39/1, 1866, vol. 8, 154–56; Peter Kolchin, *First Freedom: The Responses of Alabama's Blacks to Emancipation and Reconstruction* (Westport, Conn., Greenwood P, 1972), 58–59. Gen. Swayne's intent was superseded by the Alabama state government's declaration that all couples living together were considered married and their children legitimate.

28. Clinton B. Fisk [Brevet Maj. Gen. and Asst. Comm.], report of Jan. 23, 1866, to Gen. Howard, and "Address to Freedmen," Dec. 26, 1865; H.R., *Exec. Dos.,* 39/1, 1866, vol. 8, 231–33; see also Joel Williamson, *After Slavery: The Negro in South Carolina during Reconstruction, 1861–1877* (Chapel Hill, U

of North Carolina P, 1965), 309. Many other examples could be cited, e.g., [A-4212]. Even amidst the atrocities they often had to report in 1865–66, assistant commissioners frequently mentioned marriage problems.

29. Rev. Henry McNeal Turner, quoted in Catherine Clinton, "Bloody Terrain: Freedwomen, Sexuality, and Violence during Reconstruction," *Georgia History Quarterly*, 76:2 (Summer 1992), 31. Many scholars have commented on freedpeople's eager welcome of legal marriage, beginning with Gutman, *Black Family*, esp. 412–29, and Leon Litwack, *Been in the Storm So Long: The Aftermath of Slavery* (New.York, Random House, 1979), 240–41, both of whom stress ex-slaves' understanding of marriage as an exercise of civil rights. See, e.g., [A-1098]; Roberta Sue Alexander, *North Carolina Faces the Freedmen: Race Relations during Presidential Reconstruction, 1865–67* (Durham, Duke UP, 1985), 58–65; Davis, *Neglected Stories*, 30–40. Edwards, "'The Marriage Covenant,'" 99–111, recognizes resistance as well as positive response.

30. "Negro Suffrage and Polygamy," *New York World*, Oct. 12, 1865; untitled response in *New York Tribune*, Oct 13, 1865, 4; "Negro Suffrage and Polygamy," ibid., Oct. 14, 1865, 4. I was alerted to these articles by Gutman, *Black Family*, 297. See Kolchin, *First Freedom*, 58, on southern newspapers mocking the possibility of Negro fidelity.

31. C. W. Buckley, Asst. Supt. of Freedmen, Montgomery Co., Ala., Sept. 1, 1865, monthly report to Brig. Gen. Swayne, Comm. of Ala. [A-1604]; see also [A-9495].

32. Pension file of Joseph E. Williams, WC 471957 [P-67]; cf. Joe M. Richardson, *The Negro in the Reconstruction of Florida, 1865–1877* (Tallahassee, Florida State UP, 1965), 29–32. Monthly report, F. E. Grossman, Capt. and Subassistant Comm., Lake City, Fla., Sept. 1, 1866, to Maj. S. L. McHenry, AAG, Talahassee [A-1098]; see also the annual report from E. B. Duncan, Supt. of Education., Tallahassee, Oct. 31, 1866 [A-1061]; and George Book, Lt. V.R.C. and Supt., Staunton, Va., to Capt. R. B. Lacy, Supt. of the South District, Va., June 30, 1866 [A-7445]. Many documents show the Freedmen's Bureau ceding authority to states: e.g., Circular no. 5, Georgia Freedmen's Bureau, Brig. Gen. Davis Tillson Acting Asst. Comm., April 7, 1866 [A-10919]. Secondary sources on southern states legitimizing ex-slaves' marriages include Gutman, *Black Family*, 419–20; Alexander, *North Carolina*, 47; Howard, *Black Liberation*, 122–25.

33. A. B. Sweeney Supt., Stanardville, Va., to Maj. T. F. T. Crandon, Supt. of 4th District, April 30, 1866 [A-7434]. For other instances of white southern resistance, see J. S. Taylor, Lt. and Supt., Hamburg, Ark., to Capt. D. H. Williams, AAG, Little Rock, Sept. 5, 1866 [A-2599]; W. H. Cornelius, 1st Lt.

and Agent, St. Martinville, La., April 16, 1866, to Capt A. F. Hayden, AAG, New Orleans [A-8734]; L. D. Burwell, Agent, Rome, Ga., Mar. 12, 1866, to Davis Tillson, AAG, Augusta, Ga., [A-5313]; Samuel Martin to T. D. Elliott, Esq., Glasgow, Ky., Dec. 30, 1867 [A-36].

34. C. J. True, Supt., 5th District, Maysville, Ky., to Brevet Col. R. E. Johnston, Chief Supt., Lexington, Ky., Sept. 30, 1866 [A-4447]; James F. Bolton, Lt. V.R.C. and Supt., Columbus, Ky., Oct. 2, 1866, to [illeg.] Tice, Esq, Commonwealth Attorney [A-4601].

35. J. R. Johnson, Supt. of Marriages, 5th District, Va., to Col. S. P. Lee, Comm. for Freedmen, Alexandria, Freedmen's Village, June 30, 1866 [A-9975], reprinted in Berlin, ed., *Freedom,* ser. 2 (1982), 672–73; Philip Jones, Greensboro, N.C., to General, Sept. 4, 1866 [A-543]; J. E. Eldridge, Bladenboro, N.C., to Agent of the Freedmen's Bureau, Wilmington, N.C., July 29, 1867, in Berlin, ed., *Families,* 172–73; see also [A-642].

36. J. R. Stone, Brevet Maj. and Subassistant Comm., Petersburg, Va., to Capt. Garrick Mallery, AAAG, Richmond, Va., June 18, 1867 [A-7769]. Arkansas agents similarly reported a "deplorable state of morals," with "promiscuous cohabitation" the "universal custom." W. J. Dawes, Brevet Maj. and General Supt., Arkansas River District, Pine Bluffs, Nov. 30, 1866, to Maj. John Tyler, AAAG [A-2474]; and see [A-2471] and [A-2336].

37. W. H. Gregory to Gen. C. B. Fisk, Columbia, [Tenn.], Jan. 18, 1866 [A-6127]. An agent from Texas said he saw "an inclination on the part of man and wife to sepperate *[sic]*" when family responsibilities became "incumbrances." A. P. Delano, Subassistant Comm., to Capt C. C. Morse, AAG, Marlin Falls Co., Tex., March 26, 1866 [A-3207].

38. See Edwards, "Marriage Covenant," 106–11.

39. Report from HQ Asst. Comm. Charleston, S.C., Nov. 1, 1866, in Sen. *Exec. Docs.,* 39/2, 1866–67, vol. 1, Doc. No. 6, 124–25. Even when testifying to "numerous instances of as ardent and enduring conjugal love, instances of as true fidelity . . . as are found in other races," Mansfield French, the Freedmen's Bureau supervisor of marriage relations of the freedmen, dwelt on the difficulties of regularizing freedmen's marital responsibilities; M. French to Brevet Maj. Gen. R. K. Scott, Asst. Comm., S.C., Nov. 6, 1866 [A-7004].

40. Report of HQ Division of the Potomac, Richmond, Va., Oct. 27, 1866, in Sen. *Exec. Docs.,* 39/2, 1866–67, vol. 1, doc. no. 6, 162–63.

41. William. McCullough, Lt. and Supt., Devalls Bluff, Ark., March 31, 1866, to Capt. D. H. Williams, AAG [A-2450]; T. Sargent Free, Asst. Inspector Gen. for the state of Mississippi, to Col. Samuel Thomas, Asst. Comm. of Freedmen, Miss., Sept. 9, 1865 [A-9033].

42. General Orders No. 8, "Marriage Rules," HQ Asst. Comm., BRFAL, S.C., Ga., and Fla., Aug. 11, 1865 [A-11033].

43. W. H. Horton, Subassistant Comm., Wharton, Tex., to Lt. J. T. Kirkman, AAAG, Galveston, April 3, 1867 [A-3059]; J. W. McConaughey, Subassistant Comm., Wharton, Tex., to Col. William. Sinclair, AAG, March 28, 1866 [A-3270]; W. H. Gregory to Gen. C. B. Fisk, Columbia, [Tenn.], Jan. 18, 1866 [A-6127]; William H. Rock, Subassistant. Comm., Richmond, Tex., to Lt. J. T. Kirkman, AAAG, March 6, 1867 [A-3052]; William. L. Tidball, Capt. V.R.C. and Asst. Supt., Urbana, Va., to Capt. James A. Bates, AAAG, Richmond, April 30, 1866 [A-7433]. Additional examples of male nonsupport are in [A-10216, A-4605, A-574]; affadavit, July 24, 1866, in Berlin, ed. *Families, 7.*

44. Saxton quoted in McFeely, *Yankee Stepfather,* 146; see also 50–54, 102–03, 126–31, 320–21; Foner, *Reconstruction,* 87.

45. HQ BFRAL, New Orleans, Dec. 4, 1865, Circular No. 29, H.R. *Exec. Docs.,* 39/1, 1866, vol. 8, 30–32; Foner, *Reconstruction,* 87; Stanley, *From Bondage,* 43–45; see McFeely, *Yankee Stepfather,* 151–52, for a typical contract for family labor. See also William A. Britton, Supt., Arkadelphia, Ark., Aug. 3, 1866, to Brevet Gen. J. W. Sprague, Asst. Comm., Mo. and Ark. [A-2422]; and Daniel Mandell, "Shifting Boundaries of Race and Ethnicity: Indian-Black Intermarriage in Southern New England, 1760–1880," *JAH,* 85 (Sept. 1998), 496–98.

46. On the husband's persistent right, see Joseph Warren, "Husband's Right to Wife's Services," *Harvard LR,* 38 (Feb. 1925), part 1, 421–46, part 2, 622–50; Norma Basch, "Invisible Women: The Legal Fiction of Marital Unity in Nineteenth-Century America," *FS,* 5:2 (Summer 1979), 346–66; Richard H. Chused, "Married Women's Property Law: 1800–1850," *Georgetown LJ,* 71:5 (June 1983), 1359–1425; Amy Dru Stanley, "Conjugal Bonds and Wage Labor: Rights of Contract in the Age of Emancipation," *JAH,* 75:2 (Sept. 1988), 471–500; Reva B. Siegel, "The Modernization of Marital Status Law: Adjudicating Wives' Rights to Earnings, 1860–1930," *Georgetown LJ,* 82:7 (Sept. 1994), 2127–2211.

47. See Robert J. Steinfeld, "Property and Suffrage in the Early American Republic," *Stanford LR,* 41:2 (1989), 335–76, on the shift from property-ownership to self-ownership, or command of one's own labor, as the warrant for political participation.

48. Jacob Howard, Rep. of Mich., Jan. 30, 1866, *CG* 39/1, 504. Abolitionists had used similar rhetoric since the 1830s, to emphasize the (male) slave's deprivation; see Stanley, "Conjugal Bonds and Wage Labor" and *From Bondage,*

esp. 26–29, 50–55, 129–35; I follow her argument that Republican visions of civil rights for freedmen upheld both free labor and husbands' marital privileges.

49. Rep. Thomas D. Eliot, Rep. of Mass., May 23, 1866, *CG* 39/1, 2779.

50. On the sentimental strategy, see Laura Hanft Korobkin, "The Maintenance of Mutual Confidence: Sentimental Strategies at the Adultery Trial of Henry Ward Beecher," *Yale Journal of Law and the Humanities*, 7:1 (Winter 1995), 1–48.

51. *CG* 39/1, Jan. 30, 1966, 504. See also Rep. Ebon Ingersoll of Ill., *CG* 38/1, June 15, 1864, 2990.

52. Kasson of Iowa, *CG* 38/2, Jan. 12, 1865, 193.

53. Farnsworth, *CG* 38/2, Jan. 10, 1865, 200. See Lucie, "On Being a Free Person," 350; Lea S. VanderVelde, "The Labor Vision of the Thirteenth Amendment," *U of Pennsylvania LR*, 138:2 (Dec. 1989), 454–58, 475–81; Davis, *Neglected Stories;* and Stanley, *From Bondage.*

54. The political vocabulary of that time differentiated "natural" rights (personal security and liberty, which government was formed to protect); "civil rights" (effected by government to protect natural rights); "political rights" (suffrage, office-holding, jury, and military duty); and a fourth category, "social" rights, which was vaguer and more contested, having to do with social relations and the choice of friends and business associations, matters generally seen as beyond the reach of legislation. See Foner, *Reconstruction,* 231; Mark Tushnet, "The Politics of Equality in Constitutional Law: The Equal Protection Clause, Dr. Du Bois, and Charles Hamilton Houseton," *JAH,* 74:3 (Dec. 1987), 886–89; Nina Morais, "Sex Discrimination and the Fourteenth Amendment: Lost History," *Yale LJ,* 97 (1988), 1157–58; Sandra Rierson, "Race and Gender Discrimination: A Historical Case for Equal Treatment under the Fourteenth Amendment," *Duke Journal of Gender Law & Policy,* 1 (1994), 111–14; Robert J. Kaczorowski, "To Begin the Nation Anew: Congress, Citizenship, and Civil Rights," *AHR,* 92:1 (Feb. 1987), 48–49.

55. Trumbull, in the debate on the civil rights bill of 1866, *CG* 39/1, April 4, 1866, 1757.

56. My thanks to Akhil Amar for helpful guidance on this issue. Trumbull, ibid.; Bingham, *CG* 37/2, April 11, 1862, 1639; see also Rep. James Wilson of Iowa, *CG* 39/1, March 1, 1866, 1117; Rep. William Windom of Minn., March 2, 1866, 1159; Sen. Henry Wilson of Mass., March 7–8 1866, 1255.

57. Rowland Berthoff finds that delegates to state constitutional conventions throughout the mid-nineteenth century assigned *femes coverts,* widows, and single women all to "the self-same boat of dependency" in "Conventional

Mentality: Free Blacks, Women, and Business Corporations as Unequal Persons, 1820–1870," *JAH*, 76:2 (Dec. 1989), 760.

58. See Foner, *Reconstruction*, esp. 228–80; DuBois, "Outgrowing the Compact," esp. 844–47; Kaczorowski, "To Begin," 48–49.

59. DuBois, "Outgrowing the Compact," 847–49, quotation on 848.

60. *CG* 39/1, 63, 2767; William E. Nelson, *The Fourteenth Amendment: From Political Principle to Judicial Doctrine* (Cambridge, Harvard UP, 1988) 138.

61. Quoted in Martha Hodes, *White Women, Black Men* (New Haven, Yale UP, 1998), 169, and see generally 147–75.

62. See Rep. Samuel Cox of Ohio, *CG* 38/1, Feb. 17, 1864, 710–11, and the response of Rep. Hiram Price, March 1, 1864, 888–89; likewise Rep. William Kelley of Pa., Feb. 23, 1864, 773–74.

63. George M. Fredrickson, *The Black Image in the White Mind: The Debate on Afro-American Character and Destiny, 1817–1914* (New York, Harper & Row, 1971), 74–90, 160–74.

64. New bans were passed in Alabama, Arizona, Colorado, Idaho, Mississippi, Nevada, Ohio, Oregon, South Carolina, and West Virginia. David H. Fowler, *Northern Attitudes towards Interracial Marriage* (New York, Garland, 1987), 265–55 and appendix. The South Carolina constitution of 1868 repealed that state's ban, which was reinstated in 1879.

65. Cowan, *CG* 39/1, Feb. 2, 1866, 603.

66. James D. Richardson, ed., *A Compilation of the Messages and Papers of the Presidents*, 10 vols. (Washington, D.C., Government Printing Office, 1896–99), 6:407–8.

67. *CG* 39/1, Feb. 2, 1866, 600.

68. *CG* 39/1, Feb. 3, 1866, 632.

69. Steven A. Bank, "Anti-Miscegenation Laws and the Dilemma of Symmetry: The Understanding of Equality in Civil Rights Act of 1875," *U of Chicago Law School Roundtable*, 2:1 (1995), esp. 319–23; Bank calls this usual justification the doctrine of "symmetrical equality." See, in *CG* 39/1, Sen. Reverdy Johnson, [Dem.] of Md., Jan. 30, 1866, 505–06; Sen. Garrett Davis, [Dem.] of Ky., Sen. Lyman Trumbull of Ill., and Sen. Edgar Cowan of Pa., Feb. 2, 1866, 598–604; Rep. Samuel Marshall, [Dem.] of Ill., Feb. 3, 1866, 629; and Rep. Andrew Rogers, [Dem.] of N.J., May 10, 1866, 2538.

70. *Pace v. Alabama*, 106 U.S. 583 (1883). Cf. *Dred Scott v. Sandford*, 60 U.S. 393 (1857), 409, 413–14, citing marriage bans as evidence of the inferior civic position of blacks.

71. See Robert Hale, "Coercion and Distribution in a Supposedly Non-coercive State," *Political Science Quarterly,* 38 (1923); Morris R. Cohen, "Property and Sovereignty," *Cornell Law Quarterly,* 13 (1927); Betty Mensch, "Freedom of Contract as Ideology," *Stanford LR,* 83 (1981), 752–72.

72. Fowler, *Northern Attitudes,* 234 and appendix; Harvey Applebaum, "Miscegenation Statutes," *Georgetown LJ,* 53 (1964), esp. 56–57; Michael Grossberg, "Crossing Boundaries: Nineteenth-Century Domestic Relations Law and the Merger of Family and Legal History," *American Bar Foundation Research Journal,* 1985:4, 823; Nelson, *Fourteenth Amendment,* 152. During Reconstruction two southern state supreme courts struck down intermarriage bans on the reasoning that marriage was a contract as defined in the Civil Rights Act. *Burns v. State,* 48 Ala. 195 (1872), was quickly overruled in *Ford v. State,* 53 Ala. 150 (1875) when white Democrats returned to power on the court, and definitively overturned in *Green v. State,* 58 Ala. 190 (1877). *Hart v. Hoss and Elder,* 26 La. Ann. 90 (1874), created a longer-lasting opening in Louisiana, until the legislature reinstated a prohibition on racial intermarriage in 1894.

73. *State v. Wesley Hairston and Puss Williams,* 63 N.C. 439 (1869), quotations from 440, 441.

74. Justice Story and the decisions following are quoted in the U.S. Supreme Court decision *Maynard v. Hill,* 125 U.S. 190, 210–13 (1888). Cf. Grossberg, *Governing,* 133–44; Stanley, "Contract Rights in the Age of Emancipation," 254–56. For feminist analysis of the paradox of marriage as a contract and a status, see Carole Pateman, "The Shape of the Marriage Contract," in *Women's Views of the Political World of Men,* ed. Judith H. Stiehm (Dobbs Ferry, N.Y., Transnational Publications, 1984), 77.

75. *Maynard v. Hill,* 125 U.S. 190, 211 (1888); emphasis added. The cases affirming the contractual basis of marriage are *Meister v. Moore,* 96 U.S. 76 (1877), and *Maryland v. Baldwin,* 112 U.S. 490 (1884).

76. Kermit L. Hall, *The Magic Mirror: Law in American History* (New York, Oxford UP, 1991), 230–31.

77. The *Nation,* Dec. 3, 1868; *New York Times* (1870) quoted in Gordon, "'The Liberty of Self-Degradation,'" 844–45; on the consolidation of national power see Richard Franklin Bensel, *Yankee Leviathan: The Origins of Central State Authority in America, 1859–1877* (Cambridge, Cambridge UP, 1990).

78. Amy E. Holmes, "'Such Is the Price We Pay': American Widows and the Civil War Pension System," in *Toward a Social History of the American Civil War,* ed. Maris A. Vinovskis (Cambridge, Cambridge UP, 1990), 171–73; see Theda

Skocpol, *Protecting Soldiers and Mothers* (Cambridge, Harvard UP, 1992), 102–52.

79. Howard, *Autobiography*, 203. The Freedmen's Bureau's unprecedented intrusion of federal power into individuals' lives and property caused much opposition when it was proposed: see *CG* 38/1, e.g., Feb. 19, 1864, 761–763; March 1, 1864, 891–94; cf. Peter Charles Hoffer, *The Law's Conscience: Equitable Constitutionalism in America* (Chapel Hill, U of North Carolina P, 1990), 126.

80. I rely on Megan J. McClintock, "Civil War Pensions and the Reconstruction of Union Families," *JAH*, 83:2 (Sept. 1996), 456–480; she sees the pension system as a "family policy."

81. See Philip Corrigan and Derek Sayer, *The Great Arch: English State Formation as Cultural Revolution* (London, Basil Blackwell, 1985), esp. 4–6, on the "moral discipline effected by state formation."

5. Monogamy as the Law of Social Life

1. Brigham Young quoted in "The 'Twin Relics of Barbarism,'" *New York Times*, July 18, 1869, 4.

2. "Why Is Single Life Becoming More General?" *The Nation*, March 5, 1868, 190–91; "The Future of the Family," *The Nation*, Dec. 3, 1868, 453–54.

3. James, "Is Marriage Holy?" *Atlantic*, 25 (March 1870). *The Nation* took James to task in "Society and Marriage," March 26, 1870, 332–33; and he responded, "Mr Henry James on Marriage, *The Nation*, June 9, 1870, 366–67.

4. Theodore Woolsey, *Essay on Divorce and Divorce Legislation* (New York, Scribners, 1869), quotation on 235, and see 198–205. Woolsey's articles appeared in vols. 26 (1867) and 27 (1868) of *The New Englander*. In 1881 he founded the New England (later National) Divorce Reform League; see Glenda Riley, *Divorce: An American Tradition* (New York, Oxford UP, 1991), 108–110.

5. See *New York Times*, "Marriage and Divorce," Aug. 2, 1868, 4; "Marriage and Divorce in the Episcopal Convention," Oct. 26, 1868, 4; "Marriage and Divorce," Jan. 5, 1869, 4; untitled, Oct. 3, 1869, 4; "Divorce Made Easy," Oct. 10, 1869, 4. See also "Frequent Divorce in New England," *American Church Review*, 20 (1868), 226; "The Divine Law of Divorce," *Ladies' Repository*, Oct. 1868, 287–91; "Divorce Legislation in Connecticut," *Catholic World*, 4 (1866), 103; "The Indissolubility of Christian Marriage," *Catholic World*, 5 (1867), 684–89; "Marriage and Divorce," *The Southern Review*, 9 (Jan. 1871), 124–40; M. F. Taylor, "Marriage and Divorce," *The Southern Magazine*, 11 (July-Dec. 1872),

447–52; Hon. N. H., Davis, "Divorce," *The International Review*, 1 (1874), 794–818.

6. For cross-national comparison, see Roderick Phillips, *Putting Asunder: A History of Divorce in Western Society* (Cambridge and New York, Cambridge UP, 1988), 463–64; for cross-regional comparison within the U.S., see Riley, *Divorce*, 86–87.

7. See Hendrik Hartog, "Lawyering, Husbands' Rights, and the 'Unwritten Law' in Nineteenth-Century America," *JAH*, 84 (June 1997), 67–96; Jennifer Miller, "The Public Price of Private Life: The McFarland-Richardson Murder Scandal and New York City Political Culture, 1869," paper delivered at the Berkshire Conference on the History of Women, June 1993; Nelson Manfred Blake, *The Road to Reno: A History of Divorce in the United States* (New York, Macmillan, 1962), 101–02; Norma Basch, *Framing American Divorce* (Berkeley, U of California P, 1999), chap. 3.

8. "The End of the McFarland Trial and the Moral of It," *New York Herald*, May 11, 1870.

9. *New York Times*, Dec. 5, 1868, 4; see also May 11, 1870, 4, and May 12, 1870, 4. Cf. the editorial in the *New York Post*, May 11, 1870, calling the trial a farce; and see Miller, "Public Price." "The McFarland Case," *The Nation*, May 12, 1870, 300–02, quotation from 301; cf. *The Nation*'s first, skeptical notice of the murder, Dec. 2, 1869, 474–75.

10. Samuel W. Dike, "The Theory of the Marriage Tie," *Andover Review*, 17 (Nov. 1893), 672–80; Michael Grossberg, *Governing the Hearth: Law and the Family in Nineteenth-Century America* (Chapel Hill, U of North Carolina P, 1985), 86–99; Victor B. Howard, *Black Liberation in Kentucky: Emancipation and Freedom, 1862–1884* (Lexington, UP of Kentucky, 1983), 124; *In re McLaughlin's Estate*, 4 Wash. 570, 587, 509 (1892).

11. Indiana revoked its infamous omnibus clause. See Michael Grossberg, "Guarding the Altar: Physiological Restrictions and the Rise of State Intervention in Matrimony," *American Journal of Legal History*, 26 (July 1982), esp. 209–25; Riley, *Divorce*, 66; James Harwood Barnett, *Divorce and the American Divorce Novel 1858–1937* (New York, Russell and Russell, 1968), 21–22.

12. *New York Times*, Dec. 9, 1869, noted in Blake, *Road to Reno*, 133. A constitutional amendment to establish national uniformity in marriage and divorce laws was proposed in 1885–86; *CR* 49/1, vol. 17, 340.

13. Carroll D. Wright, *A Report on Marriage and Divorce in the United States, 1867 to 1886* (Washington, D.C., Government Printing Office, 1891); Riley, *Divorce*, 108–110; see Philip Corrigan and Derek Sayer, *The Great Arch:*

English State Formation as Cultural Revolution (London, Basil Blackwell, 1985), 134–5, on "statistics."

14. Between 1867 and 1886, Utah courts granted 4,087 divorces, and only 1,267 of the couples had been married in Utah. Riley, *Divorce,* 96–99; Sarah Barringer Gordon, "'The Liberty of Self-Degradation': Polygamy, Woman Suffrage, and Consent in Nineteenth-Century America," *JAH,* 83 (Dec. 1996), 843–45. Gordon's work stresses that antipolygamists wanted to establish a national standard of monogamy.

15. Ray Jay Davis, "Plural Marriage and Religious Freedom: The Impact of *Reynolds v. United States,*" *Arizona LR,* 15 (1973), 301, n. 69, says less than 10 percent of Mormons were polygamists; Craig Foster, "Polygamy among the Mormons," says 20 percent at the height of the practice, in *Encyclopedia of the American West,* ed. Charles Phillips and Alan Axelrod, vol. 3 (New York, Macmillan, 1996), 1310; "Polygamy," in Howard Lamar, ed., *New Encyclopedia of the American West* (New Haven, Yale UP, 1998), says 5 to 15 percent.

16. Orma Linford, "The Mormons and the Law: The Polygamy Cases," part 2, *Utah LR,* 9:2 (Winter 1964), 585.

17. McKean quoted in Van Wagoner, *Mormon Polygamy,* 110; see John L. Brooke, *Refiner's Fire: The Making of Mormon Cosmology, 1644–1844* (New York, Cambridge UP, 1994), 212–17, 283, on state-building; on subsequent presidents, see Linford, "The Mormons," 317; Grossberg, *Governing,* 123–24; Edward P. Hutchinson, *Legislative History of American Immigration Policy, 1798–1965* (Philadelphia, U Pennsylvania P, 1981), 69.

18. Gordon, "Liberty of Self-Degradation."

19. "Great Indignation Meeting of the Ladies of Salt Lake City to Protest against the Passage of Cullom's Bill," *Deseret Evening News* (Salt Lake City), Jan. 14, Jan. 15, 1870.

20. Quotations from Sarah Barringer Gordon, "'The Twin Relic of Barbarism': A Legal History of Anti-Polygamy in Nineteenth-Century America," Ph.D. diss., Princeton U, 1995, 168, 174–76.

21. Gordon, "Liberty of Self-Degradation," esp. 826–28; "The Women of Utah," *New York Times,* March 5, 1869, 6–7.

22. *Reynolds v. U.S.,* 98 U.S. 145 (1879), 164, 165–67.

23. See Carol Weisbrod and Pamela Sheingorn, "Reynolds v. United States: Nineteenth-Century Forms of Marriage and the Status of Women," *Connecticut LR,* 10:4 (Summer 1978), esp. 833, highlighting Lieber; Dorothy Ross, *The Origins of American Social Science* (New York, Cambridge UP, 1991), 37–42, 48–50, 64–69, 279–80; Michael Herz, "Rediscovering Francis Lieber: An Afterword and Introduction," in *Cardozo LR,* 16 (April 1995), 2107–34.

24. See Francis Lieber, *Essays on Property and Labor* (New York, Harper, 1841), esp. 15–16, 21–23.

25. "The Mormons: Shall Utah be Admitted into the Union?" *Putnam's Monthly*, 5 (March 1855), 234, 235–36; Weisbrod and Sheingorn, "*Reynolds.*"

26. Linford, "The Mormons" part 1, *Utah LR*, 9:1 (Summer 1964), 40–41.

27. Lieber, "Shall the Mormons?" 235–36.

28. Joan Brumberg, "Zenanas and Girlless Villages: The Ethnology of American Evangelical Women, 1870–1910," *JAH*, 69:2 (1982), 347–71.

29. Frank Gaylord Cook, "The Marriage Celebration in the United States," *Atlantic Monthly*, 61 (April 1888), 531, 529. Cf. Nathan Allen, "Divorces in New England," *North American Review*, 130 (Jan. 1880), 547–64. See Gail Bederman, *Manliness and Civilization: A Cultural History of Gender and Race in the United States, 1880–1917* (Chicago, U of Chicago P, 1995).

30. George W. Stocking, Jr., "The Turn-of the Century Concept of Race," *Modernism/Modernity*, 1 (1993), 4–16, and *Victorian Anthropology* (New York, Free P, 1987). I am indebted to Daniel A. Segal for advice and helpful discussions on pre- and post-Darwinian understandings of race and civilization.

31. "Shall We Have a New Conflict with the Mormons?" *New York Times*, Jan. 27, 1870; C. C. Goodwin, "The Political Attitude of the Mormons," *North American Review*, 132 (Jan. 1881), quotations from 276, 283, 285, 286; John Codman, "Mormonism," *The International Review*, 11 (1881), 221–34.

32. See, e.g., Goodwin, "Political Attitudes." Disfranchisement of convicted felons was practiced by more than half the states; my thanks to Alexander Keyssar for this information.

33. *Murphy v. Ramsey*, 114 U.S. 15, 43, 45 (1884)—a unanimous decision.

34. Linford, "The Mormons," 364, counts 988 convictions for unlawful cohabitation between 1882 and 1892; Davis, "Plural Marriage," 291, counts 1,300 men imprisoned during the 1880s.

35. Quotation from the governor of Utah in Report of the Secretary of the Interior, H.R. *Exec. Docs.*, 49/2, vol. 8, 70–71; Report of the Secretary of the Interior, H.R. *Exec. Docs.*, 49/1, vol. 11, 84–85; Report of the Utah Commission, H.R. *Exec. Docs.*, 49/2, vol. 9, 1063–66; *CR* 49/1, vol. 17 (History of Bills and Resolutions), 43, 140, 143, 176; Weisbrod and Sheingorn, "*Reynolds,*" 834.

36. See Gordon, "Twin Relic," 116–18, 206, and "Liberty of Self-Degradation"; Linford, "The Mormons," part 2.

37. Christopher Tiedemann's influential 1886 *Treatise on the Limitations of the Police Power in the United States* said, "the law cannot but recognize that Christianity is in the main the religion of this country," quoted in Gordon, "Twin Relic," 186; Carol Weisbrod, "Family, Church, and State: An Essay on

Constitutionalism and Religious Authority," *Journal of Family Law,* 26:4 (1987–88), 741–70; G. Edward White, *The American Judicial Tradition: Profiles of Leading American Judges* (New York, Oxford UP, 1976), 148–49.

38. *Mormon Church [or Late Corp of LDS] v. U.S.,* 136 U.S. 1 (1889), quotation at 49; see Davis, "Plural Marriage," 294. This was not a unanimous decision.

39. Brooke, *Refiner's Fire,* 290–1, including the quotation from the manifesto. On the recent recrudescence of plural marriage, see Timothy Egan, "The Persistence of Polygamy," *New York Times Magazine,* Feb. 28, 1999, 51–55.

40. Francis Paul Prucha, *Americanizing the American Indians* (Cambridge, Harvard UP, 1973); Vine Deloria, Jr. and Clifford M. Lytle, *American Indians, American Justice* (Austin, U of Texas P, 1983).

41. Report of the Secretary of the Interior, H.R. *Exec. Docs.,* 49/1, vol. 11, 23–25.

42. Report of the Secretary of the Interior, Nov. 1, 1883, reprinted in Francis Paul Prucha, *Documents of United States Indian Policy,* 2d ed. (Lincoln, U of Nebraska P, 1990), 160–61, 186–88.

43. *CR* 49/2, vol. 17, Feb. 19, 1886, 1630–33; vol. 18, Dec. 5, 1886, 189–90. Prior to the act, about 800 Indians had sought and received individual allotments by treaty and more had taken up public domain land under the Indian homestead act; Report of the Secretary of the Interior, H.R. *Exec. Docs.,* 49/2, vol. 8, 1886, 5.

44. Charles Alexander Eastman, *From the Deep Woods to Civilization* (Boston, Little Brown, 1916).

45. Round Hill quotation in Wendy Wall, "Gender and the 'Citizen Indian,'" in *Writing the Range,* ed. Elizabeth Jameson and Susan Armitage (Norman, U of Oklahoma P, 1997), esp. 214–16. Some white "squaw men" accused of crimes had tried to use their tribal marriages to evade the American justice system, by claiming to be under Indian jurisdiction; to prevent such claims, Congress in 1888 legislated that marriage to an American citizen made an Indian women an American citizen herself (without sacrificing her tribal property and interests). Congressmen were divided on whether to regard such marriages as civilizing for the Indians or degrading to the "white race." Report of the Secretary of the Interior, H.R. *Exec. Docs.,* 49/1, vol. 11, 28–29; and H.R. *Exec. Docs.,* 49/2, vol. 8, 4; "Bill Relative to Marriage between White Men and Indian Women," *CR* 50/1, vol. 19, 1887–88, 512, 6885–686, 6903, 7011.

46. *CR,* 42/3, vol. 17, 1873, 1240, 1307, 1358, 1436–37, 1524–25, 1571, 2210.

47. David Pivar, *Purity Crusade: Sexual Morality and Social Control, 1868–1900* (Westport, Conn., Greenwood, 1973); John D'Emilio and Estelle B. Freedman, *Intimate Matters: A History of Sexuality in America* (New York, Harper & Row, 1988), 145–67; Nicola Beisel, *Imperiled Innocents: Anthony Comstock and Family Reproduction in Victorian America* (Princeton, Princeton UP, 1997).

48. *Ex parte Jackson*, 96 U.S. 727 (1877), quotation from 736; see also Kermit L. Hall, *The Magic Mirror: Law in American History* (New York, Oxford UP, 1991), 161.

49. See the recent reassessment in Richard Wightman Fox, *Trials of Intimacy* (Chicago, U of Chicago P, 1999).

50. Beisel, *Imperiled Innocents*, 66.

51. James C. Mohr, *Abortion in America: The Origins and Evolution of National Policy* (New York, Oxford UP, 1978); Beisel, *Imperiled Innocents*, 40; see Linda Gordon, *Woman's Body, Woman's Right* (New York, Grossman, 1976).

52. Timothy J. Gilfoyle, "The Hearts of Nineteenth-Century Men: Bigamy and Working-Class Marriage in New York City, 1800–1890," *Prospects*, 19 (1994), 135–60.

53. *State v. Walker*, 36 Kans. 297 (1887), quotations from 299, 300, 304 (emphasis added), 310, 311, 313. The couple's marriage statements are reproduced in the opinion. On Moses Harman, see Hal Sears, *The Sex Radicals: Free Love in High Victorian America* (Lawrence, Kans., Regents P, 1977).

54. Constance Noyes Robertson, *Oneida Community: The Breakup, 1876–1881* (Syracuse, Syracuse UP, 1972), 89, 154, 76; Weisbrod and Sheingorn, *"Reynolds"*; Carol Weisbrod, "On the Break-up of Oneida," *Connecticut LR*, 14:4 (Summer 1982), 717–32.

55. *New York Times*, Feb. 15, 1879, 1; Professor John W. Mears, D.D., "Utah and the Oneida Community," *The Independent*, 31 (1879), 1584; *New York Times*, April 10, 1879, 1.

56. Robertson, *Oneida: Break-up*, 154–55; Weisbrod, "On the Break-up"; Spencer C. Olin, Jr., "The Oneida Community and the Instability of Charismatic Authority," *JAH*, 67:2 (1980), 285–300.

57. On marital rights as a site of majority/minority conflict, see Martha Minow, "We, the Family: Constitutional Rights and American Families," *JAH*, 74:3 (Dec. 1987), esp. 962–67; and on moral regulation by state action, see Corrigan and Sayer, *The Great Arch*, esp. 4–5, 198–200; and William J. Novak, *The People's Welfare: Law and Regulation in Nineteenth-Century America* (Chapel Hill, U of North Carolina P, 1996), esp. 152–56, 216.

6. Consent, the American Way

1. In *Fong Yue Ting v. U.S.*, 149 U.S. 698 (1893), the Supreme Court asserted the right of a sovereign nation to exclude or expel aliens for its own safety and independence.

2. Quotation from Rep. Richard Bartholdt of Mo., *CR* 54/1, May 19, 1896, 5423–24.

3. *Wong Kim Ark v. U.S.*, 169 U.S. 649 (1898). Two justices dissented, despite the clarity of the fourteenth amendment on this point.

4. *Shanks v. Dupont*, 3 Pet. 242 (1830); Virginia Sapiro, "Women, Citizenship, and Nationality: Immigration and Naturalization Policies in the United States," *Politics and Society*, 13:1 (1984), 1–26; Nancy F. Cott, "Marriage and Women's Citizenship in the United States, 1830–1934," *AHR*, 103:5 (Dec. 1998), 1440–74.

5. Amy Dru Stanley, *From Bondage to Contract: Wage Labor, Marriage, and the Market in the Age of Slave Emancipation* (New York, Cambridge UP, 1998).

6. Rep. Rowland Mahany, *CR* 54/1, May 20, 1896, 5474. See George W. Stocking, Jr., *Victorian Anthropology* (New York, Free P, 1987), and "The Turn-of the Century Concept of Race," *Modernism/ Modernity*, 1 (1993), 4–16; Barbara J. Fields, "Ideology and Race in American History," in *Region, Race, and Reconstruction*, ed. J. Morgan Kousser and James MacPherson (New York, Oxford UP, 1982); and Matthew Frye Jacobson, *Whiteness of a Different Color* (Cambridge, Harvard UP, 1998).

7. E.g., Sen. Henry Cabot Lodge, *CR* 54/1, March 16, 1896, 2817; John Higham, *Strangers in the Land: Patterns of American Nativism, 1860–1925* (New York: Atheneum, 1963), 153–56.

8. Petition from seventeen thousand "laboring men" of California, incorporated in a speech by Horace F. Page of Feb. 10, 1875, printed in *CR* 43/1, appendix, 44; Rep. Martin Foran, *CR* 48/2, June 19, 1884, quoted in Gwendolyn Mink, *Old Labor and New Immigrants in American Political Development: Union, Party, and State, 1875–1920* (Ithaca, Cornell UP, 1986), 109–10.

9. Petition from seventeen thousand, *CR*, 43/1, 1875, 44; "Report of the Joint Special Committee to Investigate Chinese Immigration," *CR*, 44/2, part 3, Feb. 28, 1877, 2004–05 (quotation from 2004).

10. Alexander Saxton, *The Indispensable Enemy: Labor and the Anti-Chinese Movement in California* (Berkeley, U of California P, 1975); Bill Ong Hing, *Making and Remaking Asian America through Immigration Policy, 1850–1920* (Stanford, Stanford UP, 1993), 20–26; Edward P. Hutchinson, *Legislative History of American Immigration Policy, 1798–1965* (Philadelphia, U of Pennsylvania P,

1981), 67–84, 104, 130, 431–33; Lawerence Glickman, "Inventing the 'American Standard of Living'": Gender, Race, and Working-Class Identity, 1880–1925," *Labor History,* 34 (Spring/Summer 1993), 221–35.

11. Sucheng Chan, "European and Asian Immigration into the United States in Comparative Perspective, 1820s to 1920s," in *Immigration Reconsidered: History, Sociology, and Politics,* ed. Virginia Yans-McLaughlin (New York, Oxford UP, 1990), 69, n. 16.

12. See Hutchinson, *Legislative History,* 65–66, and Gerald Neuman, *Strangers to the Constitution: Immigrants, Borders, and Fundamental Law* (Princeton, Princeton UP, 1996), esp. 19–51, on restrictions by states on in-migrants before 1875.

13. *In re Ah Fong,* 1 Fed. Cas. 213, no. 102 (C.C.C.D. Cal. 1872), quoted in a speech by Horace F. Page, Feb. 10, 1875, recorded in *CR* 43/1, appendix, 42–44. See Sucheng Chan, "The Exclusion of Chinese Women, 1870–1943," in *Entry Denied: Exclusion and the Chinese Community in America, 1882–1943,* ed. Sucheng Chan (Philadelphia, Temple UP, 1991), esp. 95–97, 105–09; Megumi Dick Osumi, "Asians and California's Anti-Miscegenation Laws," in *Asian and Pacific American Experiences: Women's Perspectives,* ed. Nobuya Tsuchida (Minneapolis, Asian/Pacific American Learning Resource Center and U of Minnesota, 1982), 8. According to Chan, prostitutes composed 22 percent to 54 percent of the Chinese female population in several different California localities in 1880, but only 14 to 16 percent in 1900; see Chan, *This Bittersweet Soil: The Chinese in California Agriculture, 1860–1910* (Berkeley, U of California P, 1986), table 34, 392–93.

14. An alternative nineteenth-century view, often linked to the Irish essayist William Lecky, contended that prostitution supported conventional marriage by allowing "respectable" men to vent their sexual aggressions apart from women of their own class, thus preserving their modest wives' image and saving their bodies.

15. See Pamela Haag, *Consent: Sexual Rights and the Transformation of American Liberalism* (Ithaca, Cornell UP, 1999), esp. 63–93.

16. "Report of the Joint Special Committee to Investigate Chinese Immigration," *CR* 44/2, part 3, Feb. 28, 1877, 2005.

17. Chan, "The Exclusion of Chinese Women," 105–09.

18. Hutchinson, *Legislative History,* 67–84, 104, 130, 431–33.

19. "Report of the Joint Special Committee to Investigate Chinese Immigration," *CR* 44/2, part 3, Feb. 28, 1877, 2004–05.

20. *Annals of Congress,* 1/2 (1st Cong., 2d sess.), 1790, 1057, 1109–1125; *CG* 41/2, (July 2, 1870, July 4, 1870), 5114–5125, 5148–177; George M.

Fredrickson, *White Supremacy: A Comparative Study in American and South African History* (New York, Oxford UP, 1981), 145; Hutchinson, *Legislative History*, 57–61.

21. Higham, *Strangers in the Land*, 99–100; Keith Fitzgerald, *The Face of the Nation: Immigration, the State, and the National Identity* (Stanford, Stanford UP, 1996), esp. 99–102; Sidney Kansas, *U.S. Immigration Exclusion and Deportation and Citizenship of the United States of America*, 2d ed. (Albany and New York, Matthew Bender, 1940), 4–6; Hutchinson, *Legislative History*, 422–23, 452. The Bureau of Immigration was established in the Treasury Department in 1891, and was moved to the Departmentt of Commerce and Labor in 1903. In 1906 it became the Bureau of Immigration and Naturalization. Immigration and Naturalization were separated and both put under the Department of Labor when it was created in 1913. They were reunited in 1933 in the Immigration and Naturalization Service, transferred in 1940 to the Justice Department.

22. Comm.-Gen. of Immigration to [the Secretary of State], April 14, 1910, and other correspondence, Jan.-April 1910, and 1913–14, U.S. Bureau of Immigration files, National Archives RG 85, entry 9, box 151, file 52737/499.

23. Mink, *Old Labor and New Immigrants*, esp. 124–28.

24. Thomas J. Curran, *Xenophobia and Immigration, 1820–1930* (Boston, Twayne, 1975), pp. 119–25.

25. Rep. Morse (Mass.), *CR* 54/1, May 19, 1896, 5434 (cf. Stanyarne Wilson of S.C. on May 20, 1896, 5471); Wilson, 1894, quoted by Mink, *Old Labor*, 223.

26. March 16, 1896, *CR* 54/1, 2817.

27. Republican Rep. Parker of NJ., *CR* 54/2, Jan. 27, 1897, 1228. He wanted to increase the number of women immigrants, arguing, "Do they compete with the labor of this country, or do they come as wives and bring families and cause money to be spent here?"

28. Passed several times by Congress, the provision was repeatedly killed by presidential veto. In 1917, Congress roused the necessary two-thirds majority to override President Wilson's veto.

29. Mink, *Old Labor*, 213, n. 24.

30. Theodore Roosevelt, *The Free Citizen: A Summons to Service of the Democratic Ideal*, ed. Hermann Hagedorn (New York, Theodore Roosevelt Association, 1956), 30–31; see also his "What Americanism Means," *Forum*, 17 (April 1894), 199.

31. See Kristin L. Hoganson, *Fighting for American Manhood: How Gender Politics Provoked the Spanish-American and Philippine-Americans Wars* (New

Haven, Yale UP, 1998), 154–55, for the general point and the quotation from Beveridge, *The Young Man and the World* (1905).

32. *CR* 59/2, vol. 41, Jan. 21, 1907, 1463–67; Feb. 27, 1907, 4116; Feb. 28, 1907, 4263–64; Cott, "Marriage and Women's Citizenship."

33. *Mackenzie v. Hare,* 239 U.S. 299 (1915), 311, 312 (an opionion written by Justice McKenna, who also wrote the opinion upholding the White Slave Traffic Act for its moral good); see also *Mackenzie v. Hare,* 165 Cal. 775 (1913) at 785, 783.

34. Hing, *Making and Remaking Asian America,* 53.

35. Hing, *Making and Remaking Asian America,* 53–55; Chan, "European and Asian Immigration," 62–63. Chan points out that another issue of realpolitik underlay this diplomatic agreement: Japan agreed to recognize U.S. interests in the Philippines and the United States agreed not to interfere with Japan's aims in Korea.

36. Nebraska, Montana, and Nevada explicitly nullified marriage between whites and Japanese or Chinese; Arizona, California, Idaho, Utah, and Wyoming banned marriage between whites and Chinese or "Mongolians." David H. Fowler, *Northern Attitudes towards Interracial Marriage* (New York and London, Garland, 1987), appendix.

37. Compare decisions on male headship determining the status of Chinese merchants' wives, in *U.S. v. Mrs. Gue Lim,* 176 U.S. 459 (1899), *Tsoi Sim v. U.S.,* 116 Fed. 920 (1902).

38. "Report on White Slavery," *CR* 61/2, vol. 45, part 8, June 25, 1910, 9040; see Haag, *Consent,* 63–93; Margit Stange, *Personal Property: Wives, White Slaves, and the Market in Women* (Baltimore, John Hopkins UP, 1998); Ruth Rosen, *The Lost Sisterhood: Prostitution, 1900–1918* (Baltimore, John Hopkins UP, 1982).

39. See *CR* 61/2, vol. 45, part 1, esp. Jan. 11, 1910, and Jan. 19, 1910, 546–47 (quotation) and 812–21 (quotation from 812).

40. See *CR* 61/2, vol. 45, part 1, esp. Jan. 11, 1910, and Jan. 19, 1910, 546–47 and 812–21; substantive debate on the bill is on 517–30, 545–51, 804–23, 1030–41.

41. Haag's unpublished Ph.D. diss., Yale University, 1995, "A History of the Private Self: Sexual Freedom, Sexual Violence, and Individual Rights in Modern American Culture," led me to these records. Report of Marcus Braun, dated Sept. 29, 1908, and A. Warner Parker, Chief of the Law Division of the Bureau of Immigration, memo to Acting Comm.-Gen., Oct. 19, 1908, National Archives Record Group 85 [Immigration and Naturalization Service], entry 9, box 110, file 52484/1A. Correspondence from and about Braun is concentrated

in the many folders in entry 9 numbered 52484 in boxes 110 and 111. "Importing Women for Immoral Purposes" [also called "Report on Harboring Women for Immoral Purposes"], Sen. Doc. 196, *Sen. Docs.* 61/2 (61st Cong., 2d sess.), vol. 63 (1909).

42. Braun's 46-page typed report from Europe, dated Oct. 2, 1909, entry 9, box 111, file 52484/1G, folder 1, quotations from 29, 32, 41; and see Immigration Service, Office of the Inspector in Charge, Seattle, Wash., to Marcus Braun, Aug. 13, 1908, entry 9, box 107, 52484/1. On Jewish prostitutes in New York City see Jenna Weissman Joselit, *Our Gang: Jewish Crime and the New York Jewish Community, 1900–1940* (Bloomington, Indiana UP, 1983), 45–50, and Edward J. Bristow, *Prostitution and Prejudice: The Jewish Fight against White Slavery, 1870–1939* (Oxford, Clarendon P, 1982). A New York grand jury funded and headed by John D. Rockefeller, Jr., also found that "white slaves" were not deceived and coerced; Stange, *Personal Property,* 85–86, and 149, n. 5.

43. Daniel Keefe, Comm.-Gen. of Immigration, to Secretary of Commerce and Labor, Jan. 12, 1910, entry 9, box 109, file 52483/1A, folder 2. See also "Suppression of the White-Slave Traffic," Sen. Doc. 214, 61/2 (1909), and "Importing Women for Immoral Purposes," Sen. Doc. 196.

44. Daniel Keefe, Comm.-Gen. of Immigration, to Secretary of Commerce and Labor, Jan. 12, 1910, entry 9, box 109, file 52483/1A, folder 2; quotation from "Suppression of the White-Slave Traffic," Sen. Doc. 214, part 2, 61/2 (1909–10), 11; and see "Importing Women for Immoral Purposes," Sen. Doc. 196. In 1910 Congress removed the three-year time limit; Hutchinson, *Legislative History,* 452. Mark Connelly, *The Response to Prostitution in the Progressive Era* (Chapel Hill, U of North Carolina P, 1980), 171, n. 7, finds that sixty-five alien prostitutes were deported between June 1907 and June 1908, and 261 in the following twelve months.

45. "Suppression of the White-Slave Trade," 10–11, replicating Daniel Keefe to the Secretary of Commerce and Labor, Jan. 12, 1910, 15–18, entry 9, box 109, folder 52483/1A.

46. Extracts from Opinions of the Attorney Gen., July 30, 1909, Aug. 27, 1909, entry 9, box 91, 52241/5.

47. Braun report dated Sept. 29, 1908, 13, entry 9, box 110, file 52484/1A. See also entry 9, box 91, file 52241/5, "Deportation of Prostitutes Married to American Citizens"; A. Warner Parker, Chief, Law Division, Bureau of Immigration, memo for the Acting Comm.-Gen., Oct. 19, 1908, entry 9, box 110, file 52484/1A.

48. "Report on Harboring Women for Immoral Purposes," 45–46, 52–53; "Suppression of the White-Slave Traffic," 10–11. Rep. Bennett commented on the small number of cases, *CR*, 64/1, vol. 53, March 20, 1916, 5172–73.

49. *Comments of Labor Dept on Bill to Regulate Immigration*, 63/2 (63d Cong., 2d sess.), 1913–14, 451, 10, quoted in Candice Bredbenner, *A Nationality of Her Own* (Berkeley, U of California Press, 1998), 40. Law of Feb. 5, 1917 (64th Cong., 2d sess.), *Statutes at Large of the U.S.A. from December 1915 to March 1917 . . .*, vol. 39, part 1 (1917), 889; Hutchinson, *Legislative History*, 452. Because of the 1917 provision, seventeen thousand European "war brides" of World War I American soldiers were scrutinized for "immorality" before acquiring citizenship by marriage; see documents in entry 9, box 294, file 54549/512.

50. Digest of Braun report of Sept. 20, 1907, entry 9, box 44, file 51630/44F; T. F. H. Larned, Acting Comm.-Gen. of the Bureau of Immigration and Naturalization, to the Comm. of Immigration., Ellis Island, N.Y., Nov. 17, 1908, entry 9, box 111, file 52484/3; see A. Warner Parker, Chief, Law Division, memo for the Acting Comm.-Gen., Oct. 19, 1908, entry 9, box 110, file 52484/1A, and Braun's report of Sept. 29, 1908, entry 9, box 110, file 52484/1A, 7–10.

51. Parker memo, 4; "History of Chinese-Exclusion Laws and Some Difficulties in the Way of their Enforcement," *CR* 61/2, March 31, 1910, 4081–84.

52. My thinking about the love match versus arranged or fraudulent marriage, and the connections of both to consent and coercion in immigration history, is deeply indebted to Pamela Haag, "History of the Private Self," chaps. 4 and 5, and *Consent*, 94–118, 131–39. Quotations from Robert S. Lynd and Helen Lynd, *Middletown* (New York, Harcourt Brace, 1929), 114–15.

53. Haag, *Consent*, 94–118.; cf. Werner Sollors, *Beyond Ethnicity: Consent and Descent in American Culture* (New York, Oxford UP, 1986).

54. Alice Yun Chai, "Picture Brides: Feminist Analysis of Life Histories of Hawai'i's Early Immigrant Women from Japan, Okinawa, and Korea," in *Seeking Common Ground: Multidisciplinary Studies of Immigrant Women in the United States*, ed. Donna Gabaccia (Westport, Conn., Greenwood, 1992).

55. Hawaii was annexed by the United States in 1898 and became a territory in 1900. Robt W. Breckons, U.S. District Attorney, Dept. of Justice, District of Hawaii, Honolulu, to E. R. Stackable, Esq., Collector of Customs, July 10, 1903, entry 9, box 32, file 51520/21; see also E. R. Stackable to the Hon. J. K. Brown, Immigrant Inspector in Charge, Honolulu, July 13, 1903, and other documents of May and June 1903 in the same file.

56. Comm. at Angel Island to Richard Taylor, Dec. 23, 1913, entry 9, box 107, file 52424/13A; Comm.. of Immiration, San Francisco, to Comm.-Gen. of Immigration, Washington D.C., June 24, 1908; see John H. Sargent, Inspector in Charge, Seattle, Wash., to Comm.-Gen. of Immigration, Washington, D.C., July 9, 1908; and Samuel Backus, Commissioner, Angel Island, to Comm.-Gen. of Immigration, Washington, D.C., Oct. 11, 1908, all in entry 9, box 107, file 52424/13, folder 1; the Bureau of Immigration's memorandum about the Braun report, Oct. 19, 1908, is in file 52484/1A.

57. F. H. Larned, Acting Comm.-Gen., to Comms. of Immigration at San Francisco and Montreal, and to Inspector-in-Charge at Seattle, Nov. 17, 1908; Comm. in San Francisco to Comm.-Gen. in Washington, D.C., Nov. 24, 1908; Inspector-in-Charge at Seattle to Comm-Gen., Dec. 14, 1908, entry 9, box 107, file 52424/13, folder 1.

58. Protest documents are in entry 9, box 107, file 52424/13A (also labeled #2).

59. Bureau figures are in entry 9, box 107, file 52424/13A. The estimate for the California population is midway between the Census figures for 1910 (2,377,549) and 1920 (3,426,861). The Phelan speech is in *CR* 64/2, Dec. 14, 1916, 314. In Seattle only 365 picture brides entered during the fiscal year July 1, 1914–June 30, 1915.

60. See Walter LaFeber, *The Clash: A History of U.S.-Japan Relations* (New York, Norton, 1997), 106–16, on U.S.-Japanese relations during World War I, including the Lansing-Ishii agreement, of Nov. 2, 1917, which upheld the U.S. "Open Door" policy in China while granting Japan "special relations" and "special interests" in areas to which it had "territorial propinquity."

61. Documents in entry 9, box 107, file 52424/13B, folders 1 and 2, including W. B. Wilson, Secretary of Labor, to Secretary of State, Aug. 20, 1917 (quotation). This decision opened a "new phase of the problem" for U.S. male citizens of Japanese descent who had married brides from Japan by the proxy method, and wanted them to enter the United States. The Bureau of Immigration refused to accept the validity of proxy marriage for U.S. citizens, though it did for Japanese subjects. Japanese-American U.S. citizens were advised to join their would-be wives outside the country, marry, and then try to reenter. But once the Asian barred zone was established later in 1917, and Asians were rendered inadmissible in 1924, this was a prescription for leaving the United States and becoming unable to reenter. See documents in 52424/13B, folder 1, esp. Asst. Secretary of Labor Louis Post to the Hon. Secretary of State, Nov. 21, 1917.

62. Hing, *Making and Remaking Asian America,* 32–33.

63. Memorandum from the Japanese ambassador dated Dec. 13, 1919; clipping from *Seattle Star,* July 30, 1919, entry 9, box 107, folder 52424/13C.

64. See the documents in entry 9, box 107, folder 52424/13C. Cf. Ernest G. Lorenzen, "Marriage by Proxy and the Conflict of Laws," *Harvard LR,* 32 (1918–19), 473–88; *Ex parte Suzanna,* 295 Fed. 713 (1924); Minor Bronaugh, "Marriage by Proxy or Correspondence," *Law Notes,* 29:4 (July, 1925), 68–71.

65. See Michael C. LeMay, *From Open Door to Dutch Door: An Analysis of U.S. Immigration Policy since 1820* (New York, Praeger, 1987). The 1924 act worsened U.S.-Japanese relations.

66. Robert A. Divine, *American Immigration Policy, 1924–1952* (New Haven, Yale UP, 1957), esp. 11–17; Mae M. Ngai, "The Architecture of Race in American Immigration Law: A Reexamination of the Immigration Act of 1924," *JAH,* 86 (June 1999), 67–92.

7. The Modern Architecture of Marriage

1. Blanche Crozier, "Constitutionality of Discrimination Based on Sex," *Boston U LR,* 15 (1935), 744–45; she saw the formal structure of marriage as still "untouched" by the "great principle of liberty and equality" in the U.S. Constitution.

2. "The New Erotic Ethics," *The Nation,* March 14, 1912, 261; Inez Milholland, "The Liberation of a Sex," *McClure's Magazine,* 1913; see Nancy F. Cott, *The Grounding of Modern Feminism* (New Haven, Yale UP, 1987), 40–49.

3. Robert S. Lynd and Helen Lynd, *Middletown* (New York, Harcourt Brace, 1929), 266–67, note the movie titles. The books mentioned are, in order, by Freda Kirchwey, Samuel Schmalhausen, Sherwood Eddy, and V. F. Calverton (the final two).

4. *Tinker v. Colwell,* 193 U.S. 473 (1904), quotation from 481. Three justices dissented, but without offering reasons. Rogers Smith, *Civic Ideals: Conflicting Visions of Citizenship in U.S. Law* (New Haven, Yale UP, 1997), 456–59, usefully summarizes conservative court decisions on women at the turn of the century.

5. *U.S. v. Bitty,* 208 U.S. 383 (1908), quotations from 401; cf. the view of vice reformers analyzed in Mark Thomas Connelly, *The Response to Prostitution in the Progressive Era* (Chapel Hill, U of North Carolina P, 1980), 16–19.

6. Robert G. McCloskey, ed., *The Works of James Wilson* (Cambridge, Harvard UP, 1976), 602–3.

7. *State v. Oliver,* 70 N.C. 60, 61–62 (1874), and other judges' opinions quoted in Reva B. Siegel, " 'The Rule of Love': Wife Beating as Prerogative and Privacy," *Yale LJ,* 105:8 (June 1996), 2117–2207, esp. 2140–155, which my

interpretation follows; see also Elizabeth B. Clark, "'The Sacred Rights of the Weak': Pain, Sympathy, and the Culture of Individual Rights in Antebellum America," *JAH*, 82:3 (Sept. 1995), 463–93.

8. *Thompson v. Thompson*, 218 U.S. 611 (1911), quotations on 619, 618.

9. Gail Bederman, *Manliness and Civilization: A Cultural History of Gender and Race in the United States, 1880–1917* (Chicago, U of Chicago P, 1995), 1–5, 8–10, 41–42; Pamela Haag, *Consent: Sexual Rights and the Transformation of American Liberalism* (Ithaca, Cornell UP, 1999), 121–32; Paul R. Spickard, *Mixed Blood: Intermarriage and Ethnic Identity in Twentieth-Century America* (Madison, U of Wisconsin P, 1989), 288; Randy Roberts, *Papa Jack: Jack Johnson and the Era of White Hopes* (New York, Free P, 1983).

10. David H. Fowler, *Northern Attitudes towards Interracial Marriage* (New York and London, Garland, 1987), 302–13; Haag, *Consent*, 122–32; *The Crisis: A Record of the Darker Races* (New York), April 1916, 306; June 1921, 65–66; April 1925, 251; Feb, 1928, 50 (quotation); April 1928, 118.

11. Fowler, *Northern Attitudes*, xi–xii, 267–68, 286–313, 322–23; Kermit L. Hall, *The Magic Mirror: Law in American History* (New York, Oxford UP, 1991).

12. John Rogers, *CR* 67/2, vol. 62, part 2, June 20, 1922, 9047.

13. Cable Act debate, *CR* 67/2, vol. 62, part 9, 9039–9067. See Sophonisba P. Breckinridge, *Marriage and the Civic Rights of Women* (Chicago, U of Chicago P, 1931), 23–25; Blanche Crozier, "The Changing Basis of Women's Nationality," *Boston U LR*, 14 (1934), 132–33. Waldo Emerson Waltz, *The Nationality of Married Women: A Study of Domestic Policies and International Legislation* (Urbana, U of Illinois P, 1937), 43–44; Luella Gettys, *The Law of Citizenship in the United States* (Chicago, U of Chicago P, 1934), 124–25; J. Stanley Lemons, *Woman Citizen: Social Feminism in the 1920s* (Urbana, U of Illinois P, 1973), 63–68, 235–37; Virginia Sapiro, "Women, Citizenship, and Nationality: Immigration and Naturalization Policies in the United States," *Politics and Society*, 13:1 (1984), 1–26; Candice Dawn Bredbenner, *A Nationality of Her Own: Women, Marriage, and the Law of Citizenship* (Berkeley, U of California P, 1998); Nancy F. Cott, "Marriage and Women's Citizenship in the United States, 1830–1934," *AHR*, 103:5 (Dec. 1998), 1440–74.

14. Rep. Isaac Siegel of N.Y., June 20, 1922, *CR* 67/2, vol. 62, part 9, 9047. On revisions, see Lemons, *Woman Citizen*, 235–37; Bredbenner, *Nationality of Her Own;* Cott, "Marriage and Women's Citizenship."

15. Lemons, *Woman Citizen*, 69–73; Linda K. Kerber, "A Constitutional Right to Be Treated like American Ladies: Women and the Obligations of Citizenship," in *U.S. History as Women's History*, ed. Linda K. Kerber et al. (Chapel Hill, U of North Carolina P, 1995), 29–32, and *No Constitutional Right to Be*

Ladies: Women and the Obligations of Citizenship (New York, Hill and Wang, 1998), 136–39; Blayne H. Cutler, "When Women Became Peers: A Century's Struggle for Equal Jury Access in America, 1870–1975," Ph.D. diss., Yale U, 1996, 32 (the 1938 figure); Joan Hoff, *Law, Gender, and Injustice: A Legal History of U.S. Women* (New York, New York U, 1991), 224–27; on the doubled judicial readings, which she calls the "emancipatory" and the "incremental," see Jennifer K. Brown, "The Nineteenth Amendment and Women's Equality," *Yale LJ,* 102 (June 1993), 2175–2204.

16. See Alice Kessler-Harris, *Out to Work* (New York, Oxford UP, 1982), 217–49; Cott, *Grounding,* 129–34, 215–28.

17. Cott, *Grounding,* 162–64, 204–08.

18. Phyllis Blanchard, *New Girls for Old* (1930), quoted in Cott, *Grounding,* 157–58; Christina Simmons, "Companionate Marriage and the Lesbian Threat," *Frontiers,* 4 (Fall 1979), 54–59.

19. For examples of women's irony and criticism of marriage in the 1920s and 1930s see *These Modern Women,* ed. Elaine Showalter (Old Westbury, N.Y., Feminist P, 1978), quotation from Sue Shelton White (1927) on 52; Cott, *Grounding,* 187–89, 200–02; novels such as Tess Schlesinger's *The Unpossessed* or Mary McCarthy's *The Group;* Anne duCille, *The Coupling Convention* (New York, Oxford UP, 1993), esp. 66–109; and Angela Davis, "I Used to Be Your Sweet Mama," in *Sexy Bodies,* ed. Elizabeth Grosz and Elspeth Probyn (New York, Routledge, 1995), 231–65.

20. See the summary of married women's laws as of 1900 in Hoff, *Law, Gender, and Injustice,* 128–35; and Chester G. Vernier, *American Family Laws: A Comparative Study of the Family Law of the Forty-Eight American States . . .,* vol. 3, *Husband and Wife* (Stanford, Stanford UP, 1935), esp. the introduction and 193–94.

21. Vernier, *American Family Law,* 3:195. Both the husband's legal duty to support his wife and hers to serve him stayed in place through mid-century. See Joseph Warren, "Husband's Right to Wife's Services," *Harvard LR,* 38 (Feb. 1925), part 1, 421–46, part 2, 622–50; Robert C. Brown, "The Duty of the Husband to Support the Wife," *Virginia LR,* 18 (June 1932), 823–49; Blanche Crozier, "Marital Support," *Boston U LR,* 15 (1935), 28–58; Paul Sayre, "A Reconsideration of Husband's Duty to Support and Wife's Duty to Render Services," *Virginia LR,* 29 (1943), 857–75; Monrad G. Paulsen, "Support Rights and Duties between Husband and Wife," *Vanderbilt LR,* 9 (June 1956), 709–42; Reva B. Siegel, "The Modernization of Marital Status Law: Adjudicating Wives' Rights to Earnings, 1860–1930," *Georgetown LJ,* 82:7 (Sept. 1994), 2127–2211.

22. On husbands' desertion and courts' enforcement of support obligations, I have relied on Martha May, "The 'Problem of Duty': Family Desertion in the Progressive Era," *Social Service Review*, 62 (March 1988), 40–60; Annette Igra, "Male Providerhood and the Public Purse: Anti-Desertion Reform in the Progressive Era," in *The Sex of Things*, ed. Victoria de Grazia (Berkeley, U of California P, 1996), 188–211 (especially on the reformers' critique of households); Elizabeth Pleck, *Domestic Tyranny: The Making of Social Policy against Family Violence from Colonial Times to the Present* (New York, Oxford UP, 1987), 136–43.

23. The support laws' purpose of disciplining working-class men is stressed in Pleck, *Domestic Tyranny*, 108–110, 141–43; Reva B. Siegel, " 'The Rule of Love': Wife Beating as Prerogative and Privacy," *Yale LJ*, 105:8 (June 1996), 2136–39; Igra, "Male Providerhood"; and May, "Problem of Duty." Cf. Paulsen, "Support Rights," 140: "In practice, the criminal penalty was reserved for those 'on the lowest rung of the economic ladder.' "

24. Crozier, "Marital Support," 41; cf. Paulsen, "Support Rights," 735: "A wife living with her husband has almost no remedy to enforce her right to support except her personal persuasiveness." A husband generally went free upon mending his behavior.

25. For centuries earlier, private groups and local authorities had dispensed charity to poor single mothers with dependent children (and other paupers), either by assigning them to the workhouse or by dispensing "outdoor relief," small amounts of money or goods for them to use on their own.

26. My discussion of mothers' pensions relies on Molly Ladd-Taylor, *Mother-Work: Women, Child Welfare, and the State, 1890–1930* (Urbana, U of Illinois P, 1994); Linda Gordon, *Pitied But Not Entitled: Single Mothers and the History of Welfare* (New York, Free P, 1994), 37–64, 100–07, quotation from Mary Richmond on 100; Gwendolyn Mink, "The Lady and the Tramp: Gender, Race, and the Origins of the American Welfare State," in *Women, the State, and Welfare*, ed. Linda Gordon (Madison, U of Wisconsin P, 1990), and *The Wages of Motherhood: Inequality in the Welfare State, 1917–1942* (Ithaca, Cornell UP, 1995); Theda Skocpol, *Protecting Soldiers and Mothers* (Cambridge, Harvard UP, 1992), 311–479.

27. Ladd-Taylor, *Mother-Work*, 49.

28. For the impact of the Depression on women workers, see Ruth Milkman, "Women's Work and the Economic Crisis: Some Lessons from the Great Depression," *Review of Radical Political Economics*, 8:1 (1976), 73–95; Lois Scharf, *To Work and to Wed: Female Employment, Feminism, and the Great De-*

pression (Westport, Conn., Greenwood, 1980); Kessler-Harris, *Out to Work*, 250–72; Cott, *Grounding*, 209–11, 222–25.

29. Mirra Komarovsky et al., *The Unemployed Man and His Family* (New York, Dryden Press for the Institute for Social Research, 1940); Roosevelt quoted in William E. Forbath, "Race, Class, and Equal Citizenship," paper prepared for the annual convention of the Organization of American Historians, April 17–20, 1997, San Francisco, 76, 80; see Holly Allen, "Fallen Women and Forgotten Men: Gendered Concepts of Community, Home, and Nation, 1932–1945," Ph.D. diss., Yale U, 1996, on the "masculinist" orientation of the New Deal.

30. On the Social Security Act (including women reformers' part in designing the gender-differentiated outcome), I have relied on Barbara Nelson, "The Gender, Race, and Class Origins of Early Welfare Policy and the Welfare State," in *Women, Politics, and Change*, ed. Louise A. Tilly and Patricia Gurin (New York, Russell Sage Foundation, 1990), 413–35; Mink, *Wages of Motherhood;* and especially Gordon, *Pitied But Not Entitled.*

31. Kenneth Casebeer, "The Workers' Unemployment Insurance Bill: American Social Wage, Labor Organization, and Legal Ideology," in *Labor Law in America: Historical and Critical Essays*, ed. Christopher L. Tomlins and Andrew J. King (Baltimore, Johns Hopkins UP, 1992), 231–260.

32. My discussion of the 1939 amendments relies on Alice Kessler Harris, "Designing Women and Old Fools: The Construction of the Social Security Amendments of 1939," in *U.S. History as Women's History*, ed. Linda K. Kerber et al. (Chapel Hill, U of North Carolina P, 1995), 87–106; see also Grace Ganz Blumberg, "Adult Derivative Benefits in Social Security: A Women's Issue," in *Women and the Law: A Social Historical Perspective*, ed. D. Kelly Weisberg (Cambridge, Schenkman, 1980), 2:187–221, esp. 191–92; the 1996 figures are in Jill Elaine Hasday, "Federalism and the Family Reconstructed," *UCLA LR*, 45:5 (June 1998), 1384, n. 343.

33. Kessler-Harris, "Designing Women." As a result of *Weinberger v. Wiesenfeld*, 420 U.S. 636 (1975) (argued by Ruth Bader Ginsburg), Social Security spousal benefits became gender-neutral, so either a husband or wife could benefit from the other's higher earnings and gain survivor's benefits.

34. Linda Gordon, "Black and White Visions of Welfare: Women's Welfare Activism, 1890–1945," *JAH*, 78 (Sept. 1991), 559–590, and *Pitied*, 67–143; and see Susan Ware, *Beyond Suffrage: Women in the New Deal* (Cambridge, Harvard UP, 1981).

35. Vernier, *American Family Laws*, 3:65, 247.

8. Public Sanctity for a Private Realm

1. *United States v. One Package*, 13 F. Supp. 334 (E.D. N.Y. 1936); affirmed 86 F.2d 737 (2d Cir. 1936); James Reed, *From Private Vice to Public Virtue* (New York, Basic Books, 1978), 120–21.

2. Paul Glick, "Types of Families: An Analysis of Census Data," *American Sociological Review*, 6:6 (Dec. 1941), 830–38. Thanks to Jim Scott for bringing this to my attention.

3. Glen Elder, *Children of the Great Depression* (Chicago, U of Chicago P, 1974).

4. More than half of Americans lived below below the poverty line during the Depression; at the end of World War II, this proportion was reduced to about one third. Alan Brinkley, "The New Political Paradigm: World War II and American Liberalism," in *The War in American Culture: Society and Consciousness during World War II*, ed. Lewis A. Erenberg and Susan E. Hirsch (Chicago, U of Chicago P, 1996), 317.

5. Brinkley, "New Political Paradigm," 315; John D'Emilio, *Sexual Politics, Sexual Communities* (Chicago, U of Chicago P, 1983); Allan Berube, *Coming Out under Fire* (New York, Free P, 1990); Leisa Meyer, "Creating GI Jane: The Regulation of Sexuality and Sexual Behavior in the WACs during World War II," *FS*, 18:3 (Fall 1992), 581–602.

6. Reed Ueda, "The Changing Path to Citizenship: Ethnicity and Naturalization during World War II," in Erenberg and Hirsch, ed., *War*, 202–216; Bill Ong Hing, *Making and Remaking Asian America through Immigration Policy, 1850–1990* (Stanford, Stanford UP, 1993), 36–40; Robert A. Divine, *American Immigration Policy, 1924–1952* (New Haven, Yale UP, 1957), 146–54; Elfrieda Berthiaume Shukert and Barbara Smith Scibetta, *War Brides of World War II* (Novato, Calif., Presidio P, 1988), 198–200.

7. Shukert and Scibetta, *War Brides*, 209–18; Paul R. Spickard, *Mixed Blood: Intermarriage and Ethnic Identity in Twentieth-Century America* (Madison, U. of Wisconsin P, 1989), 132–35.

8. The petitioners in California, both Catholic, contended that the statute prevented them from receiving the sacrament of marriage and thus invaded freedom of religion. The court, citing a difference between freedom to believe and freedom to act, instead addressed the right to marry as a fundamental right; *Perez v. Sharp*, 32 Cal.2d 711, 198 P.2d 17 (1948). See Megumi Dick Osumi, "Asians and California's Anti-Miscegenation Laws," in *Asian and Pacific American Experiences: Women's Perspectives*, ed. Nobuya Tsuchida (Minneapolis, Asian/Pacific American Learning Resource Center and U of Minnesota, 1982),

24–25; David H. Fowler, *Northern Attitudes towards Interracial Marriage* (New York and London, Garland, 1987), xii–xiii; Spickard, *Mixed Blood*, 295. See *Loving v. Virginia*, 388 U.S. 1, 6, n. 5 (1967), for a review of state changes since *Perez*.

9. Divine, *American Immigration Policy*, 146–85. On expressions of 1940s cultural diversity, see Michael Denning, *The Cultural Front* (London and New York, Verso, 1996), esp. 445–54.

10. The preceding two paragraphs are indebted to Susan M. Hartmann, *The Home Front and Beyond: American Women in the 1940s* (Boston, Twayne, 1982); Carolyn C. Jones, "Split Income and Separate Spheres: Tax Law and Gender Roles in the 1940s," *Law and History Review*, 6:2 (Fall 1988), 263–64.

11. Kenon Breazeale, "In Spite of Women: *Esquire* Magazine and the Construction of the Male Consumer," *Signs*, 20 (Autumn 1994), 1–22.

12. My discussion of pin-ups, including the words quoted, is indebted to Robert Westbrook, "'I Want a Girl, Just like the Girl That Married Harry James': American Women and the Problem of Political Obligation in World War II," *AQ*, 42 (Dec. 1990), 587–614, and "Fighting for the American Family: Private Interests and Political Obligation in World War II," in *The Power of Culture*, ed. Richard W. Fox and T. J. Jackson Lears (Chicago, U of Chicago P, 1993), 195–221.

13. Quoted in Elaine Tyler May, "Rosie the Riveter Gets Married," in Erenberg and Hirsch, ed., *War*, 137.

14. Quoted in Westbrook, "Fighting for the American Family," 201–02.

15. See David Gerber, "Heroes and Misfits: The Troubled Social Reintegration of Disabled Veterans in *The Best Years of Our Lives*," *AQ*, 46 (Dec. 1994), 545–74; and Sonya Michel, "Danger on the Home Front: Motherhood, Sexuality, and Disabled Veterans in American Postwar Films," *Journal of the History of Sexuality*, 3:1 (1992), 109–28.

16. On the readjustment literature, I rely on Susan M. Hartmann, "Prescriptions for Penelope: Literature on Women's Obligations to Returning World War II Veterans," *Women's Studies*, 5 (1978), 223–239.

17. Hartmann, *Home Front*, 7–8, 43–45, 67–69, 105–08, 165–66, 212–13. The GI Bill reopened a nearly closed gap in men's and women's educational attainments by streaming many more men than women into higher education. Women gained 40 percent of all B.A. or higher degrees in 1940, but only 25 percent in 1950.

18. On this point and in my following discussion of the innovation of the joint return, I rely on Jones, "Split Income and Separate Spheres"; Alice Kessler-Harris, "'A Principle of Law But Not of Justice': Men, Women, and Income Taxes in the United States, 1913–1948," *Southern California Review of*

Law and Women's Studies, 6 (Spring 1997), 331–60; and Edward J. McCaffery, *Taxing Women* (Chicago, U of Chicago P, 1997). See also Linda K. Kerber, *No Constitutional Right to Be Ladies: Women and the Obligations of Citizenship* (New York, Hill and Wang, 1998), 121–23.

19. Susan M. Hartmann, "Women's Employment and the Domestic Ideal in the Early Cold War Years," in *Not June Cleaver: Women and Gender in Postwar America, 1945–1960,* ed. Joanne Meyerowitz (Philadelphia, Temple UP, 1994), 89–90.

20. See David J. Langum, *Crossing over the Line: Legislating Morality and the Mann Act* (Chicago, U of Chicago P, 1994).

21. *Cleveland v. U.S.* 329 U.S. 14 (1946); Murphy's dissent is on 24–29.

22. A Supreme Court case of 1906 had allowed states to set their own terms on out-of-state divorces. Katherine L. Caldwell, "Not Ozzie and Harriet: Postwar Divorce and the American Liberal Welfare State," *Law and Social Inquiry,* 23:1 (Winter 98), 45–51; Hendrik Hartog, *Man and Wife in America: A History* (Cambridge, Harvard UP, 2000), chap. 9.

23. A section on divorce set up by the American Bar Association for the National Conference on Family Life (which was called together by President Truman in 1948) stated as its founding premise that "the family is a legal unit, created by law, protected by law, and involving a legal status which can be dissolved only by law." Quoted in Caldwell, "Not Ozzie," 27.

24. Caldwell, "Not Ozzie," 28–30.

25. Rebecca M. Ryan, "The Sex Right: A Legal History of the Marital Rape Exemption," *Law and Social Inquiry,* 20:4 (1995), 109–13. On the emergence of "public discourse on nonmarital nonprocreative sexuality," see also Estelle B. Freedman, "'Uncontrolled Desires': The Response to the Sexual Psychopath, 1920–1960," *JAH,* 74 (June 1987), 83–106.

26. Ryan, "The Sex Right," 109–13.

27. On the "kitchen debate," see Elaine Tyler May, *Homeward Bound: American Families in the Cold War Era* (New York, Basic Books, 1988), 16–18; Sonya Michel, "American Women and the Discourse of the Democratic Family in World War II," in *Behind the Lines: Gender and the Two World Wars,* ed. Margaret Randolph Higonnet et al. (New Haven, Yale UP, 1987).

28. *Poe v. Ullman,* 367 U.S. 497 (1960), quotations from 519–22, 548.

29. In *Prince v. Massachusetts,* 321 U.S. 158 at 166 (1944), the court had acknowledged "the private realm of family life which the state cannot enter," adding, "but the family itself is not beyond regulation in the public interest."

30. *Griswold v. Connecticut,* 381 U.S. 479 at 486, 495 (1965) (Goldberg's

concurrence). See Thomas C. Grey, "Eros, Civilization, and the Burger Court," *Law and Contemporary Problems*, 43:3 (1979–80), 83–100; Martha Minow, "We, the Family: Constitutional Rights and American Families," *JAH*, 74:3 (Dec. 1987), 959–83.

31. *Loving v. Virginia*, 388 U.S. 1 (1967). In *Meyer v. Nebraska*, 262 U.S. 390 at 399 (1923), the court had first called the right to marry fundamental. The 1955 opportunity left aside was *Naim v. Naim*, 197 Va. 80, 87 S.E. 2d 749; the 1964 case, *McLaughlin v. Florida*, 379 U.S. 184, which overruled *Pace v. Alabama*. The opinion in *Loving* notes, p. 6, n. 5, that sixteen states still prohibit and punish marriage on the basis of racial classification: Ala., Ark., Del., Fla., Ga., Ky., La., Miss., Mo., N.C., Okla., S.C., Tenn., Tex., Va., and W. Va. Maryland repealed its law after the *Loving* case was initiated. See Peter Wallenstein, "Race, Marriage, and the Law of Freedom: Alabama and Virginia, 1860–1960s," *Chicago-Kent LR*, 70:2 (1994), 371–437, on the background to *Loving*.

32. *Eisenstadt v. Baird*, 405 U.S. 438, 453 (1972).

33. See Alice Kessler-Harris, *Securing Equity: Women, Men, and the Pursuit of Economic Citizenship*, forthcoming from Oxford UP.

9. *Marriage Revised and Revived*

1. On Roussel's findings, see Mary Ann Glendon, *The Transformation of Family Law: State, Law, and Family in the United States and Western Europe* (Chicago, U of Chicago P, 1989), 144–45.

2. The figures here and in following paragraphs come from the *Statistical Abstract of the United States*, 1995; Robert Joseph Taylor, James S. Jackson, and Linda M. Chatters, ed., *Family Life in Black America* (Thousand Oaks, Calif., Sage, 1997), 39–42, 47–50; "Single Motherhood: Stereotypes vs. Statistics," *New York Times*, Feb. 11, 1996; "Women and Work," *The Economist*, July 18, 1998; Frank Furstenberg, "Family Change and Family Diversity," in *Diversity and Its Discontents*, ed. Neil J. Smelser and Jeffrey C. Alexander (Princeton, Princeton UP, 1999), 152; and Peter Kilborn, "Shifts in Families Reach a Plateau, Study Says," *New York Times*, Nov. 27, 1996. Unmarried-couple figures for 1998 come from the U.S. Bureau of the Census "Current Population Survey," Internet version, release date Jan. 7, 1999; and the most recent proportions for unmarried couples and not-marrieds come from Tom W. Smith, "The Emerging Twenty-first Century American Family," General Social Survey Social Change Report no. 42, National Opinion Research Center, University of Chicago, released Nov. 24, 1999.

3. In 1993, 61 percent of black women and 58 percent of black men were not married, and so were 41 percent of white women and 38 percent of white men. Preliminary national figures for 1993 show 9 marriages and 4.6 divorces per 1,000 people; Pacific states show 7.1 marriages and 5.1 divorces per 1,000. Since California, Indiana, and Lousiana figures are lacking, both the national and the Pacific divorce ratios are probably understated. (In 1980, California's marriage rate was 8.9, its divorce rate 5.6; Indiana's marriage rate was 10.5, its divorce rate 7.3; Louisiana's marriage rate was 10.5, its divorce rate 4.3.) In preliminary figures for the first half of 1997 released by the Centers for Disease Control and Prevention, the ratio of the divorce rate to the marriage rate is 1 to 2 only in the mid-Atlantic and the east south central regions; elsewhere it is higher.

4. Kate Millett, *Sexual Politics* (Garden City, N.Y., Doubleday, 1970).

5. See, e.g., Robin Morgan, ed., *Sisterhood is Powerful* (New York, Vintage, 1970).

6. See Barbara Babcock et al., *Sex Discrimination and the Law: History, Practice, and Theory,* 2d ed. (Boston, Little Brown, 1996).

7. On divorce reforms noted in this and the following paragraph I have relied on Stephen D. Sugarman and Herma Hill Kay, ed., *Divorce Reform at the Crossroads* (New Haven, Yale UP, 1990); Milton C. Regan, Jr., *Family Law and the Pursuit of Intimacy* (New York, New York UP, 1993); Mary Ann Glendon, *Abortion and Divorce in Western Law: American Failures, European Challenges* (Cambridge, Harvard UP, 1987). Glendon points out, 66–67, that virtually every country of western Europe moved to allow divorce by mutual consent between 1969 and 1985.

8. Herbert Jacob, "Women and Divorce Reform," in *Women, Politics, and Change,* ed. Louise A. Tilly and Patricia Gurin (New York, Russell Sage Foundation, 1990), 482–503.

9. On incentives and requirements for welfare mothers to earn, see Joanne L. Goodwin, " 'Employable Mothers' and 'Suitable Work': A Re-evaluation of Welfare and Wage-earning for Women in the Twentieth-Century United States," *Journal of Social History,* 29:2 (Winter 1995), esp. 262–70.

10. *Marvin v. Marvin,* 134 Cal. Rptr. 815, 557 P.2d 106 (Cal. 1976); Judith Areen, *Family Law: Cases and Materials,* 3d ed. (Westbury, N.Y., Foundation P, 1992), 900–08; see Grace Blumberg, "Cohabitation without Marriage: A Different Perspective," *UCLA LR,* 28 (1981), 1125–39.

11. *Borelli v. Brusseau,* 12 Cal. App. 4th 667, 16 Cal. Rptr. 2d 16 (1993), excerpt reprinted and discussed in *Family Law,* ed. Leslie Harris, Lee Teitelbaum, and Carol Weisbrod (Boston, Little Brown, 1996), 70–75; additional thanks to Carol Weisbrod.

12. *Roe v. Wade*, 410 U.S. 113 (1973). The decision conceded the state's interest in regulating abortion after the first trimester, for health reasons.

13. See Elizabeth Schneider, "The Violence of Privacy," *Connecticut LR*, 23 (Summer 1991), 973–99. In raising awareness of domestic battery and marital rape, Susan Schechter, *Women and Male Violence* (Boston, South End P, 1982), and Diana E. H. Russell, *Rape in Marriage* (New York, Macmillan, 1982), were important public clarions.

14. Quoted in Rebecca Ryan, "The Sex Right: A Legal History of the Marital Rape Exemption," *Law and Social Inquiry*, 20:4 (1995), 996, n. 215.

15. *People v. Liberta*, 474 N.Y.2d 567 (1984), cited in Ryan, "The Sex Right."

16. Ryan, "The Sex Right"; Lisa Eskow, "The Ultimate Weapon? Demythologizing Spousal Rape and Reconceptualizing Its Prosecution," *Stanford LR*, 48 (1996), 677–708; see also Jill Elaine Hasday, "Contest and Consent: A Legal History of Marital Rape," *California LR*, 88 (Oct. 2000).

17. Words such as dejuridification, delegalization, deregulation, and privatization are used for the same phenomena in Glendon, *Transformation*, and "Marriage and the State: The Withering Away of Marriage," *Virginia LR*, 62 (May 1976), 663–720; Stephen Parker, *Informal Marriage, Cohabitation, and the Law, 1750–1989* (New York, St. Martin's, 1990); and Milton C. Regan, *Family Law and the Pursuit of Intimacy* (New York, New York UP, 1993).

18. See Timothy Egan, "The Persistence of Polygamy," *New York Times Magazine*, Feb. 28, 1999, 51–55.

19. See Goodwin, " 'Employable Mothers' and 'Suitable Work,' " 264–78, on the trend since the 1960s toward urging employment and job training on mothers receiving welfare (as well as unemployed fathers, who were added to AFDC in 1962).

20. Smith, "The Emerging Twenty-first Century American Family."

21. "More Clergy Members Giving Blessing to Ceremonies Uniting Gay Couples," *New York Times*, April 17, 1998, A1, A20.

22. *Bowers v. Hardwick*, 478 U.S. 186 (1986); see Scalia's dissent in *Romer v. Evans*, 517 U.S. 620 (1996), in which the majority prevented Colorado from nullifying civil rights protections for homosexuals.

23. *Jay Brause and Gene Dugan v. Bureau of Vital Statistics, Alaska . . .*, Peter Michalski, Judge of Superior Court for the State of Alaska, 3d Jud District, Feb. 27, 1998 [1998 WL 88743, Alaska Super.], case 3AN-95-6562 CI. My thanks to Sarah Hammond for giving me an early copy of this decision.

24. Joel Prentiss Bishop, *Commentaries on the Law of Marriage and Divorce*, 4th ed. (Boston, Little Brown, 1864), 1:2.

25. *Baehr v. Lewin*, 852 P 2d 44, 58 (1993).

26. Lambda Legal Defense and Education Fund, "2000 Anti-Marriage Bills Status Report," online at <www.lambdalegal.org>; "Ballot Test for Gay Marriage in Alaska, Hawaii," *San Francisco Chronicle*, Oct. 26, 1998, 1, 9; "Hawaii's High Court Rules Gay Marriage Issue Closed," *Los Angeles Times*, Dec. 11, 1999, 17; "Vermont High Court Backs Rights of Same-Sex Couples," *New York Times*, Dec. 21, 1999, 1; *Stan Baker et al. v. State of Vermont et al.*, filed Dec. 20, 1999, Supreme Court of Vermont, Lexis 406; "Vermont's House Backs Wide Rights for Gay Couples," *New York Times*, March 17, 2000, 1; "California Votes to Ban Recognition of Gay Marriages," *Washington Post*, March 8, 2000, 21; "Vermont Gives Final Approval to Same-Sex Unions," *New York Times*, April 26, 2000, A14.

27. The most extensive debates on the Defense of Marriage Act (Public Law 104–199, Sept. 21, 1996) are in *CR* 104/2, vol. 142 no. 63, May 8, 1996; vol. 142, no. 102, July 11, 1996; vol. 142, no. 103, July 12, 1996; vol. 142, no. 122, Sept. 9, 1996.

28. Speakers are Y. Tim Hutchinson of Ark., Bob Barr of Ga., Tom Coburn of Okla., Charles Canaday of Fla., and Steve Largent of Okla., *CR* 104/2, vol. 142, no. 102, July 11, 1996, 7441–47.

29. James M. Talent of Mo., *CR* 104/2, vol. 142, no. 102, July 11, 1996, 7446.

30. Dave Weldon of Florida, *CR* 104/2, vol. 142, July 12, 1996, 7493.

31. E.g., Patrick Kennedy of R.I., Barney Frank of Mass., Sheila Jackson-Lee of Texas, Sam Farr of Calif., John Lewis of Ga., *CR* 104/2, vol. 142, no. 102, July 11, 1996, 7441–47; Barbara Boxer of Calif., vol. 142, no. 122, Sept. 9, 1996, 10065.

32. H.R., July 12, 1996; Sen., Sept. 10, 1996.

33. *CR* 104/2, vol. 142, no. 63, May 8, 1996.

34. Public Law 104–193, Aug. 21, 1996.

35. Quotation from *Prince v. Mass*, 321 U.S. 158, 166 (1944); see Martha A. Fineman, "Intimacy outside of the Natural Family: The Limits of Privacy," *Connecticut LR*, 23 (Summer 1991), 955–72.

36. Dorothy A. Brown, "The Marriage Bonus/Penalty in Black and White," in *Taxing America*, ed. Karen B. Brown and Mary Louise Fellows (New York, New York UP, 1996), 45–57. See also Anne L. Alstott, "Tax Policy and Feminism: Competing Goals and Institutional Choices," *Columbia LR*, 96 (Dec. 1996), 2001–2082.

37. See opinions on all sides in Andrew Sullivan, ed., *Same-Sex Marriage: Pro and Con* (New York, Vintage, 1997).

38. See "The Wedding Dress That Ate Hollywood," *New York Times*, Aug. 30, 1998, sect. 9, 1–2.

ACKNOWLEDGMENTS

Writing this book has taken far longer than I imagined when I began, and I have accumulated many debts of gratitude along the way, all of which I'm delighted to acknowledge, as if they could be repaid in words. First, there are other historians to whose scholarship I returned again and again, relying on it more than individual citations can convey. I am grateful to Linda Gordon, Michael Grossberg, Pamela Haag, Hendrik Hartog, Linda Kerber, Alice Kessler-Harris, Jan Lewis, Amy Dru Stanley, Carol Weisbrod, and Robert Westbrook for inspiring and aiding me with their evidence and ideas. I benefited from the contributions of research assistants: More than a decade ago, Jane Kamensky produced superbly efficient notes on dozens of books; then Jessica Steigerwald's creativity and conscientiousness in research tasks helped me and the project in substantial ways; and I counted on Leah Newkirk's intelligence and reliability during my fellowship at Radcliffe. Hearty thanks to them and also to Professor Leslie Rowland, who generously facilitated my research in the Freedmen and Southern Society collection at the University of Maryland, and to Lisa Cardyn, Ariela Dubler, and Beth Hillman, who divined the mysteries of Westlaw for me on crucial occasions. For encouragement at early stages of the project, I am indebted to Linda Gordon, Linda Kerber, and Peggy Pascoe; for stimulating conversations over several years of thinking and writing, I want to thank Reva Siegel. I am grateful to William Deverell, Eric Foner, Alexander Keyssar, and Robert Westbrook for reading parts of the book-in-progress during 1998–99 and giving me crucial feedback. My research and writing were greatly assisted by two grants from the A. Whitney Griswold Fund of Yale University, a National Endowment for the Humanities Fellowship, a Liberal Arts Fellowship in Law at the Harvard Law School, and a Visiting Research Scholarship at the Schlesinger Library of Radcliffe College. I also appreciate the privilege I had in being appointed William Clyde DeVane Professor at Yale for the spring of 1998, which helped—or forced—me to write twelve lectures and thus map out the book.

A fellowship at the Center for Advanced Study in the Behavioral Sciences, a bicyclist's as well as a scholar's paradise, enabled me to write a full draft in 1998–99. I remain supremely grateful for that opportunity, for the support of the Andrew W. Mellon Foundation, for the helpful advice of the Center's staff (especially Patrick Goebel, Cynthia Bacon, and Jean Michel), and for the wise counsel and sustaining camaraderie of other fellows, especially Jeff Alexander, Alex Keyssar, Hilda Sabato, Jim Scott, and Dan Segal. Neil Smelser, the director of the Center, was the first person to read the whole first draft of the manuscript; he offered generous and astute commentary, as did Lisa Cardyn, Richard W. Fox, Hendrik Hartog, Robert Johnston, Alice Kessler-Harris, Martha Minow, and Peggy Pascoe later. To all, I am obliged for your constructive responses. I gained enormously from the presence of Joyce Seltzer's critical editorial genius at my shoulder, bracing and comforting at the same time; my gratitude to her for enlivening the process of writing and publication. Hearty thanks also to Nancy Clemente, whose wit and long experience made her an ideal manuscript editor, and to Jill Breitbarth, a *simpatica* designer, at Harvard University Press; and to Lynn Walterick, whose scrupulous reading detected and prevented several blunders just in time.

INDEX

Abortion, 126, 210, 213, 222

Adams, John, 20–21

Adultery, 28, 29–30, 32, 37, 106, 112, 208–209, 215. *See also* Infidelity, marital

Aid to Families with Dependent Children. *See* Public assistance

African Americans, 4, 122, 185; as ex-slaves, 5, 80–94, 98–99; and marriage across the color line, 40–46, 98–102; and "marriage penalty," 224; marriage rate among, 203, 282n3; as single mothers, 204, 221, 224; as slaves, 32–35, 37, 57–63; as Union soldiers, 83–84, 103; as voters, 96–97, 98, 164. *See also* Citizenship; Husband's role; Slavery

Alabama, 40–41, 87, 88–89, 100–101, 253n27

Alaska, 216–217

Amalgamation, 98. *See also* Intermarriage; "Race mixture"

American Bar Association, 196, 205–206

American Law Institute, 196–197

American Revolution: conception of virtue in, 18–19; familial analogies cited in, 14–15; marital analogies cited in, 16–17

Americanization, 150–151

Anarchists, 139, 165

Anthony, Susan B., 67, 97

Antislavery protest, 56–58, 75–76, 116–117

Arkansas, 83, 91–92

Arranged marriage, 149–151

Asians, 4; and citizenship, 132–133, 138–139, 145–146, 165, 183–184, 272n61; excluded, 138, 154–155; and fraud in marriage, 149–155; linked to polygamy, 114–116, 137, 149; and prostitution, 136–138, 149. *See also* Chinese; Immigration; Japanese

Astell, Mary, 65

Banns, 31, 39

Beecher, Catharine, 70

Beecher, Henry Ward (Rev.), 108, 125

The Best Years of Our Lives (film), 188–190

Bibb, Henry, 83

Bigamy, 28, 30, 32, 38–39, 126–127; among ex-slaves, 88–89, 90–92

Birth control, 125–126, 129, 181–182, 197, 198–199, 202, 216

Birth rate, 203

Bishop, Joel, 46–47, 217

Blackwell, Antoinette Brown, 64, 66

Bradley, Joseph (Justice), 119–120

Braun, Marcus, 146–150

Brennan, William J. (Justice), 199

Buchanan, James (Pres.), 56

Buckley, C. W., Chaplain, 83, 88–89

Bureau of Indian Affairs, 25, 27, 120–123

Bureau of Refugees, Freedmen, and Abandoned Lands, 83–94, 103, 104, 105, 113, 122, 158, 174, 222

DISCARDED
from
New Hanover County Public Library

NEW HANOVER COUNTY PUBLIC LIBRARY
201 CHESTNUT STREET
WILMINGTON, NC 28401

GAYLORD S

ML